A guide to contemporary French usage

A guide to contemporary French usage

R. E. BATCHELOR
Senior Lecturer in Modern Languages
University of Nottingham

M. H. OFFORD
Lecturer in French
University of Nottingham

CAMBRIDGE UNIVERSITY PRESS
Cambridge
London   New York   New Rochelle
Melbourne   Sidney

Published by the Press Syndicate of the University of Cambridge
The Pitt Building, Trumpington Street, Cambridge CB2 1RP
32 East 57th Street, New York, NY 10022, USA
296 Beaconsfield Parade, Middle Park, Melbourne 3206, Australia

© Cambridge University Press 1982

First published 1982

Printed in Great Britain by Spottiswoode Ballantyne Ltd

Library of Congress catalogue card number: 82–4558

British Library cataloguing in publication data

Batchelor, R.E.
A guide to contemporary French usage.

1. French language
I. Title II. Offord, M.H.
448   PC2112

ISBN 0 521 28037 0

Contents

Foreword

This book provides the student with an essentially practical guide to the contemporary French language. It is practical first because it attempts to deal with many of the major aspects of the language by defining and illustrating them through everyday examples. Second, its practical nature may be seen in the attention paid to the levels of register in French, a feature of this book which breaks new ground. It not only clarifies points of usage and grammar, but shows the circumstances in which words, expressions, grammatical constructions, and so on, are most appropriate. Third, a serious and systematic attempt has been made to help the English student work his/her way through the complex web of *faux amis*, paronyms, prepositions, etc., where English language patterns can easily provoke error. It will be understood once and for all that a French person says 'La clef est *sur* la porte', and 'Le boxeur est *sur* le ring', that *lier* and *relier* are not the same, and that *sous*, *au-dessous de*, *en dessous de*, and *à travers*, *en travers de*, *au travers de* are more complicated than may first appear.

The book is unusual in that it combines a survey of both vocabulary and grammar. Traditional French grammar books for English students are naturally largely confined to matters of grammar; books on vocabulary, *faux amis* and other aspects of lexis are not concerned with grammar. The inextricable association of grammar and vocabulary in language is implicit in the conception of this book.

The authors do not claim to provide a comprehensive guide to all aspects of the French language. For example, no section on adverbs is included, partly because it is felt that adverbs do not present the same problems as, for instance, prepositions. Neither is space given to the definite and indefinite articles. Adjectives are not given a section to themselves, but are found in the chapter on word order, for instance. The whole point of the book is that it is less concerned with the prescriptive rules of grammar than with the way the language is actually used. It has been conceived on the basic assumption that the student has already acquired a certain expertise in the French language. Indeed some readers may well be acquainted with many, if not all, of the concepts presented in the section on register. In that section we have deliberately avoided discussion and criticism of previous work on the subject and have attempted to provide as simple and straightforward a model of register as possible, in keeping with the aims of this book.

Much of the material in the book has been set out in tabular form for the sake of clarity. It is hoped that the student will be able to seize and memorise the essential points more easily through the visual impact.

Authors' Acknowledgements
We are immeasurably indebted to the following:

Mme N. Jolivet	Mlle S. Lescop
Mlle A. Le Bohec	Mme D. Chang
M. P. Lanoë	Mme A. Arguile

We should also like to thank Rosemary Davidson for her help and encouragement. Finally, we should like to thank all our students whose generous mistakes over the years have provided us with the raw material for this book.

R. E. Batchelor
M. H. Offord

Abbreviations

adj	adjective	qn	*quelqu'un*
F (f)	feminine	R1	see **1.4**
fig	figurative	R2	see **1.4**
gen	generally	R3	see **1.4**
impers	impersonal	sb	somebody
intr	intransitive	sg	singular
M (m)	masculine	st	sometimes
occ	occasionally	sth	something
pft	perfect	subj	subjunctive
ph	past historic	trans/tr	transitive
pl	plural	usu	usually
pp	past participle	/	or
pres	present	(...)	non-use of preposition
qch	*quelque chose*		(see **3.4.1.1**)

1 Register

In order to appreciate fully what is meant by the term register and how vital it is in the advanced study of a foreign language, it is necessary first of all to consider it against the general background of what are known as varieties of language.

1.1 Varieties of language

Students talking among themselves would use a different type of vocabulary and even different grammatical structures from those they would use when addressing their teacher, or when being interviewed for a job, or when talking to a young child – or a dog. They would use different vocabulary and structures when writing an essay on 20th-century French literature, when talking about pop music or feminism with friends in a pub, or when visiting grandparents. A person can speak formally or informally, or can use an appropriate shade of formality. The intention can be to persuade, to encourage, to inform, to amuse. One can express oneself in writing, in conversation, in a speech. A person can speak in a professional role, for instance as a teacher, a lawyer or a doctor. It is clear that people have at their command many different ways of expressing themselves depending upon circumstances. Language is used for a variety of purposes, in a variety of situations and is expressed by a variety of means. A language should not therefore be seen as a homogeneous whole, but as a collection of varieties. There exist varieties of English; there are also varieties of French, German, Spanish, and so on.

At the same time as children acquire the grammar, vocabulary and pronunciation systems of their own language, they acquire in addition an increasing intuitive awareness of the varieties available in their language and of when to use them appropriately. However, for the foreign-language learner, acquiring the capacity to operate within an appropriate variety of language is a more conscious matter, although even here, with increasing competence, selection of the appropriate variety becomes increasingly automatic.

A variety of language is determined by a number of factors; some are peripheral, others central in importance. In this book we are not concerned with varieties themselves, but with one of the essential factors which constitute them, register.

1.2 Peripheral factors

The way French speakers use their language is affected by such matters as their sex (a woman may have different general speech characteristics from a man), their age (for example whether they are adolescents or octogenarians), where they come from (for example a Parisian, a Marseillais, and a Martiniquan will all have idiosyncracies of speech which are due to their places of origin), and their socio-economic standing (that is to say the degree of education they have received and their social and professional status). These are factors over which the speaker has little, if any, control, as they are deep-rooted ingredients of his or her individuality. They are, therefore, of secondary importance in an analysis of varieties of language.

1.3 Central factors

Of much greater immediate importance in determining the composition of varieties are the following factors: subject matter, purpose, medium and register.

1.3.1 Field

What one is talking about affects the way one expresses oneself. For example, when the French discuss politics they will draw upon a certain vocabulary which would be quite inappropriate in a discussion on zoology, although, of course, there are certain 'common core' features which are used whatever the topic under discussion. The term 'field' is used to denote the subject matter of a conversation, speech, etc. It means a collection of words and expressions relating specifically to a certain topic, for example politics, and covers the many types of situations in which politics may be discussed. It may be politics as practised by a politician, or as reported by a political correspondent in the press, or as debated over a glass of wine between friends in a bar. The field includes, therefore, not only the technical vocabulary of the professional but also the less technical vocabulary used by the non-specialist talking about the same subject.

1.3.2 Purpose

Whatever the status of the speaker – whether he or she is a politician, or the political correspondent of a daily newspaper, or simply a layman talking politics with a friend – language is used with a purpose. The politician will attempt to persuade; the political journalist to inform, comment and/or evaluate; the layman may simply chat, or may adopt the stance of the politician or journalist depending upon knowledge, inclination or intention.

1.3.3 Medium

The medium of communication also needs to be taken into account. By medium is meant the vehicle through which the subject matter is conveyed to a listener or an audience. In politics it may be a speech made in parliament or at the hustings, it may be a written report of a debate or a manifesto, a piece of propaganda used in an election campaign, or simply a conversation. The spontaneous expression of a conversation will contrast with the carefully prepared wording of a speech: the medium therefore places constraints on the way one expresses oneself.

1.3.4 Register

The final factor to consider in this analysis of varieties of language is register. Register is concerned with the relationship that exists between a speaker and the person he or she is speaking to. In other words it is the degree of formality or informality which a speaker accords the listener. This degree of formality/informality depends in turn upon four variable factors, in increasing order of importance: sex, age, status and intimacy. The sex of the speaker or listener, the least important of the variables, may not even be relevant in certain situations. However, sometimes it is: exclusively male or female gatherings often have their own peculiar speech habits which are a direct result of the company present; a young man talking to his girl friend may use a different standard of language from that which he will use when he is chatting to his male friends; it may involve only a slight adjustment – does he swear in the presence of women? The age of a speaker has already been mentioned in **1.2** as having a bearing upon the way he or she speaks – elderly speakers have different speech habits from younger ones – but in this section it is the possibility of varying the way one speaks, according to the age of the person spoken to, that is relevant. Parents talking to young children will use a different, simpler, vocabulary and grammar from that which they would use when talking to colleagues or contemporaries. In the same way, a teacher will use a different level of language in classroom and common room. Status also plays an important role in determining register. When discussed in 1.2, status was used to refer to the degree of education and the social and professional standing of the speaker. In this section it refers to the ability of a person to adjust his or her speech according to the status of the person addressed: an employee in a factory talking to a director, the director in turn talking to an employee, a shop assistant serving a customer, will use different registers because of their respective positions in the social or professional hierarchy. Finally and most important, intimacy, the degree to which speakers know and trust each other, affects the way they speak to each other. A first encounter between two persons requires a different register from that required by a conversation between a husband and wife celebrating their fourth wedding anniversary. These four factors, sex, age, status and intimacy, combine to produce register, the relationship of formality/informality existing between speakers.

The relationship between these factors, particularly those of age and status, and the peripheral factors mentioned briefly in 1.2, needs to be considered briefly. There is, of necessity, some interaction between the two types of factor. To examine first the relationship between the age of the speaker (peripheral) and the age of the person addressed (central), it is clear that in certain cases the age of the speaker will override his or her ability to adjust to the level of the person addressed: for example, a child will not have the necessary linguistic sophistication to adjust its speech in order to address an adult in an adult way; at the other end of the age range, an elderly person may lose the expertise he or she once possessed to adjust his or her speech to become comprehensible to a child, or such a person may never have had sufficient experience of children's language to realise what adjustments should be made. Similarly for status: it is well known that, for certain people, the linguistic patterns peculiar to their class or profession are so indelibly ingrained that they are unable or would consider it demeaning to vary their speech: it is unlikely that a poorly-educated person will be in a position to produce the appropriate level of language when conversing with a person of higher social standing; conversely a person of aristocratic stock may find it extremely difficult to eliminate from his or her speech those linguistic elements which are all but innate, when addressing someone of lower social rank. There are circumstances, therefore, when a certain neutralisation of the effects of the various factors occurs.

A corollary of register concerns the character of the language actually produced, more precisely the degree of explicitness which is necessary for communication within a given situation. In particular, the more intimately one knows someone, the more similar the socio-economic status and to a lesser degree the ages involved, the more information that can be taken for granted in conversation and the less need for formal structuring of language (**1.6.1**): there is no need to be explicit about family matters within the family or about business affairs with close colleagues, because in these cases so much is common knowledge and may be left unspecified. On the other hand, strangers meeting for the first time or students attending an induction course require detailed explanations of every aspect of this new experience or undertaking and an elaborate, grammatically correct structuring of what is said (**1.6.4** and **1.6.5**).

It is now possible to show in diagrammatic form how all these factors combine to constitute a variety of language.

a variety of language

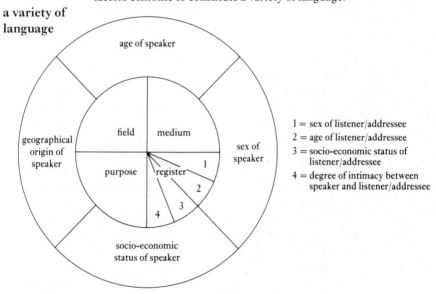

1 = sex of listener/addressee
2 = age of listener/addressee
3 = socio-economic status of listener/addressee
4 = degree of intimacy between speaker and listener/addressee

---

1.4   Register as used in this book

According to the definition of the previous section (**1.3.4**), register involves the relationship of formality/informality existing between the two participants in a conversation or any other situation in which language is used. The most accurate way of representing register would be to envisage it as a scale extending from extreme informality at one end to extreme formality at the other, with a multitude of different shades of formality in between. However, for ease of reference and use in this book, the scale will be divided into three distinct sections, each of which will cover a third of the scale of formality. These three sections will be known as R1, R2 and R3 and their major characteristics may be summarised in the following way:

extreme
informality

extreme
formality

←——→

R1	R2	R3
very informal, casual, colloquial, familiar, careless, admitting new terms almost indiscriminately, certain terms short-lived, at times truncated, elliptical, incorrect grammatically, prone to redundant expressions, includes slang expressions and vulgarisms, likely to include regional variations	standard, polite, educated, equivalent of 'BBC English', compromise between the two extremes	formal, literary, official, with archaic ring, language of scholars and purists, meticulously correct, reluctant to admit new terms

It must be stressed once more that these sections are the result of an artificial division and that the reality behind them consists of subtle, imperceptible shifts, not of rigidly defined categories. (We have confined these register divisions to three, as being more practicable to handle, although scholars in the field often distinguish five.)

A few comments on the above schematisation of register are called for. Because the divisions are arbitrary some examples (**2.10.1**) do not fit exactly into one of the sections (an example might be more accurately classified as R1½): in such circumstances it has been necessary to place the examples in the section below the more accurate classification (therefore R1½ becomes R1). Whereas R2 and R3 appear more homogeneous as divisions of register, R1 covers a rich range of informal language, stretching, for example, from obscene interjections to unobjectionable ones (**2.10.1**); at times language included in R1 is in fact grammatically incorrect and frequently swings from elliptical usage to an extensive use of unnecessary repetition.

Looking towards the future it is possible that some of what at present are deemed incorrect usages contained in R1 will become socially acceptable language. It is interesting to observe that the *tolérances* – lists of grammatical and orthographical usages previously condemned but now accepted – issued by the French government for the benefit of examiners quite frequently concern matters of register (although this is not explicitly acknowledged by the authorities). What was considered typically R1 usage, and therefore shunned by the users of 'correct' R2/R3 French, is raised by decree to at least R2 status:

eg   an examiner may now accept:
   c'est là de beaux résultats
   as well as the traditionally only acceptable
   ce sont là de beaux résultats
   similarly, in the matter of sequence of tenses with the subjunctive (3.7.1),
   j'avais souhaité qu'il vienne sans tarder
   is now tolerated as well as
   j'avais souhaité qu'il vînt sans tarder

Although the *tolérances* have official backing, they do not always find universal acceptance outside such circles:

eg   **la fillette, obéissante à sa mère, alla se coucher**
   j'ai recueilli cette chienne errante dans le quartier
   étant données les circonstances (3.6.3.2)

Another characteristic of R1 usage which should be stressed is the fact that many items of its vocabulary are ephemeral in nature. In slang and popular speech there are noticeable preferences for certain types of words, namely those which are striking by their sound or by the manner in which they are created (usually as a result of a metaphorical extension of meaning). Such words are frequently victims of the ravages of fashion and within a relatively short period of time tend to become overworked, thus losing their impact and appeal, and need to be replaced. A rapid turnover in vocabulary is the result: words that are on everyone's lips one year, or even for part of a year, seem terribly dated the following year, and using an out-of-date term may well mark a speaker as being 'past it' or at least old-fashioned. (For this reason a number of the terms included in 2.10.1 will have a limited life-span.)

The phenomenon of register switch should also be illustrated. It is likely that uneducated speakers will use only R1 whatever social situation they find themselves in, whereas an educated speaker will be able to command all three with equal ease, passing from one end of the scale to the other without great difficulty. To go further than was possible in section 1.3.4 and to give a specific example drawn from higher education, a formal lecture would normally be delivered in R3, whereas a seminar would normally be conducted in R2, and, depending upon the degree of friendliness existing between lecturer and student, it is conceivable that a one-to-one tutorial might be carried on in R1: linguistic distinctions based upon differences of sex, age and status disappear with deepening intimacy. It is not, of course, only lecturers who have the ability to switch register! A native speaker's ability to adjust his or her register in various circumstances is the key to avoiding offence and to gaining acceptance in any given situation. The degree to which a foreign learner can achieve that ability to adjust his or her register is a mark of competence in, and mastery of, the foreign language.

1.5 Illustration of register

Register affects all aspects of language: pronunciation, vocabulary and grammar. Although vocabulary and grammar are the major preoccupations of this book, it is worthwhile considering briefly some of the effects of register upon the pronunciation of French.

1.5.1 Pronunciation and liaison

The making of valid general comments upon the issues raised by pronunciation is fraught with risks. Pronunciation is the least stable, most variable aspect of a person's speech habits, and it is well known that a single individual will not necessarily always pronounce the same word in the same way. Consequently the observations that follow must be appreciated in the light of such a reservation. Another problem is that certain tendencies of pronunciation are restricted to a particular region; in such cases disentangling accent from register is very difficult.

On the whole, as might be expected, an R1 speaker tends to be less careful about his pronunciation than an R2 and particularly an R3 speaker. In what follows, R1 usage is contrasted with R2 and R3 usages, and regionalisms will be kept as far as possible to a minimum.

The most obvious general characteristic of R1 pronunciation is a relative laziness of articulation, resulting in, amongst other things, the loss of certain sounds or the introduction or change of others. This is illustrated in the following ways. It should be noted that it is not always a matter of, for example, the clear-cut presence or absence of /r/ (ie /kat/ versus /katr/), but of a gradual movement from precise articulation to more indistinct articulation of the sound.

Register marked in treatment of	R1 and example		R2+R3	written form
consonants:				
reduction of groups of consonants	/gʒ/ → /ʒ/ /ks/ → /s/	/syʒɛsjɔ̃/ /ɛskyz/ /ɛspedisjɔ̃/ /ɛsplwa/	/sygʒɛstjɔ̃/ /ɛkskyz/ /ɛkspedisjɔ̃/ /ɛksplwa/	*suggestion* *excuse* *expédition* *exploit*
	/lk/ → /k/ /st/ → /s/ /tr/ → /t/	/kɛkʃoz/ /ʒɛsjɔ̃/ /ptɛt/ /kat/ /vɔt/	/kɛlkəʃoz/ /ʒɛstjɔ̃/ /pɸtɛtr/ /katr/ /vɔtr/	*quelque chose* *gestion* *peut-être* *quatre* *votre*
dropping of consonants	/l/	/i fɛ bo/ /i vjɛ̃/	/il fɛ bo/ /il vjɛ̃/	*il fait beau* *il vient*
	/r/	/rəgade/	/rəgarde/	*regarder*
change of consonant	/s/ → /z/	/ãtuzjazm/ /idealizm/ /sɔsjalizm/	/ãtuzjasm/ /idealism/ /sɔsjalism/	*enthousiasme* *idéalisme* *socialisme*
vowels:				
confusion of *e*-sounds	/ə/ → /e/	/rekɔ̃stitɥe/ /reose/	/rəkɔ̃stitɥe/ /rəose/	*reconstituer* *rehausser*
	/e/ → /ə/ /e/ → /ɛ/	/rəbɛljɔ̃/ /ʒə pɸ vu lasyrɛ/ /dəgrɛ/ (Parisian)	/rebɛljɔ̃/ /ʒɔ pɸ vu lasyre/ /dəgre/	*rébellion* *je peux vous l'assurer* *degré*
	/ɛ/ → /e/	/me/ /frãse/ /rezɔ̃/	/mɛ/ /frãsɛ/ /rɛzɔ̃/	*mais* *français* *raison*
treatment of mute *e*	pronounced where normally silent	/apəle/ /ãsɛɲəmã/ /evɛnəmã/ /mɛ̃tənã/	/aple/ /ãsɛɲmã/ /evɛnmã/ /mɛ̃tnã/	*appeler* *enseignement* *événement* *maintenant*
	silent where normally pronounced	/fra/ /frɔ̃/ /fzɛ/	/fəra/ /fərɔ̃/ /fəzɛ/	*fera* *feront* *faisait*
	introduction of /ə/	/arkə də trijɔ̃f/ /avɛkə/ /lɔrsəkə/	/ark də trijɔ̃f/ /avɛk/ /lɔrskə/	*Arc de Triomphe* *avec* *lorsque*
lengthening of /a/	/a/ → /aː/	/gaːto/	/gato/	*gâteau*
confusion of *o*-sounds	/o/ → /ɔ/	/ɔt/ /o ʃɔd/ } South- /sɔte/ ern /vɔʒ/ }	/otr/ /o ʃod/ /sote/ /voʒ/	*autre* *eau chaude* *sauter* *Vosges*

Liaison – the phenomenon which, in closely linked groups of words, causes the normally silent final consonant of a word to be sounded before the initial vowel of the next word – may also be affected by considerations of register. However, first of all it should be stressed that in certain circumstances liaison is compulsorily applied and in others it is prohibited; in other words all speakers, regardless of their normal register of speech, are obliged to observe these rules of liaison as briefly illustrated in the following table:

	circumstance	examples	
liaison compulsory	between qualifier + noun	*ses amis*	/sez ami/
		deux ans	/døz ã/
		de grands arbres	/də grãz arbr/
		NOTE: an adjective ending in a nasal vowel is denasalised in liaison and is pronounced like the corresponding F form: *le prochain arrêt:* /lə prɔʃɛn arɛ/	
	between pronoun + verb/ verb + pronoun	*elles ont*	/ɛlz ɔ̃/
		nous avons	/nuz avɔ̃/
		allez-y	/alez i/
	between monosyllabic adverb or preposition + article, noun, pronoun, adjective or adverb	*sous une chaise*	/suz yn ʃɛz/
		moins utile	/mwãz ytil/
		plus important	/plyz ɛ̃pɔrtã/
	after the conjunction (not interrogative) *quand*	*quand il vient*	/kãt il vjɛ̃/
	after the following words ending in a nasal vowel: *en, on, un, mon, ton, son, bien, rien*	NOTE: partial denasalisation occurs with *en, on, un, mon, ton, son*, the degree of denasalisation depending upon a variety of factors (eg register, place of origin): *mon ami* /mɔ̃n ami/ or /mɔn ami/ This does not apply to *bien* and *rien*: *bien indisposé* is always /bjɛ̃ ɛ̃dispose/.	

	circumstance	examples	
liaison prohibited	before numeral beginning with a vowel	*les onze* *cent un crayons*	/le ɔ̃z/ /sɑ̃ œ̃ krɛjɔ̃/
	after *et*	*et alors*	/e alɔr/
	before *oui*	*mais oui*	/mɛ wi/
	between singular subject + verb	*le soldat est parti*	/lə sɔlda ɛ parti/
	after words ending in a nasal vowel not specified above	*selon eux* *bon à rien* NOTE: however, when *bon à rien* is a noun, liaison occurs	/səlɔ̃ ø/ /bɔ̃ a rjɛ̃/
	before words with aspirate *h*	*un héros* *le hibou* NOTE: R1 speakers tend to disregard the aspirate *h* in: *les handicapés* *les haricots* *les Hollandais*	/œ̃ ero/ /lə ibu/

There are on the other hand, circumstances where liaison is optional. Practice may be summed up in the following simple formula: the more formal the language, the more liaisons are made; the more informal, the fewer liaisons. The dividing line may normally be situated within R2: a slightly higher register is struck when liaison is made. Use of liaison is often accompanied by an element of emphasis.

	circumstances	examples	R1+R2	R2+R3
liaison optional	between plural noun + verb, adjective or adverb	*des mots impossibles à comprendre* *les trains arrivent*	/mo ɛ̃pɔsibl/ /trɛ̃ ariv/	/moz ɛ̃pɔsibl/ /trɛ̃z ariv/
	between verb + past participle, infinitive, adjective, adverb or prepositional expression	*je suis en retard* *je suis heureux* *je suis assez content*	/sɥi ɑ̃ rətar/ /sɥi œrø/ /sɥi ase kɔ̃tɑ̃/	/sɥiz ɑ̃ rətar/ sɥiz œrø/ /sɥiz ase kɔ̃tɑ̃/

circumstances	examples	R1 + R2	R2 + R3
after polysyllabic adverbs and prepositions and monosyllabic conjunctions (except *et* and *quand*)	*extrêmement assidu* *pendant une semaine* *mais il riait*	/ɛkstrɛməmɑ̃ asidy/ /pɑ̃dɑ̃ yn səmɛn/ /mɛ il riɛ/	/ɛkstrɛməmɑ̃t asidy/ /pɑ̃dɑ̃t yn səmɛn/ /mɛz il riɛ/

1.5.2 Vocabulary and grammar

As already stated, it is with vocabulary and grammar that this book is primarily concerned. The following tables give a preliminary picture of the repercussions of considerations of register upon French vocabulary and grammar.

In the interpretation of the tables it is important to draw a distinction between those concerning vocabulary and those concerning grammar. In the former, terms that are designated R2 are not necessarily confined exclusively to R2 usage and may also occur in R1 and R3 usages, without disconcerting an addressee. On the other hand, R1 and R3 terms are normally (that is, with the reservations mentioned earlier) restricted to the relevant register. For example, *boue*, recorded in the table as R2, is a neutral term as far as register is concerned, and may be used not only in R2 but also in R1 and R3 usages, whereas *gadoue*, recorded as R1, immediately evokes an R1 context and *fange*, recorded as R3, evokes an R3 context, both terms being rarely used outside those register-divisions. In other words, an R1 speaker may choose between a distinctive R1 term, *gadoue*, and a neutral, 'common core' term *boue*; similarly an R3 user may opt for a term redolent of R3 usage, *fange*, or the neutral term *boue*.

It will be noticed that there are not in all cases terms for each of the three register-divisions: no vocabulary of any language is characterised by perfect regularity. The occasional gaps in the tables, therefore, under R1 and R3 (eg *bruit* and *faire (du) mal à/vexer*) may be accounted for by the fact that there is no distinctive R1 and R3 term in those cases, and that the term recorded as R2 should be understood as being appropriate there as well.

However, the same flexibility is not applicable in the case of the tables concerning grammar. In some cases, there are three distinct forms (eg R1: *fermez la porte*; R2: *(vous) fermez la porte, s'il vous plaît*; R3: *je vous prie de fermer la porte*). In such cases the R2 form is characteristic of the middle register-division, as opposed to the two outer divisions, and R1 and R3 speakers would not have recourse to it, except as a deliberate attempt to improve, in the case of an R1 speaker, or downgrade, in the case of an R3 speaker, their normal speech habits. On the other hand it sometimes happens that a particular form is perfectly appropriate for two or even all three divisions. This is indicated by arrows across the columns in the tables. Thus *au début de janvier* may occur quite normally in both R2 and R3 usages, and no particular effect would be produced; if it were used in R1 speech it would immediately imply a desire on the part of the speaker to converse in a higher register.

There are also gaps in the grammar tables. These should be interpreted as implying that in such cases there is no closely corresponding version available or that in that particular register-division speakers are unlikely to express that idea at all.

There is, of course, nothing exclusive about these divisions. An R3 speaker is perfectly at liberty to use an R1 form in his speech; the effect will be arresting, probably humorous, evoking momentarily a situation which is quite foreign to the speaker. Similarly if an R1 speaker suddenly uses an isolated R3 form, the result is that his speech will briefly acquire a pedantic tone.

All the foregoing remarks hold good for the two major parts of the book. In **Part 2: Vocabulary**, sections 2.1 to 2.5, R2 terms may generally be used in R1 and R3 usages as well; in later sections concerning the vocabulary, restricting comments are sometimes made. In **Part 3: Grammar**, the tables and comments specify how usages are to be applied.

Register marked in treatment of vocabulary	R1	R2	R3
		accorder/donner/ remettre	conférer/ décerner
	donner un coup de main	aider	assister/seconder
	sympa	aimable/gentil/ plaisant/sympathique	affable/amène
	crevant/marrant/ rigolo/tordant	amusant/drôle	cocasse
	gadoue	boue	fange
	j'en ai marre/ j'en ai ras-le-bol	j'en ai assez	j'en suis saturé
		baser	fonder
		bâtir/construire	édifier/ériger

Register marked in treatment of vocabulary

	R1	R2	R3
	boucan/chahut	bruit	
	d'acc/O.K.	d'accord	entendu
		dire au revoir/ saluer	faire ses adieux/ prendre congé
	embêter/emmerder/ enquiquiner	ennuyer	importuner
		enterrement	obsèques
		faire (du) mal à/ vexer	blesser/offusquer
	bonne femme	femme = *lady*	dame
		femme = *wife*	épouse
	gueule/trogne/bouille/ binette/tronche	figure/visage	face
	fille	jeune fille	demoiselle
	gars	garçon/jeune homme	
		honnête	intègre/probe
		il y a des rom- anciers qui	il est des rom- anciers qui
	balancer/bazarder/ flanquer/foutre en l'air	jeter	
	dégueulasse/infect	malpropre/sale	immonde
	louper/rater	manquer	
	homme (*as in*: mon homme)	mari	époux
	bonhomme/mec/type	monsieur/homme	
	se foutre de/ mettre en boîte	se moquer de	se gausser de
		mort	décès/trépas
		obscurité	ténèbres
		pour	afin de
		raconter/rapporter	narrer/relater
		remplir	emplir
	réaliser	se rendre compte de	prendre conscience de
	paie	salaire/traitement	rémunération
	je me rappelle de	je me souviens de/ je me rappelle	j'ai souvenance de/ il me souvient de
	se casser la figure	tomber	

Register marked in treatment of grammar	R1	R2	R3
ellipsis	malade, lui? impossible	il n'est pas malade, ce n'est pas possible	
		←——— il est impossible/ n'est pas possible ———→ qu'il soit malade	
	(à la) fin mai	←——— à la fin (du mois) de mai ———→	
	(au) début janvier	←——— au début de janvier ———→	
redundancy of expression	comme par exemple	←——— par exemple ———→	
	mais ils ont cependant	←——— mais/cependant ils ont ———→	
	et puis après	←——— et puis/et après ———→	
	descendre en bas	←——— descendre ———→	
	monter en haut	←——— monter ———→	
	prévoir à l'avance	←——— prévoir ———→	
imperative	fermez la porte	(vous) fermez la porte, s'il vous plaît	je vous prie de fermer la porte
	fermez pas la porte	ne fermez pas la porte, s'il vous plaît	je vous prie de ne pas fermer la porte
exclamation	ça alors, il est déjà là	quelle surprise, il est déjà là	cela m'étonne/ surprend qu'il soit déjà là/je m'étonne qu'il soit déjà là
	ce qu'il a grandi/ qu'est-ce qu'il a grandi	←——— comme/qu'il a grandi ———→	
highlighting	l'objectif, c'est de	←——— l'objectif est de ———→	
	le whisky, ça j'aime pas	←——— je n'aime pas le whisky ———→	
	je la casse, la vitre	←——— je casse la vitre ———→	
inversion	←——— il est à peine arrivé ———→		
	←——— à peine est-il arrivé ———→		
	←——— elle est du moins la meilleure de la classe ———→		
	←——— du moins est-elle la meilleure de la classe ———→		
	←——— on peut dire tout au plus ———→		
	←——— tout au plus peut-on dire ———→		
	←——— j'ai vu une voiture qu'un vieillard conduisait ———→		
	←——— j'ai vu une voiture que conduisait un vieillard ———→		

Register marked in treatment of grammar	R1	R2	R3
subjunctive	←——————— après qu'il soit venu ———————→		après qu'il est venu
	←——— le seul/dernier/premier homme que je connais ———→		
		←——— le seul/dernier/premier homme que je connaisse ———→	
	aucun pays ne permet ça	il n'y a aucun pays qui permet cela	il n'y a aucun pays qui permette cela
	c'est pas vrai qu'elle est arrivée	il n'est pas vrai qu'elle est arrivée	il n'est pas exact qu'elle soit arrivée
tense of subjunctive		le fait qu'il soit (= *was*) le premier à partir	(le fait) qu'il fût le premier à partir
past tenses	c'était qui le premier ministre?	qui était le premier ministre?	qui fut le premier ministre?
	Louis XIV, il était roi de France quand?	quand est-ce que Louis XIV a été roi de France?	quand Louis XIV fut-il roi de France?
agreement with *c'est*	c'est eux	←——————— ce sont eux ———————→	
	c'est les meilleures voitures	←——— ce sont les meilleures voitures ———→	
interrogatives	vous dites quoi?	qu'est-ce que vous dites?	
		←——— que dites-vous? ———→	
	hein?/quoi?	comment?/pardon?	plaît-il?
	elle vient?	est-ce qu'elle vient?	vient-elle?
	vous venez d'où/ d'où vous venez?	d'où est-ce que vous venez?	d'où êtes-vous originaire?
	pourquoi (qu') il vient?	pourquoi est-ce qu'il vient?	
		←——— pourquoi vient-il? ———→	
	elle vient quand?	quand est-ce qu'elle vient?	
		←——— quand vient-elle? ———→	
	il le fait comment?	comment est-ce qu'il le fait?	
		←——— comment le fait-il? ———→	
	c'était qui le premier ministre?	qui était le premier ministre?	qui fut le premier ministre?

Register marked in treatment of grammar	R1	R2	R3
que versus inversion	peut-être qu'il viendra		
		←———— il viendra peut-être ————→	
		←——— peut-être viendra-t-il ———→	
	sans doute qu'elle a raison		
		←———— elle a sans doute raison ————→	
			sans doute a-t-elle raison
pronouns	ça		cela (celui-ci/celui-là) ←————————————————→
	on est content, les gens nous aident	on est content d'être aidé par les gens	nous sommes heureux que les gens nous viennent en aide
	c'est difficile de		←———— il est difficile de ————→
	je vois la maison – c'est grand		←—— je vois la maison – elle est grande ——→
pronouns and possessive adjectives with parts of the body	une pierre est tombée sur ma tête		←—— une pierre m'est tombée sur la tête ——→
prepositions	le chapeau à Marc	←———— le chapeau de Marc ————→	
	il va en vélo	←———— il va à vélo/bicyclette ————→	
	←———— dans l'église ————→		en l'église
negation	j'ose pas le faire	je n'ose pas le faire	je n'ose le faire
		il n'a pas cessé de pleuvoir	il n'a cessé de pleuvoir
	(je) sais pas (moi)/j'en sais rien	je ne sais pas	je ne sais
	ça vaut pas le coup de le faire/ c'est pas la peine (de le faire)	ce n'est pas la peine de le faire	
		←—— il n'est pas nécessaire de le faire ——→	

Register marked in treatment of grammar	R1	R2	R3
partitive article with adjective before plural noun	←———	je vois des grands arbres, des grosses carottes ———→	
		←——— je vois de grands arbres, de grosses carottes	———→
infinitive versus *que*-clause	←——— demande à ton père de venir ———→		demandez au ministre qu'il vienne
	←——— dis à ta sœur de venir ———→		dites au ministre qu'il vienne
euphony	←——— si on constate que ———→		si l'on constate que

As has already been implied in the preceding tables, R1 speech is occasionally (sometimes frequently) characterised by a certain grammatical or lexical carelessness, which may in fact involve significant departure from the grammatical rules accepted in R2 and R3 usage. The following table illustrates a few of the most widespread examples; the standard forms in R2 and R3 are also given.

R1 characterised by grammatical carelessness	R2 + R3
je m'en rappelle	je me le rappelle
du point de vue littérature	du point de vue littéraire
un espèce de fou	une espèce de fou
neuf francs chaque	neuf francs chacun
se fâcher après	se fâcher contre
aller au dentiste/docteur	aller chez le dentiste/docteur
nous avons convenu de (= *we agreed to*)	nous sommes convenus de NOTE: *this is being replaced by* nous avons convenu de
ce n'est pas de sa faute	ce n'est pas sa faute
il fait pareil que vous	il fait comme vous
partir à Lyon/en Italie/à la campagne	partir pour Lyon/l'Italie/la campagne
	NOTE: *the distinction between* à/en *and* pour *is blurred here. Many R2 speakers would readily use* à/en.

R1 characterised by grammatical carelessness	R2+R3
la chose que j'ai besoin	la chose dont j'ai besoin
lire sur le journal	lire dans le journal
la lettre dans laquelle je vous annonce	la lettre par laquelle je vous annonce
une avion	un avion
une élastique	un élastique
un autoroute	une autoroute
la mode d'emploi	le mode d'emploi
revenant de voyage, notre père est venu nous chercher à la gare	notre père est venu nous chercher à la gare à notre retour

R1 characterised by lexical carelessness	R2+R3
on oppose son véto	on met son véto
cette nouvelle s'est avérée fausse	cette nouvelle s'est révélée fausse
messieursdames	mesdames et messieurs
il risque de gagner	il a des chances de gagner
de l'argent plein les poches	les poches pleines d'argent
j'ai très faim	R3: j'ai grand-faim
	NOTE: *although* très *is frowned upon by purists, it is widely used in such circumstances in R2 speech*

In the body of this book unless it is specifically stated otherwise, the word or expression or grammatical construction under discussion will belong to R2.

1.6 Passages illustrating levels of register

NOTE: *From the first to the last passage there is a gradual movement from R1 to R3.*

1.6.1 Au sortir du cinéma

Sylvie: Oh, c'est vachement bien.
Philippe: Ah, bon?
Sylvie: Ah ouais, terrible.

Philippe: Qu'est-ce qu' t'as trouvé de terrible dans ce film?

Sylvie: Oh, chais pas ce qu'i't'faut, toutes les cascades et tout. Il est doué le mec.

Philippe: Ouais, d'accord, il est doué mais j'en ai ras-le-bol. C'est toujours la même chose.

Sylvie: Ah non, c'est pas vrai. J'trouve pas.

Philippe: Ouais, les petites aventures, les cascades, les petits flirts, d'accord, euh ... Ça m'a pas très, très emballé comme film.

Sylvie: Tu vas au ciné pourquoi?

Philippe: Chais pas. C'est pas le genre de film que j'aime. Je m'attendais à aut'chose un petit peu, euh, quelque chose d'un petit peu plus sérieux, mais enfin, oh, c'est Belmondo, j'aurais dû m'y attendre.

Sylvie: Oh, pourtant Belmondo, c'est aut'chose à côté de Delon.

Philippe: Vous êtes toutes pareilles, les filles, Belmondo, Belmondo, y a que Belmondo.

Sylvie: C'est vrai. Y a que lui.

Philippe: Ouais, d'accord.

Sylvie: Chais pas ce qu'i't'faut. C'est vachement bien, j'trouve.

Philippe: Qu'est-ce que t'as trouvé d'bien dans ce film? Oh, d'accord, certaines cascades, euh, des poursuites de bagnoles.

Sylvie: Euh, ouais, y a des cascades, y a le paysage, c'est vachement beau le Mexique, et puis la musique.

Philippe: Bon, à ce moment-là tu vas voir des documentaires sur le Mexique.

Sylvie: Ah non!

Philippe: Et puis y a des truquages dans ce film.

Sylvie: Evidemment y a des truquages. Chais bien.

Philippe: Au point de vue documentaire j'trouve pas ça terrible. D'accord, y avait du suspense.

Sylvie: Ah non, c'était bien, euh, j'l'ai bien aimé.

Philippe: Enfin j'aurais mieux fait d'dépenser mes vingt balles dans un café.

Sylvie: Ça c'est sûr.

Vocabulary	vachement bien	= damn good
	terrible	= marvellous
	ouais	= yes
	chais	= je (ne) sais
	mec	= bloke
	j'en ai ras-le-bol	= I'm fed up with it
	emballer	= to get excited (trans)
	bagnole	= car
	balle	= new franc (in this passage) also
		= *centime* for older people
	ça	= it/that

Form of address	t'(u)

Verbs	restricted range of tenses	only present, perfect, 1 imperfect, 1 conditional perfect; complete absence of subjunctive mood
Elision/ ellipsis	t'as trouvé chais pas i' t' J'trouve c'est pas	ça m'a pas aut'chose y a que d'bien y a des j'l'ai d'dépenser
Highlighting	il est doué le mec vous êtes toutes pareilles, les filles	
Interjections	Oh, ah, bon, d'accord, ah non, euh, mais enfin	
Manner of speech	short, sharp sentences concentrating upon personal feelings	

1.6.2 Une agence de voyages

Monsieur: Bonjour, mademoiselle.

Mademoiselle: Monsieur, vous désirez?

Monsieur: Oui, voilà, j'aimerais passer mes vacances en Israël.

Mademoiselle: Euh, oui, quel genre de voyage exactement?

Monsieur: C'est-à-dire, je ne suis pas très fixé, vous voyez.

Mademoiselle: C'est-à-dire, nous pouvons vous proposer trois solutions. Soit un voyage que nous établissons pour vous seul. A ce moment-là ça risque d'être assez cher, parce que nous n'avons pas tous les avantages et toutes les réductions que peut apporter un voyage de groupe.

Monsieur: Oui.

Mademoiselle: Ou, alors, pour un voyage de groupe soit un circuit . . .

Monsieur: Oui.

Mademoiselle: Vous visitez des villes sur un plan établi d'avance ou, euh, carrément un séjour dans un hôtel près de la mer, et vous restez, euh, le temps que vous voulez, avec possibilité, bien sûr, de faire des excursions, mais à ce moment-là c'est à votre charge, en plus du séjour.

Monsieur: Ah, je vois, non, en fait, le problème est très simple. Bon, je voudrais passer quinze jours en Israël, hein, euh, un prix tout à fait raisonnable, et puis voir le maximum de choses.

Mademoiselle: Oui.

Monsieur: C'est-à-dire profiter au maximum de mon séjour.

Mademoiselle: A ce moment on peut vous proposer le grand tour d'Israël où vous voyez, bien sûr, de nombreux monuments. Enfin, évidemment vous passez par Jérusalem. Euh, vous pouvez également voir la vie de certains kibboutz.

Monsieur: Oui.

Mademoiselle: Euh, avec séjour dans quelques kibboutz le long du parcours et la Mer Morte.

Monsieur: Euh, on bénéficie d'un guide?

Mademoiselle: Oui, bien sûr, ça se passe dans un autocar climatisé et chaque soir, on s'arrête, vous arrêtez, dans un hôtel, euh, de très bonne classe avec nourriture continentale. Bien sûr, si vous voulez, vous pouvez également avoir de la nourriture typique. De temps en temps vous assisterez à des danses folkloriques, et le prix, en ce moment, c'est trois mille huit cents francs pour quinze jours.

Monsieur: D'accord, et vous m'avez bien dit que le voyage se faisait en car?

Mademoiselle: Oui, en car.

Monsieur: Cela doit être assez fatigant, je suppose.

Mademoiselle: Euh, non, ce n'est pas fatigant.

Monsieur: Bien, nous sommes le combien aujourd'hui? Le quinze juin, euh, bon, j'aimerais partir, euh début août, hein, euh, pour les réservations? Enfin si je vous donne la réponse, si je reviens disons la semaine prochaine, est-ce qu'il sera trop tard pour faire les réservations? J'aimerais réfléchir.

Mademoiselle: Oui, euh, à ce moment-là, si vous voulez partir un peu plus tard parce que ça nous laisse, euh, à peine trois semaines, euh, un mois pour faire les réservations.

Monsieur: Oui. Il faudrait que je vous donne la réponse, disons, euh . . .

Mademoiselle: Le plus tôt possible. Et à ce moment-là je vous demanderais de verser, euh, environ, dix pour cent de la somme.

Monsieur: Hmm.

Mademoiselle: Et ensuite, le reste environ une semaine avant de partir.

Monsieur: Bien, euh, vous avez quelques prospectus?

Mademoiselle: Ah, oui, tout ce qu'il vous faut, prenez.

Monsieur: Je vous remercie. Bon, très bien, merci. Au revoir, Mademoiselle.

Mademoiselle: Au revoir, Monsieur.

Vocabulary	Business-like: the customer is enquiring about a holiday. The vocabulary is quite formal, but colourful.	désirez	parcours
		proposer	Mer Morte
		soit	bénéficie
		établissons	autocar
		réductions	climatisé
		établi d'avance	également
		carrément	danses
		à votre charge	folkloriques
		raisonnable	réservations
		maximum	verser
		monuments	dix pour cent
		kibboutz	prospectus

Grammar	The pleasant, yet respectful, atmosphere of a travel agency gives the grammar an R2 tone. As is to be expected, it contains nothing unusual.
Form of Address	**vous**
Interjections	**voilà, euh, oui, c'est-à-dire, alors, ah, en fait, bon, hein, d'accord, enfin, Hmm**
Ellipsis	R2 usage does not allow ellipsis. The situation is quite formal.
Verbs	Variety of tenses corresponds to quite sophisticated atmosphere, present, conditional (**voudrais, aimerais, demanderais, faudrait**) which tones down feelings, and future. Inversion is also used: **que peut apporter**.
Manner	Formal, quite elegant. The travel agent tends to speak like the brochure: **avec possibilité, avec nourriture continentale, verser dix pour cent de la somme**.

1.6.3 Part of a debate between Michèle-Laure Rassat and Georges Kiejman organized by *L'Express*

L'Express: Il n'y avait plus un seul condamné à mort dans les prisons françaises. Et puis, le 14 juin, le jour même où la Commission des lois votait en faveur de l'abolition de la peine capitale, la cour d'assises du Tarn prononçait une condamnation à mort. On pouvait penser que la France allait vers une abolition de facto, comme en Belgique et en Grèce. Ce verdict relance le débat de fond: faut-il aller jusqu'à l'abolition, dans la loi, de la peine de mort?

Mme Michèle-Laure Rassat: Il ne faut pas confondre l'existence de la peine de mort et son utilisation effrénée. Le problème est de savoir s'il n'y a pas des cas où il faut exécuter. C'est une question de principe. Le système du maintien a sur le système purement abolitionniste l'avantage de ne pas éliminer tout recours possible à la peine de mort en présence de personnalités criminelles exceptionnelles. Dans la perspective qui est la mienne, il pourrait s'agir d'une exécution tous les cinq ou six ans, ou peut-être moins.

Maître Georges Kiejman: Ceux qui croient à l'utilité de la peine de mort ne cessent de faire des concessions défensives: à les entendre, ce qui importe, c'est qu'elle existe, quitte à ne l'appliquer que très rarement. Comment la justifier sans croire à son caractère dissuasif, exemplaire? Or, elle ne peut avoir un effet dissuasif que si elle est appliquée assez largement . . .

M.-L. Rassat: Non, si elle est simplement applicable.

Maître Kiejman: La peine de mort simplement virtuelle ne peut avoir

23

d'effet dissuasif, c'est évident. Or, les partisans de son maintien admettent qu'elle ne doit être prononcée que pour un nombre de crimes de plus en plus réduit. C'est la position du garde des Sceaux, qui propose de faire la toilette du Code pénal. C'est un fait, aussi, qu'on souhaite l'appliquer le moins souvent possible, puisque le ministère public la requiert beaucoup moins qu'autrefois. Si bien que, finalement, la peine de mort n'est plus qu'un symbole – un symbole politique, j'en suis persuadé – bien plus qu'elle n'est nécessaire à la répression criminelle.

L'Express: Selon la théorie traditionnelle, la peine de mort aurait quatre fonctions : l'amendement du criminel, l'expiation, l'intimidation, l'élimination. Que valent ces justifications ?

Peine de mort : que faire ?
L'Express, 30 juin, 1979, p.76

Vocabulary	much legal vocabulary	**Commission des lois**
		cour d'assises = Assize Court
		prononçait
		condamnation à mort
		abolition
		verdict
		peine capitale/de mort
		personnalités criminelles
		exécution
		garde des Sceaux = Lord Chancellor
		Code pénal
		requiert (a form often used by lawyers, but not by average French speakers; past participle **requis** is the only form of **requérir** generally used)
Grammar	very formal	inversion	**faut-il aller ?**
			que valent ces justifications ?
		loss of **pas** in negation	**ne cessent de faire**
		expletive *ne*	**bien plus qu'elle n'est nécessaire**
Form of address	no direct form	**il ne faut pas**
	the impersonal viewpoint gives rise to impartial language	**dans la perspective qui est la mienne**
		on
		comment la justifier ?
		à les entendre

Manner	the tone is highly rhetorical and impersonal	the 2 elements of the exceptive expression ne ... que are widely separated, creating a sense of balance	**elle ne peut avoir un effet dissuasif que si ...** **elle ne doit être prononcée que ...**
		repeated use of **or** marks passage from one idea to another in a formal way	
		logical thought processes are apparent in use of abstract nouns	**l'amendement du criminel** **l'élimination**

	Sentences here are invariably longer than in the previous passages. However there is still some spontaneity associated with ordinary speech.	**et puis, le 14 juin** **à les entendre, ce qui importe, c'est** **c'est un fait, aussi, qu'on ...**

1.6.4   Passage from de Gaulle's *Mémoires*

Ce fut fait le 23 mars. M. Peake vint me rendre visite. Il me remit une note m'annonçant que son gouvernement n'insistait pas pour que Muselier restât commandant en chef et veillerait à ce que, pendant un mois, l'amiral ne pût prendre contact avec aucun élément des forces navales françaises. Le Gouvernement britannique le recommandait, toutefois, à ma bienveillance pour une affectation conforme à ses services. Sur ces entrefaites, Auboyneau, arrivé du Pacifique, prit en main l'administration et le commandement de la marine. Au mois de mai, voulant offrir à l'amiral Muselier une chance de servir encore, je l'invitai à venir me voir pour régler avec lui les conditions d'une mission d'inspection que je comptais lui confier. Il ne vint pas. Quelques jours plus tard, cet officier général, qui avait beaucoup fait pour notre marine, me notifia que sa collaboration à la France Libre était terminée. Je l'ai regretté pour lui.

C. de Gaulle, *Mémoires de Guerre*, vol. 1, Plon, Paris, 1959, p. 233

Vocabulary	strong diplomatic and military associations	**remettre une note** **annonçant** **commandant en chef** **amiral** **forces navales françaises** **affectation** **notifia**

Grammar	stringently precise	slightly ponderous constructions involving imperfect subjunctive; 3rd person sg forms only are used	n'insistait pas pour que veiller à ce que
		omission of **pas** in negation	l'amiral ne pût prendre
Verbs	This is a narrative passage, hence the pervasive use of the past historic, which also suits the impartial viewpoint, creating a distance between the writer and the events he describes. The sudden change to the perfect tense links the narrative to the present moment.	ce fût fait vint remit prit invitai notifia	
Manner	an elegantly written, lofty passage, characteristic of de Gaulle's refined style; at the same time, a personal touch recurs with **me**, **ma**, **je**, etc.		

1.6.5 Passage from Albert Camus' *La Peste*

L'intention du narrateur n'est cependant pas de donner à ces
formations sanitaires plus d'importance qu'elles n'en eurent. À sa
place, il est vrai que beaucoup de nos concitoyens céderaient
aujourd'hui à la tentation d'en exagérer le rôle. Mais le narrateur est
plutôt tenté de croire qu'en donnant trop d'importance aux belles
actions, on rend finalement un hommage indirect et puissant au mal.
Car on laisse supposer alors que ces belles actions n'ont tant de prix
que parce qu'elles sont rares et que la méchanceté et l'indifférence
sont des moteurs bien plus fréquents dans les actions des hommes.
C'est là une idée que le narrateur ne partage pas. Le mal qui est dans
le monde vient presque toujours de l'ignorance, et la bonne volonté
peut faire autant de dégâts que la méchanceté, si elle n'est pas éclairée.
Les hommes sont plutôt bons que mauvais, et en vérité ce n'est pas la
question. Mais ils ignorent plus ou moins, et c'est ce qu'on appelle
vertu ou vice, le vice le plus désespérant étant celui de l'ignorance qui
croit tout savoir et qui s'autorise alors à tuer. L'âme du meurtrier est
aveugle et il n'y a pas de vraie bonté ni de bel amour sans toute la
clairvoyance possible.

La Peste, Gallimard, 1947, Paris,
p. 106

Vocabulary	very abstract, dealing with moral preoccupations	**belles actions** **mal** **ignorance** **bonne volonté**	**bons** **mauvais** **vertu** **vice**
Grammar	few or no unusual expressions, even more lofty than the previous passage, an excellent example of clear French prose	expletive **ne**	**n'en eurent**
		balancing of the idea with the exceptive negative	**n'ont tant de prix que**
		repetition of **parce que** by **que**	
		use of **ni**	**il n'y a pas ... ni**
Verbs	The present tense is usually used. The conditional tense **céderaient** increases the impersonal tone; the past historic **eurent** fixes the idea in time. The impartial viewpoint is underlined by the past participles of semi-auxiliary verbs, **tenté** and **laissé**, and is given more general stress by the infinitives **donner**, **exagérer**, **croire** and **supposer**.		
Manner	Camus adopts an elevated and impartial tone to convey the validity of his argument.		

1.6.6 *France-Soir* and *Le Monde*

UNE JEUNE FEMME ABAT UN POLICIER
d'une balle de 11,43

Froidement, un pistolet 11,43 en main, une femme a ouvert le feu sur un policier hier vers 17 heures. Le gardien Francis Violeau, trente-cinq ans, s'est écroulé, la gorge traversée par le projectile, devant le 22, rue de la Chaise (7e) . . .

Quelques minutes plus tôt, elle circulait sur un cyclomoteur. Elle roulait sans casque. Rue de l'Arrivée à Montparnasse, des gardiens de la paix debout près de leur cyclomoteur esquissent un geste pour la stopper : elle passe en trombe. Les deux policiers se lancent à sa poursuite. Ils ont déjà plus de cent mètres de retard, mais dans le flot des voitures, ils parviennent à la repérer.

Elle s'enfuit vers le XVe arrondissement. Sa Yamaha est un peu plus rapide que les engins des gardiens qu'elle tente de 'lâcher' en tournant à chaque carrefour. Comble de malchance, un des policiers tombe en panne. L'autre, Francis Violeau, continue la poursuite . . .

A pied, elle retraverse le boulevard Raspail quand arrive le gardien Violeau qui lance un appel radio : 'Du renfort rue de la Chaise'.

Toujours sur son deux roues, le policier rattrape la jeune femme et hurle: 'Arrêtez!' Elle se retourne. Elle brandit le 11,43 et, sans un mot, tire. Une seule fois. Francis Violeau chancelle, il tombe en arrière ...

France-Soir, mercredi 5 août, 1981

Un policier blessé

Un gardien de la paix cyclomotoriste, M. François Violeau, trente et un ans, a été grièvement blessé, mardi 4 août en fin d'après-midi à Paris (7e) par une jeune femme qui a tiré sur lui avec un pistolet de calibre 11,43. Cette jeune femme qui, elle-même, circulait à cyclomoteur, avait pris la fuite pour éviter un contrôle près de Montparnasse. Poursuivie et rejointe rue de la Chaise à Paris (7e) par le gardien de la paix, l'inconnue, âgée d'une trentaine d'années, selon les témoins, sortit de son sac à main le pistolet et tira une balle. Atteint à la tête, M. Francis Violeau a été admis à l'hôpital Saint-Michel où son état est jugé préoccupant.

Le Monde, jeudi 6 août, 1981

FRANCE-SOIR

Vocabulary	sensationalised, colourful	**froidement**	**engins**
		ouvert le feu	**'lâcher'**
		s'est écroulé	**Comble de malchance**
		la gorge traversée	**son deux roues**
		stopper	**hurle**
		passer en trombe	**brandit**
		sa Yamaha	**chancelle**

Verbs	begins with perfect and imperfect; at **esquissent un geste** changes to present until end; this heightens the effect, dramatising the event; in this passage the verbs are much stronger and more striking than in *Le Monde*

Manner of reporting	the event is recounted in an anecdotal manner, building up suspense; dwells on sensational details that are not reported in *Le Monde*
	sentences are short, broken up, especially towards the end
	very few conjunctions, thus accelerating the narrative
	sentences introduced by adverbs and adverbial phrases:

> **Froidement, un pistolet 11,43 en main, une femme ...**
>
> **Comble de malchance, un des policiers ...**
>
> **A pied, elle retraverse ...**

verbless sentence: **Une seule fois.**

snatches of speech, giving the report more verve: **et hurle: 'Arrêtez!'**

LE MONDE

Vocabulary	more factual and objective	**grièvement blessé**	**éviter un contrôle**
	evokes police report	**mardi 4 août**	**l'inconnue**
		Paris (7e)	**atteint à la tête**
		de calibre 11,43	**admis à l'hôpital**
			jugé préoccupant

Verbs	perfect tenses in 1st sentence, imperfect and pluperfect in 2nd, past historic in 3rd, perfect and present in last
	a number of verbs in passive mood, absent from *France-Soir*

Manner of reporting	As opposed to the more violent approach of *France-Soir*, the article flows more easily. The reporting is more formal and neutral: the facts, details of identity, place and the result of the incident are given without comment, in keeping with the general informative tone of *Le Monde*. Attention is focussed upon the victim rather than upon the perpetrator of the crime and the action itself.
	It contains comparatively more relative pronouns and the sentences are more complex in structure than in *France-Soir*.

2 Vocabulary

2.1 Misleading similarities: deceptive cognates

Apparent similarities between words in the English and French languages are a constant source of confusion. Words which look the same or very similar in the two languages, but which have different meanings, are called 'deceptive cognates' or more commonly '*faux amis*'. Deceptive cognates may be divided into two types: 1. deceptive cognates proper, in which the meanings are completely unconnected, and 2. partial deceptive cognates, in which only part of the meanings of the words coincides. Partial deceptive cognates will be discussed and illustrated in **2.1.2**.

2.1.1 Deceptive cognates proper

'Faux ami'	English translation	English	French translation
achèvement (m)	*completion*	achievement	***accomplissement*** (m), ***exploit***(m)
achever	*to complete*	to achieve	***accomplir***
actuel	*present*	actual	***véritable***
agenda (m)	*diary (for future events)*	agenda	***ordre***(m) ***du jour***
agonie (f)	*death pangs*	agony	***angoisse***(f)
agoniser	*to be suffering death pangs*	to agonise	***être au supplice***
agréer	*to suit (impers), accept with approval*	to agree	***être d'accord, convenir (2.4*** *agreeing)*
agrément (m)	*pleasure*	agreement	***accord***(m), ***traité*** (m)
allée (f)	*path, as in garden*	alley	***ruelle***(f)
s'altérer	*to change for the worse*	to alter	***changer***

'Faux ami'	English translation	English	French translation
avertissement (m)	*warning*	advertisement	**annonce**(f), **publicité**(f)
balancer	*to sway, to rock; R1 to chuck*	to balance	**se tenir en équilibre**
blouse (f) (2.3)	*smock (usually extending to the knees), overall*	blouse	**chemisier**(m)
car (m)	*coach*	car	**auto**(f), **voiture**(f)
cargo (m)	*cargo-boat*	cargo	**cargaison**(f)
caution (f)	*security, guarantee*	caution	**précaution**(f)
cave (f)	*cellar*	cave	**caverne**(f), **grotte**(f)
change (m), échange (m)	*exchange*	change	**changement**(m), **monnaie**(f)
chips (mpl)	*potato crisps*	chips	**pommes frites**(fpl)
comédien (m)	*actor*	comedian	**comique**(m)
commando (m)	*commando platoon or terrorist gang*	commando	**membre**(m) **d'un commando**
complainte (f)	*lament (song)*	complaint	**plainte**(f), **grief**(m)
complexion (f)	*constitution (2.2.5.2), temperament*	complexion	**teint**(m)
conducteur (m)	*driver*	conductor	**receveur**(m) (*on bus*), **chef**(m) **d'orchestre**
conférence (f)	*special lecture*	conference	**congrès**(m)
conforter R3	*to strengthen, to confirm*	to comfort	**réconforter**
conséquent	*rational, consistent*	consequent	**résultant**
content	*happy*	content	**satisfait**
convenance (f)	*convention, agreement*	convenience	**commodité**(f) (*but inconvenience = **inconvénient**(m)*)
course (f)	*race*	course	**série**(f) **de cours** (m), **stage**(m)
courtier (m)	*broker (in commerce)*	courtier	**courtisan**(m)
débonnaire	*easy-going, good-natured*	debonair	**jovial, insouciant**
déception (f)	*disappointment*	deception	**tromperie**(f)
délai (m)	*time allowed (but **sans délai** = without delay)*	delay	**retard**(m)
demander	*to ask for*	to demand	**exiger**
destituer	*to dismiss*	destitute	**indigent**
destitution (f)	*dismissal*	destitution	**dénûment**(m)

'Faux ami'	English translation	English	French translation
disgrâce (f)	*lack of attractiveness*	disgrace	**honte**(f), **déshonneur**(m) (*but to be in disgrace* = **être en disgrâce, défaveur**)
disgracieux	*ungainly*	disgraceful	**honteux, infâme**
donjon (m)	*castle keep*	dungeon	**cachot**(m)
drôle	*funny*	droll	**falot, saugrenu**
effectif (m) (usually pl)	*equipment, personnel*	effective	**efficace**
effectivement	*in reality, sure enough*	effectively	**efficacement**
énerver	*to annoy*	to enervate	**affaiblir**
engin (m)	*device*	engine	**moteur**(m)
entretenir	*to maintain in good condition*	to entertain	**amuser, divertir**
étable (f)	*cowshed*	stable (**2.2.5.2**)	**écurie**(f)
éventuel	*possible*	eventual	**final**
éventuellement	*possibly*	eventually	**à la longue, en fin de compte**
évidence (f)	*obviousness, fact*	evidence	**témoignage**(m), **preuve**(f)
évincer R3	*to remove (sb from office)*	to evince	**exprimer, manifester**
exténuer	*to exhaust*	to extenuate	**atténuer**
facile	*easy*	facile	**complaisant**
fastidieux	*boring, wearisome*	fastidious	**délicat, difficile à satisfaire**
fou	*mad*	fool	**idiot, sot**
gala (m)	*variety show, spectacle*	gala	**fête**(f), **compétition**(f) **de natation**
génial	*inspired, full of genius*	genial	**bienveillant, doux**
grief (m)	*grievance, complaint*	grief	**douleur**(f)
groin (m)	*snout (of animal)*	groin	**aine**(f)
habileté (f)	*skill*	ability	**capacité**(f)
hagard	*wild-eyed*	haggard	**les traits tirés**
halle (f)	*covered market*	hall	**vestibule**(m)
harasser	*to exhaust*	to harass	**harceler**
hardi	*bold*	hardy	**dur, robuste**
hurler	*to howl (animal), to roar or yell*	to hurl	**jeter, lancer**
incessamment	*immediately*	incessantly	**sans cesse**
incidence (f)	*repercussion*	incidence	**récurrence**(f), **taux** (m)
ingénu	*ingenuous*	ingenious	**ingénieux**

'Faux ami'	English translation	English	French translation
ingénuité (f)	*ingenuousness*	ingenuity	*ingéniosité* (f)
injure (f)	*insult*	injury	*blessure* (f)
intoxiquer	*to poison (food, etc)*	to intoxicate	*enivrer, soûler*
large	*wide*	large	*grand*
lecture (f)	*reading (a book, etc)*	lecture	*cours* (m)
libraire (m, f)	*bookseller*	librarian	*bibliothécaire* (m, f)
librairie (f)	*bookshop*	library	*bibliothèque* (f)
licence (f)	*(university) degree; licentiousness*	licence	*permis* (m)
logeur (m) (logeuse more common)	*landlord*	lodger	*locataire* (m, f)
luxure (f)	*lust*	luxury	*luxe* (m)
luxurieux	*lustful*	luxurious	*luxueux*
machiniste (m)	*props man, scene shifter (in theatre)*	machinist	*mécanicien* (m)
malice (f)	*mischievousness*	malice	*malveillance* (f), *méchanceté* (f)
maniaque	*finicky*	maniac	*dément*
marron	*brown*	maroon	*carmin*
molester	*to manhandle, to knock about*	to molest	*importuner*
monnaie (f)	*change (money)*	money	*argent* (m)
motoriste (m)	*car/aeroplane mechanic*	motorist	*automobiliste* (m)
notoire	*well-known*	notorious	*mal famé, mal réputé* (m)
ombrelle (f)	*parasol, sunshade*	umbrella	*parapluie* (m)
pantomime (m)	*mime show*	pantomime	*spectacle* (m) *de Noël*
parking (m)	*car-park*	parking	*stationnement* (m)
parloir (m)	*reception room (in school, etc)*	parlour	*salon* (m)
passer (un examen)	*to sit (an exam)*	to pass (an exam)	*être reçu (à un examen)*
performant (of high-performing machine/technique)	*highly efficient*	performing	*qui accomplit, remplit (un devoir)*
pétulant	*lively, frisky*	petulant	*irritable*
physicien (m)	*physicist*	physician	*médecin* (m)
pièce (f)	*room; special item (as in* pièce d'identité, pièce à conviction)	piece	*morceau* (m)
pondre	*to lay (an egg)*	to ponder	*méditer*
portier (m)	*doorman*	porter	*porteur* (m), *concierge* (m)

'Faux ami'	English translation	English	French translation
précipice (m)	*a chasm, abyss (eg* **on tombe dans un précipice,** *but = Eng precipice in such expressions as* **il était au bord du précipice)**	precipice	**paroi**(f) **abrupte**
préjudice (m)	*detriment*	prejudice	**préjugé**(m), **prévention**(f)
présentement	*at present*	presently	**tout à l'heure**
prétendre	*to claim, to assert*	to pretend	**faire semblant, feindre**
prévariquer	*to betray trust*	to prevaricate	**tergiverser**
procès (m)	*trial*	process	**processus**(m) **(2.3)**
râper	*to grate (food)*	to rape	**violer**
rente (f)	*(unearned) income, pension*	rent	**loyer**(m)
replacer	*to put back (again)*	to replace	**remplacer**
reporter	*to postpone, to delay*	to report	**rapporter**
ressentir	*to feel (an emotion)*	to resent	**être irrité, offensé** NOTE: but **ressentiment** = *resentment*
résumer	*to summarise*	to resume	**reprendre**
rétribution (f)	*remuneration, reward*	retribution	**châtiment**(m)
rude	*rough*	rude	**impoli**
sensible	*sensitive, perceptible*	sensible	**sensé, raisonnable, sage**
sentence (f)	*maxim; sentence (in law)*	sentence **(2.2.5.2)**	**phrase**(f); **sentence** (f) **juridique**
stage (m)	*training period*	stage	**scène**(f); **estrade** (f); **étape**(f)
starter (m)	*choke (for car)*	starter	**démarreur**(m)
studio (m)	*small flat (but* **studio d'émission** = *broadcasting studio)*	studio	**atelier**(m), **studio** (m)
trivial	*commonplace, vulgar*	trivial	**insignifiant**
trouble (m)	*agitation, confusion*	trouble	**peine**(f), **difficulté** (f)
truculent R3	*highly-coloured (of speech, face, etc)*	truculent	**brutal, féroce**
user	*to use up, to wear out;* R3 *to use*	to use	**employer, se servir de**
valable	*valid*	valuable	**précieux, de valeur**
venue (f)	*arrival*	venue	**rendez-vous**(m)

'Faux ami'	English translation	English	French translation
verbaliser (intrans)	*to book (of police)*	to verbalise	***traduire en paroles***
vers (m)	*line of verse*	verse	**strophe**(f), **verset** (m)
vicaire (m)	*curate*	vicar	*no exact equivalent:* **pasteur** (m) *(de l'église anglicane)*

2.1.2 Partial deceptive cognates

Partial deceptive cognates arise because of an ambiguity in a French or English word: for example the meaning of a French word may be included amongst the meanings of a similar-sounding English word, with the result that the two words have the same meaning in some but not all circumstances. In some respects this is a more troublesome and problematic area than that involving deceptive cognates proper, since, because in these cases there is overlap between the meanings of the French and English words, it is not possible to dismiss categorically the '*faux ami*', as on occasions it may be a true equivalent. The asymmetry of the meanings of certain French and English words may be illustrated by the following examples. The English word in the upper right quarter section of the diagrams provides the normal equivalent of the French word in the upper left section. It is in the lower part that the problem posed by partial deceptive cognates is highlighted. In the lower left section, the word in parenthesis implies occasional equivalence with the English word in the lower right quarter, while beneath it is given the more usual equivalent of the English word.

French	English
assistance (f)	audience (2.2.5.2)
(assistance (f) R3) aide (f)	aid
corps (m)	body
(corps (m)) cadavre (f)	corpse
emphase (f)	bombast
(emphase (f)) force (f)	emphasis

French	English
emphatique	bombastic
(emphatique) **énergique**	emphatic
fameux	notorious
(fameux) **célèbre,** **distingué, bien** **connu**	famous

Many other examples of deceptive cognates proper and partial deceptive cognates are to be found in **2.2** Homonyms and ambiguity, **2.3** Paronyms and **2.4** Synonyms, where they are indicated by a *.

2.2   Homonyms and ambiguity

Pairs and occasionally groups of words which are identical in sound but which are different in meaning are called homonyms, and are an obvious cause of ambiguity in a language. French in fact seems to be particularly affected by homonymy. However, various means of overcoming such ambiguity exist, the principal ones being context, gender and spelling. Because context is infinitely variable and is therefore not easily classified, the following sections show how gender and spelling, both singly and in combination, help distinguish between homonyms.

2.2.1   Homonyms differentiated by gender but with identical spelling

aide	M	assistant
	F	help; female assistant
aigle	M	male eagle (also general); insignia bearing an eagle (eg **l'aigle blanc de Pologne**)
	F	female eagle; heraldic sign; standard surmounted by eagle (eg **les aigles romaines**)
chose	M	R1 = thingummybob
	F	thing

crêpe	M	crepe (material)
	F	pancake
critique	M	critic
	F	criticism
drama-tique	M	drama (ie what is dramatic)
	F	short play on TV
finale	M	finale (in music)
	F	final (in football, etc)
garde	M	guard, warden
	F	protection; guards; private nurse
gîte	M	resting place, lodging (used largely in **Les Gîtes de France**)
	F	list of ship
greffe	M	record office
	F	graft, transplant
guide	M	guide (person or book)
	F	rein; girl guide
livre	M	book
	F	pound (weight or money)
manche	M	handle (of broom, etc)
	F	sleeve; **la Manche** = English Channel
manœuvre	M	labourer
	F	manoeuvre
martyre	M	martyrdom
	F	female martyr
mémoire	M	long dissertation, report; pl = memoirs
	F	memory
mode	M	method, mood (linguistic)
	F	fashion
mort	M	dead person
	F	death
moule	M	mould (for making sth)
	F	mussel

mousse	M	ship's boy
	F	moss; froth (on beer etc); rubber foam
office	M	function (**2.2.5.1**), role
	F	butler's pantry
œuvre	M	R3 = collected works
	F	(individual) work; R1, R2 = collected works
ombre	M	grayling (fish)
	F	shade, shadow
page	M	page-boy
	F	page of book or newspaper
pendule	M	pendulum
	F	clock
physique	M	physique
	F	physics
poêle	M	stove
	F	frying pan
poste	M	job, station; set (radio, TV)
	F	postal services
pupille	M	ward (as in **les pupilles de la nation**)
	F	pupil of the eye
somme	M	snooze
	F	amount, sum
tour	M	trick; turn
	F	tower; rook (chess)
vague	M	vagueness
	F	wave
vapeur	M	steamer
	F	steam
vase	M	vase
	F	slime
voile	M	veil
	F	sail

2.2.2 Homonyms differentiated by both gender and spelling

air	M	air
ère	F	era
aire	F	playing area; threshing floor; eyrie
bal	M	ball (dance)
balle	F	ball (spherical), shot; bale; R1 franc
bar	M	bar (for serving drinks)
barre	F	bar (of wood, metal, etc); tiller
but	M	aim, goal
butte	F	hillock
capital	M	capital, assets
capitale	F	capital city; capital letter
central (téléphonique	M	telephone exchange
centrale (électrique, nucléaire)	F	(generating) station
chêne	M	oak tree
chaîne	F	chain
col	M	collar; pass (in mountain)
colle	F	paste, glue
coq	M	cock
coque	F	shell, hull
cours	M	course; waterway
cour	F	court, yard
court (de tennis, de squash, etc)	M	court
fait	M	fact
faîte	M	apex of roof
fête	F	festival
foie	M	liver
foi	F	faith
fois	F	time, occasion

maire	M	mayor
mer	F	sea
mère	F	mother
pair	M	peer
paire	F	pair
père	M	father
parti	M	party (political, etc); decision
partie	F	part
surprise-partie R3	F	social party
pois	M	pea
poids	M	weight
poix	F	pitch
pot	M	pot
peau	F	skin
sel	M	salt
selle	F	saddle

2.2.3 Homonyms differentiated by spelling only

In these cases and also in those in **2.2.4** where no external distinction exists either by gender or spelling, the danger of ambiguity arises only if the words belong to the same word-class (part of speech) or closely related word-classes. In other words, it is unlikely for *vers* the preposition to be confused with *vert* the adjective, or for *tends* the imperative to be confused with *taon* the noun, whereas the identical pronunciation of *dessein* and *dessin*, and *tache* and *tâche* could well cause difficulty in understanding. In this section and the next, only those examples of homonyms involving words belonging to the same word-class or closely related word-classes (eg noun and adjective) are given.

censé		supposed
sensé		sensible
chair	F	flesh
chaire	F	throne, pulpit
cher/chère		dear
compte	M	account
comte	M	count, earl
conte	M	story

censé	supposed	
sensé	sensible	
cou	M	neck
coup	M	blow
coût	M	cost
dégoûter	to disgust	
dégoutter R3	to drip	
dessein	M	plan
dessin	M	drawing
être	M	being
hêtre	M	beech tree
faim	F	hunger
fin	F	end
haler	to tow, haul	
hâler	to tan (of sun)	
hâlé	sunburnt	
martyr	M	martyr
martyre	M	martyrdom
pain	M	bread
pin	M	pine tree
saut	M	jump
sceau	M	seal (wax)
seau	M	bucket
sot	M	fool
sain		healthy
saint	M	saint, holy (adj)
sein	M	breast, bosom; (also fig, eg **le sein de la terre**)
seing	M	signature
tache	F	spot, stain
tâche	F	task
vair	M	squirrel fur
ver	M	worm
verre	M	glass
vers	M	line of verse
vert	M	green

2.2.4 Homonyms with no external distinction either of gender or spelling

balle	F	ball (spherical)
balle	F	bale
goûter (noun)	snack	
goûter (verb)	to taste	
limon	M	fertile alluvium, silt
limon	M	lime (fruit)
louer	to hire	
louer	to praise	
ressortir conjugated like **sortir**		to go out again
ressortir conjugated like **finir**		to be under the jurisdiction of
son also **taches de**	M	bran
son		freckles
son	F	sound
timbre	M	stamp
timbre	M	bell
vol	M	flight
vol	M	theft
voler	to fly	
voler	to steal	

2.2.5 Words with more than one meaning: incommensurability of French and English

Similar problems arise when a single word in one language has two distinct meanings, or denotes two shades of meaning, each of which is expressed by a different word in the other language. When the words in the two languages sound alike, this frequently produces partial deceptive cognates (**2.1.2**): such cases are indicated by an asterisk. The important point to grasp is that the words in the two languages do not cover precisely the same areas of meaning, and confusion can arise and the innocent speaker appear ridiculous.

2.2.5.1 French examples

allumer	to light (fire) to switch on (TV, etc)
amusant*	amusing enjoyable
appréhender	to arrest to fear
arrêter	to stop to decide, to fix (decree, rules)
assassinat* (m)	assassination murder
assister*	to attend R3 = to help, to assist
balancer	to swing R1 = to chuck
bandit* (m)	bandit crook, ruffian
bâtiment (m)	building boat
chasser*	to go hunting to chase away
complaisance* (f)	complacency willingness
confronter*	to compare to confront (legally)
conscience* (f)	conscience consciousness
contrôler*	to control to verify, to check
conventionnel*	conventional according to decorum
cynique*	R3 = entirely scornful of social convention (as in black humour) cynical (with regard to human goodness)
découper	to cut out (from newspaper, etc) to cut up (meat)

French examples

découvrir*	to discover to uncover (eg **se découvrir** = to take one's hat off)
délivrer*	to free from captivity to deliver (heavy goods)
dénoncer*	to reveal to denounce
émotion* (f)	emotion agitation, excitement
évoluer*	to develop, evolve to move around, along (fish in pool, cars on track, dancers in hall)
excéder*	R3 = to exceed to tire out
expérience* (f)	experience experiment
fermer	to shut to switch off (TV, etc)
figure (f)	face shape
formation* (f)	formation training
hôte* (m)	host guest
ignorer*	not to know (of things) to ignore
important*	important, outstanding serious (eg damage)
incliner*	to bow (**s'incliner**) to be inclined to (**incliner à, être enclin à**)
instruction* (f)	instruction judicial investigation (likewise **instruire**)
intelligence* (f)	intelligence R3 = understanding (with sb)
livrer	to place in custody to deliver (parcel, furniture)

French examples

loyal*	frank faithful
moral* (m)	moral (adj) morale, state of mind
morale* (f)	morals moral of story
office* (m)	function, office (2.2.5.2) agency, bureau (eg l'**Office National du Tourisme**)
opportunité* (f)	opportuneness R1 = opportunity
orphelin* (m)	orphan lacking one parent (eg **il est orphelin de père**)
parents (m pl)	members of a family mother and father
percevoir	to perceive to receive money (official)
place (f)	(market) square, position seat, room (space)
prétendre	to claim, to be a candidate to assert
sanctionner	to approve, validate to penalise
sensible*	sensitive perceptible
susceptible	touchy; sensitive capable of, able to
terrible*	frightening, terrible extraordinary R1 = great, fantastic
trafic* (m)	trading (eg drugs) traffic (2.2.5.2)
tronc* (m)	trunk (of body, tree) collecting box in church

French examples

vain*	R3 = vain
	empty, sham
vicieux*	vicious
	faulty (eg reasoning, expression)
voix (f)*	voice
	an individual's vote

2.2.5.2 English examples

*to abuse**	to insult	**insulter, injurier**
	to take advantage of	**abuser de**
*accomplishment**	completion	**accomplissement** (m)
	artistic attainment	**talent** (m)
*application**	diligence	**application** (f)
	for a job	**demande** (f)
*audience**	with pope	**audience** (f)
	in cinema, etc	**assistance** (f),
		spectateurs (m pl)
to balance	to keep in equilibrium	**maintenir en équilibre,**
		équilibrer
	of accounts, etc	**dresser le bilan**
*ball**	spherical	**boule** (f), **balle** (f)
		(**2.4** *ball*)
	dance	**bal** (m)
*bank**	of river	**rive** (f) (**2.4** *bank*)
	for money	**banque** (f)
*bar**	for serving drinks	**bar** (m)
	of metal, wood	**barre** (f)
*change**	transformation	**changement** (m)
	money	**monnaie** (f)
*character**	distinctive nature	**caractère** (m),
		caractéristique (f)
	person (in book, etc)	**personnage** (m)
*comfortable**	of person	**bien à l'aise**
	of thing	**confortable**
*competition**	rivalry	**concurrence** (f)
	contest in sport	**compétition** (f)
	academic	**concours** (m)
*consistent**	in reasoning	**conséquent, logique**
	in food	**consistant**

English examples

*constitution**	political	**constitution** (f)
	of body	**composition** (f)
*to cry**	to shout	**crier**
	to weep	**pleurer**
*cure**	restoration to health	**guérison** (f)
	course of treatment	**cure** (f)
*decent**	of wage, etc	**correct, décent, honnête**
	of moral quality	**honnête**
*editor**	of book	**éditeur** (m)
	of newspaper	**rédacteur** (m)
*epic**	noun	**épopée** (f)
	adj	**épique**
figure	of body	**taille** (f)
	number	**chiffre** (m)
*invalid**	unwell	**invalide, infirme, alité**
	not valid	**non-valable** (eg of train ticket)
to marry	to get married (**2.4** *marrying*)	**épouser, se marier à/avec**
	to give in marriage	**marier**
*modest**	humble	**modeste, humble**
	chaste	**pudique** (**2.3**)
*office**	place of work	**bureau** (m)
	function	**office** (m) (**2.2.5.1**)
*to order**	in commerce, restaurant	**commander**
	to command	**ordonner, commander**
*organ**	of the body	**organe** (m)
	musical	**orgue** (m)
*pathetic**	moving	**attendrissant, émouvant, pathétique**
	pitiful	**pitoyable**
*place**	location	**endroit** (m), **lieu** (m)
	room, space	**place** (f) (**2.2.5.1**)
*to preserve**	to keep in good condition, to maintain	**conserver**
	to protect	**préserver**
to realise	to understand	**réaliser, se rendre compte**
	to fulfil	**réaliser, créer**

	English examples	
*to recover**	to get better	**guérir**
	to retrieve	**R3 = recouvrer**
	to cover again, to cover over	**recouvrir**
*relations**	connections, relationships	**relations** (f pl), **rapports** (m pl)
	members of family	**parents** (m pl)
*to save**	to rescue	**sauver**
	money	**épargner, économiser,** **R3 = thésauriser**
sensible	aware	**conscient**
	well-behaved	**sensé**
*sentence**	in language	**phrase** (f)
	legal	**sentence** (f), **jugement** (m)
*square**	market square, large square	**place** (f)
	square with garden in centre	**square** (m)
	geometrical	**carré** (m)
*stable**	noun	**écurie** (f)
	adj	**stable, ferme**
study	intellectual	**étude** (f)
	room	**cabinet** (m) **d'étude**
*to succeed**	to be successful	**réussir**
	to follow	**succéder, suivre**
*traffic**	on roads	**circulation** (f)
	air, sea, road usage	**trafic** (m)
trunk	of body	**torse** (m), **tronc** (m)
	of tree	**tronc** (m)
	of car	**coffre** (m)
	for packing	**coffre** (m), **malle** (f)
	of elephant	**trompe** (f)

2.3 Paronyms

It quite frequently happens that certain pairs or groups of words are easily confused in French because, although they are not homonyms, they nevertheless sound very similar to one another. Such sets of words are called paronyms. The problem of confusion is further compounded when the meanings of the words are related to some extent. Such is often the case in the examples that follow. However, in a number of cases, a set of paronyms, linked by form and meaning is also related to other words, but by meaning only. Such cases are treated in section **2.4** Synonyms, to which reference is made after the appropriate words, eg

accroître	s'accroître	croître

The example is treated in the section on Synonyms because of the connection with *agrandir*, *augmenter* and *grandir*.

abaisser	**baisser**	**rabaisser**
to reduce height of (eg wall), also fig	to lower (general, eg head, blind)	to lower (eg price)
absorber*	**résorber**	
to absorb (eg liquid, ideas)	to absorb (an excess, eg of traffic)	
accroissement (m)	**croissance** (f)	
increase (in number, amount)	growth (organic, eg of plant, child, economics)	
accroître	**s'accroître** R3	**croître**
(see **2.4** *to increase*)		
achever R3	**parachever**	
to finish	to finish (more effort implied)	
affaiblir	**s'affaiblir**	**faiblir**
trans, to weaken	same as **faiblir**, to weaken	intrans, to weaken
affronter	**confronter**	
to face sb, sth	to place face to face; to compare	
agrandir	**grandir**	
(see **2.4** *to increase*)		
alpin*	**alpestre**	
alpine (of plant, sport, etc)	alpine (of view)	
amener	**ramener**	
(see **2.4** *to bring*)		
an (m)	**année** (f)	
year (general and specific)	year (emphasis on duration)	
anoblir	**ennoblir***	
to confer nobility upon	to exalt	

| **apercevoir** | **s'apercevoir** | **percevoir** |
| to perceive (visually and mentally) | to become aware | to perceive with senses |

| **aplanir** R3 | **aplatir** |
| to level (eg land); to smooth away (fig, eg difficulties) | to flatten (eg pastry) |

| **apparition** (f) | **parution** (f) |
| (see **2.4** *appearance*) | |

| **apporter** | **rapporter** |
| (see **2.4** *to bring*) | |

| **approcher** | **s'approcher** | **se rapprocher** |
| (see **2.4** *to approach*) | | |

| **arc** (m) | **arche** (f) |
| arc; style, shape of arch | arch (of bridge, etc) |

| **argenté** | **argentin** |
| silver-plated, silvery (colour) | silvery (of quality, sound) |

| **argument** (m) | **argumentation** (f) |
| argument supporting idea, fact | line of reasoning, way of arguing |

| **arrivage** (m) | **arrivée** (f) |
| arrival of goods | arrival of person |

| **assembler** | **rassembler** |
| (see **2.4** *to gather*) | |

| **attacher** | **rattacher** |
| to tie (eg horse to post) | to connect (eg two pipes) |

| **attentif*** | **attentionné** |
| paying attention to what is said | full of consideration |

| **attractif** | **attrayant** |
| (see **2.4** *attractive*) | |

| **au-dessous (de)** | **en dessous (de)** | **sous** |
| (see prepositions, eg **au-dessous de 3.4.4.1** and **beneath 3.4.4.2** and **2.4** *under*) | | |

| **au-dessus (de)** | **par-dessus** | **sur** |
| (see prepositions, eg **au-dessus de 3.4.4.1** and **above, over 3.4.4.2** and **2.4** *on, over*) | | |

auprès de near in space (suggests *with*, as in daughter staying *with* mother; R3 **il travaillait auprès de l'ambassade de France,** ie *with*)	**près de** near in space (**3.4.4.1**)
avance (f) military advance; financial advance	**avancement** (m) military and career advance
avare greedy for money	**avaricieux** = **avare** (less common)
baiser R3 = to kiss; R1 = to have intercourse with (indecent)	**baisser** to lower, see above **abaisser**
balle (f) (see **2.4** *ball* and **2.2.4**)	**ballon** (m)
balle (f) bale (of cotton, merchandise, etc)	**ballot** (m) packet, bundle; R1 = fool
banc (m) (see **2.4** *seat*)	**banquette** (f)
baril* (m) small barrel	**barrique** (f) barrel (size variable, according to province)
barre* (f) bigger and stronger than **barreau** (eg **barres parallèles**) (see **2.2.2**)	**barreau** (m) bar filling a specific space (eg chair, window)
se battre (see **2.4** *to fight*)	**combattre**
beugler to moo	**meugler** to moo
blouse (f) smock (usu to knees)	**blouson** (m) short jacket
bord (m) edge (general)	**bordure** (f) edge (of road), edging (of dress)

boule (f) (see **2.4** *ball*)	**boulet** (m)	
cabane* (f) hut (of wood)	**cabanon** (m) habitable cabin (in S of France)	**cabine** (f) cabin (of ship); call-box (telephone)
calculateur* (m) calculator, adding machine (as in shop)	**calculatrice** (f) calculator (small, for pocket)	
camp (m) group of tents (but a **camp militaire** does not necessarily consist of tents)	**campement** (m) encampment, suggesting family group (eg gypsies, bedouin)	**camping** (m) camp-site
cantatrice (f) opera singer, etc (no M form)	**chanteur** (m) singer (general)	**chantre** (m) bard (eg **chantre de la Révolution**)
capot (m) bonnet of car	**capote** (f) military great-coat, hooded coat; hood (of car)	
capter to intercept, to receive (as on radio)	**capturer** to capture	**captiver** to captivate
capuche (f) hood (of anorak)	**capuchon** (m) monk's hood, hood, top (of pen, etc)	
caractère* (m) person's character, main feature	**caractéristique** (f) particular feature	
carnassier flesh-eating (animals, characterised by ferocity)	**carnivore** flesh-eating	
carré (m) geometrical square	**carreau** (m) window pane, tile	
cavalier horse-rider; R3 also = partner, escort (for dance)	**chevalier** knight	
cave (f) cellar	**caverne** (f) large, natural cave	

cerveau (m) intellectual capacity	**cervelle** (f) brain (organic)	
chaire* (f) pulpit; professor's chair	**chaise** (f) chair (general)	
change (m) currency exchange (see **2.1**)	**changement** (m) passing from one state to another	
char (m) tank	**chariot** (m) wagon (in Western films); fork-lift truck; supermarket trolley	**charrette** (f) farmer's cart
charge (f) (see **2.4** *load*)	**chargement** (m)	
chasser to go hunting, to chase away (see **2.2.5.1**)	**pourchasser** to pursue, to chase in order to catch	
se chauffer to warm oneself (eg near the fire)	**s'échauffer** to warm up, to prepare self (eg athlete)	
chercher to look for (general)	**rechercher** to look for (more effort, more formal than **chercher**)	
cheveux (m pl) hair (general)	**chevelure** (f) R3 hair	**cheveu** (m) a single hair; R3 = hair (in hairdressing profession)
chute (f) fall (general)	**rechute** (f) relapse (as in illness); error	
cisailles (f pl) shears (for cutting hedge, metal, etc)	**ciseaux** (m pl) scissors	
cloche (f) (see **2.4** *bell*)	**clochette** (f)	
coasser (**coassement** (m)) to croak (of frog)	**croasser** (**croassement** (m)) to caw (of crow)	
coffre (m) chest (box)	**coffret** (m) small, ornate chest	

col (m)	collet (m)	collier (m)
collar	trap for small animals	necklace

colorer*	colorier	
to give colour (natural or artificial)	to apply different types of colour (technical)	

compréhensible	compréhensif	
understandable	inclusive; understanding	

concilier	réconcilier*	
to reconcile (ideas, etc)	to reconcile (people)	

confiance (f)	confidence (f)*	
confidence	secret, item of confidence	

congeler/surgeler	geler	
to freeze (food)	to freeze (general, of weather, etc)	

conserver	préserver	
to keep in good condition	to protect	

consommer	consumer*	
to consume (food)	to consume (with passion)	

conter	raconter	
(see 2.4 *to relate*)		

coquillage (m)	coquille (f)	
(see 2.4 *shell*)		

cordage (m)	corde (f)	
ropes, rigging	rope	

couler	s'écouler	
to flow (water)	to flow (time), to flow away (water)	

cour (f)	cours (m)	course (f)
court, yard	class (eg in school); course of river, river	race

créateur	créatif	
creative (general)	creative (modern literary jargon)	

décade* (f)	décennie (f) R3	
period of 10 days (often = decade also)	decade	

dédicace (f) handwritten dedication	**dédication** (f) dedication (of book, monument, etc, general)
dédicacer* to make hand-written dedication in book	**dédier** to dedicate (book, monument, etc, general)
défaut (m) blemish, defect (in machine, etc), failing (in character)	**faute** (f) error, misdeed, offence (in sport)
défectueux defective (general)	**défectif*** grammatical term (eg **verbe défectif**)
dégoutter R3 to drip (of liquid)	**s'égoutter** to drip (of crockery, etc)
délivrer (see **2.2.5.1**)	**livrer**
dentaire relating to teeth	**dental*** dental (phonetic term)

dépasser to overtake (car); to surpass (hopes, etc)	**outrepasser** as **surpasser**, but stronger	**surpasser** to go beyond (in most senses)

déposer to set down (eg **déposer une requête/qn à la gare**)	**poser** to put down (eg **poser un objet**)
désert* deserted, uninhabited	**désertique** with desert conditions
désespérance (f) R3 despair (literary)	**désespoir** (m) despair (general)
désintérêt (m) lack of interest	**désintéressement** (m) unselfishness
desservir to serve town, etc (as with bus, train); to clear away (table)	**servir** to serve person, country
destin (m) (see **2.4** *fortune*)	**destinée** (f)

dévotion* (f)	**dévouement** (m)		
devotion (usu religious)	devotion (general)		

différence* (f)	**différend** (m)
difference	dispute

difforme	**informe**
deformed	shapeless

dormir	**endormir**	**s'endormir**	**se rendormir**
to sleep (general)	to put to sleep	to fall asleep	to go back to sleep

durcir	**(s') endurcir**
trans and intrans more concrete than **endurcir**, suggests hardening of materials (eg soil) and attitudes (eg political)	used largely in abstract sense (eg of emotions)

éboulement (m)	**éboulis** (m)
landslide in motion	result of landslide

échapper à	**s'échapper de**
to avoid (eg **échapper à un danger**)	to get out of (eg **s'échapper de la maison**)

éclairer	**éclaircir**
to give light	to explain

économe	**économique***
thrifty (of persons)	relating to economics, economic (of things)

effarant	**effrayant**
bewildering; scary	frightful; terrifying

embûche (f)	**embuscade** (f)
ambush	ambush

emmêler/mêler	**mélanger**
to mix up, to muddle (eg **les cheveux emmêlés/mêlés**)	to mix, with suggestion of homogeneity (eg **mélanger de l'eau et du vin**)

emplir R3	**remplir**
to fill	to fill (general)

s'empresser R3	**se presser**
to hasten	to hasten

enchérir R3	renchérir	surenchérir
to go one better (less common)	to go one better	to offer a higher sum

énergique	énergétique*	
energetic	pertaining to energy (eg **la crise énergétique**)	

enfantin	infantil	
childlike	relating to childhood	

enfermer	renfermer	
to shut in	to shut in (more effort + intention)	

(s') enfler	(se) gonfler	
to swell (often involuntarily, eg leg, arm)	to swell (often voluntarily, eg lungs)	

entretenir	maintenir*	soutenir
to maintain, keep in good condition (eg a car)	to hold in a fixed position (eg **se maintenir en bonne forme**, seldom fig)	to support sth which might fall (both literally and figuratively (eg beam, argument, idea); more effort is required than with **maintenir**)

entrevue (f) R3	interview (f)	
(see **2.4** *interview*)		

envahissement (m)	invasion* (f)	
progressive occupation, encroachment (eg **l'envahissement du pouvoir central**)	brutal, rapid occupation (eg **l'invasion de la France en 1940**)	

épreuve (f)	preuve* (f)	
trial; proof of book	proof (general)	

éruption (f)	irruption (f)	
eruption	sudden entry or exit	

escadre (f)	escadrille (f)	escadron (m)
squadron in navy	squadron in airforce; flotilla of small ships	squadron in army

espérance (f) R3	espoir (m)	
hope (more permanent, eg **l'espérance est une grande consolation**)	hope (more precise, eg **il est très malade, il n'y a plus d'espoir**)	

éveiller to rouse from sleep	**réveiller** to wake up fully	
exciter (see **2.4** *to excite*)	**surexciter**	
exhibition* (f) spectacle (of animals or people)	**exposition** (f) exhibition (of objects)	
exploitant sb who exploits (eg **exploitant agricole**)	**exploiteur** sb who exploits illegally	
facilité* (f) ease	**faculté** (f) amenity; university faculty (**fac R**1)	
finlandais Finnish	**finnois R**3 Finnish (less common)	
fondation (f) (see **2.4** *foundation*)	**fondement** (m)	
fosse (f) pit, grave	**fossé** (m) ditch	
fourche (f) fork (in road, for gardening)	**fourchette** (f) fork (for eating); range or margin (statistics)	
fourgon (m) large van	**fourgonnette** (f) small van	
froid (m) cold (general)	**froideur** (f) cold temperament (of person)	**froidure** (f) **R**3 coldness of air
garde (m) guard (military)	**gardien** (m) warden, keeper (of prison, building)	
gel (m) (see **2.4** *frost*)	**gelée** (f)	
gentilhomme (m) **R**3 man of noble descent	**gentleman** (m) affected term for *gentleman*	
glacé frozen (eg earth, hands; fig eg reception)	**glacial** icy (usu of wind)	

glissade (f)	**glissière** (f)
slide (on ice, etc)	as in **porte à glissières**
	(= sliding door)
grain (m)	**graine** (f)
grain	seed
grogner	**grommeler**
to grumble	to speak gruffly,
	inarticulately
grosseur (f)	**grossesse** (f)
size	pregnancy
groupe (m)	**groupement** (m)
group (general)	grouping (eg **groupement**
	politique)
guérilla* (f)	**guérillero** (m)
guerrilla war	guerrilla
hache (f)	**hachette** (f)
axe (general)	small axe
humeur (f)	**humour** (m)
mood	humour
idiome* (m)	**idiotisme** (m)
dialect; language	idiom
immeuble	**immobilier**
real, fixed, of property; each restricted to certain fixed expressions	
(eg **biens immeubles/**	(eg **société de crédit**
immobiliers)	**immobilier** = building
	society, **agence**
	immobilière = housing
	agency)
immigrant (m)	**immigré** (m)
immigrant	immigrant (more common
	than **immigrant** as adj, eg
	les travailleurs
	immigrés)
inclination (f)	**inclinaison** (f)
action of will	incline, slope
infecter	**infester**
to infect	to infest

influencer	**influer sur** R3
to influence (general)	to influence (technical)
ingénieux*	**ingénu** R3
ingenious	ingenuous
ingéniosité (f)	**ingénuité*** (f)
ingenuity	ingenuousness
intérêt (m)	**intéressement** (m)
interest (general)	industrial involvement (eg **l'intéressement des travailleurs** = worker participation)
interrogation* (f)	**interrogatoire** (m)
question	interrogation (by police, etc)
isolation* (f)	**isolement** (m)
insulation	isolation
Israélien (m)	**Israélite** (m)
Israeli	Israelite (biblical)
joindre (see **2.4** *to join*)	**se joindre** **rejoindre**
jour (m)	**journée** (f)
day (general)	day (emphasis on duration)
labeur (m)	**labour*** (m)
labour	ploughing
lagon (m)	**lagune*** (f)
lagoon (formed by coral)	lagoon (general)
langage* (m)	**langue** (f)
language as means of communication, variety of **langue**	language of a country
lanterne (f)	**lanterneau** (m)
lantern (general)	small lantern (eg in dark part of a building)
lécher	**pourlécher**
to lick (general)	usu restricted to **se pourlécher les babines** (= to lick one's chops)

lier to tie up (eg a parcel)	**relier** to connect (eg 2 roads)	
livre (m) book (general)	**livret** (m) small book (bank book, school record book)	
logement (m) place where one stays	**logis** (m) R3 dwelling	
luire (see **2.4** *to shine*)	**reluire**	
luxueux luxurious (likewise **luxe** (m))	**luxurieux*** lecherous (likewise **luxure** (f) = lust)	**luxuriant** lush (of vegetation)
main d'œuvre (f) manpower, work force	**manœuvre** (m/f) manoeuvre; labourer (**2.2.1**)	
manier to handle deftly	**manipuler** to handle, using broader movements	
manque (m) lack	**manquement** (m) failure, weakness	
marais (m) marsh	**marécage** (m) marsh	
matériau (m) (see **2.4** *material*)	**matériel** (m)	
matin (m) morning (general)	**matinée** (f) morning (emphasis on duration)	
meuble (m) item of furniture	**mobilier** (m) suite of furniture, furniture in general	
mitraillette (f) (see **2.4** *gun*)	**mitrailleuse** (f)	
moral (m) moral (adj), morale (**2.2.5.1**))	**morale*** (f) morality, moral (of story (**2.2.5.1**))	
musée (m) museum (general)	**muséum*** (m) natural history museum	

natif R3 (see **2.4** *native*)	**natal**	

nuage (m) cloud (general)	**nuée** (f) R3 large cloud (suggesting a content, eg hail, locusts)	**nues** (f pl) R3 clouds (limited to certain expressions) (eg **porter qn aux nues** = to praise sb to the skies, **tomber des nues** = to arrive out of the blue)

offenser to offend (personally)	**offusquer** to offend (but not necessarily in a personal way)

officiel official	**officieux** semi-official, officious

offrande (f) offering, with religious connotation	**offre** (f) offer (general)

oppresser* to upset (eg **l'asthme l'oppresse**)	**opprimer** to oppress with violence (eg **un régime qui opprime ses citoyens**)

originaire coming from (a place)	**original*** peculiar, unusual	**originel** going back to the origins (eg **le péché originel**)

os (m) bone of man, animal	**ossements** (m pl) bones of dead person

paie (f) (see **2.4** *pay*)	**paiement** (m)

palace* (m) luxury hotel	**palais** (m) palace

paraître to seem	**apparaître** to appear physically (but **il apparaît** = it seems)	**comparaître** to appear (in law)

part* (f) share, portion	**parti*** (m) party (political, etc)	**partie*** (f) part of a whole (**2.2.2**)

partial* biassed	**partiel** partial, incomplete

peser	soupeser
to weigh with machine	to estimate weight

pétrolier	pétrolifère
related to oil (adj), oil-tanker (noun)	oil-bearing (strata, etc)

plier	ployer R3
to bend (general)	to bend (more formal)

plongée (f)	plongeon (m)
dive below surface (eg submarine)	dive from a height (eg in diving competition)

point (m)	pointe (f)
dot, speck	sharp point

poitrail (m)	poitrine (f)
breast or chest of animal	female breast (bosom), chest (of human being)

porteur (m)	portier (m)
porter	doorman, gatekeeper

poule (f)	poulet (m)
hen	chick, chicken when eaten

poussier (m)	poussière (f)
coal dust	dust (general)

préjudice* (m)	préjugé (m)
moral injury, wrong	bias, prejudice

préparatifs (m pl)	préparation* (f)
(only in pl)	

no clear distinction, although former more general than latter, eg **les préparatifs du mariage** (= all the work concerned with organising a wedding); **la préparation au mariage** (= last-minute preparations); **la préparation du budget, d'un plat**

procédé (m)	processus (m)	procès (m)	procédure (f)
technique	process	trial (in law), R3 = process of literary composition	procedure

proche	prochain
(see **2.4** *near*)	

prolongation (f)	**prolongement** (m)
act of prolonging beyond	increase in length (eg **le**
normal time (eg **la**	**prolongement d'une**
prolongation d'un	**rue**); consequences (eg **les**
congé, jouer les	**prolongements d'une**
prolongations = to play	**affaire**)
extra time)	
pudibond	**pudique**
easily shocked, prudish	modest, chaste
rabattre	**rebattre**
to fold down, to reduce	to hit again (eg **rebattre**
	les oreilles à qn = to
	repeat)
radier R3	**rayer**
usu to cross off name on	as **radier** but more
list	general; to scratch, to score
radoucissement (m)	**redoux** (m)
softening of mood, voice;	movement towards milder
movement towards milder	weather
weather	
raie (f)	**rayure** (f)
streak (general)	stripe, wider than **raie**
rang (m)	**rangée** (f)
(see **2.4** *row*)	
rêche	**revêche**
(see **2.4** *harsh*)	
reconstituer	**reconstruire**
to rebuild using same	to build all over again
elements	
recouvrer R3	**recouvrir**
(see **2.2.5.2**)	
refléter	**réfléchir**
(see **2.4** *to reflect*)	
reformer	**réformer**
to re-form (eg soldiers'	to change sb's ideas, etc
ranks); to reshape (more	with view to improvement;
concrete than **réformer**)	to discharge a soldier
	prematurely for health or
	other reasons

régler	**régir** R3	**réglementer**	**régulariser**
to regulate, to adjust (eg machine)	to rule, to govern	to make rules for	to regularise, to put into order (eg passport)

remplacer	**replacer**
to put sth in the place of sth else	to put back in place

renom (m)	**renommée** (f)
renown	renown

renoncement (m)	**renonciation** (f) R3
renunciation	renunciation

repartir	**répartir**
to leave (once more)	to share out, to distribute

répons* (m) R3	**réponse** (f)
response (in church liturgy)	answer

résonner	**sonner**
(see **2.4** *to ring*)	

(se) ressentir	**(se) sentir**
to feel (usu of emotions, intimate feelings)	to feel (general but often physical, as with blow)

restaurer*	**restituer**
to repair (eg house); to restore (eg king)	to restore to original state

retrait (m)	**retraite** (f)
withdrawal (of troops, not necessarily forced); withdrawal (from bank)	retreat (of troops, forced); religious retreat; pension, retirement (eg **prendre sa retraite**)

réunir	**unir**
(see **2.4** *to join*)	

rivage (m)	**rive** (f)
(see **2.4** *bank*)	

roc (m)	**roche** (f)	**rocher** (m)
rock, the substance	a stone, a rock (of granite, chalk, etc)	large rock (on mountain), rock (on sea-shore)

roman*	**romain**
Romanesque/Norman architectural style	Roman

séculaire* century-old	**séculier** secular		
séducteur (see **2.4** *to attract*)	**séduisant**		
sensé possessing good sense	**sensible*** sensitive; perceptible		
servant (m) (see **2.4** *servant*)	**serveur** (m)	**serviteur** (m)	
soir (m) evening (general)	**soirée** (f) evening (emphasis on duration)		
taper (see **2.4** *to knock*)	**tapoter**		
teindre to tint (hair, etc); to dye	**teinter*** to tinge (also fig and literary)		
teint* (m) colour/complexion (of face)	**teinte** (f) colour produced by mixing several colours; hue		
tendresse* (f) tenderness (of emotion)	**tendreté** (f) R3 tenderness (of meat)		
terrain (m) (see **2.4** *land*)	**terre** (f)		
toit (m) roof	**toiture** (f) roofing (ie roof + supports)		
tombe* (f) grave (general)	**tombeau** (m) tomb (more imposing than **tombe**, suggests monument)		
tourner to turn (eg a page)	**se tourner** to turn (of person)	**retourner** to turn over (eg earth)	**se retourner** to turn right round
triomphal triumphal (of things)	**triomphant** triumphant (of persons)		
trou (m) hole, gap (general)	**trouée** (f) hole (in hedge, wall, wood)		

val (m) R3 large valley (restricted use eg **Val de Loire**)	**vallée** (f) valley (general)	**vallon** (m) small valley
valable* valid (more common than **valide** in this sense)	**valide** valid, able-bodied	
veille (f) eve, day before; watch, vigil	**veillée** (f) staying up at night after evening meal	**réveillon** (m) late night supper, celebration; Christmas Eve, New Year's Eve
vénéneux poisonous to eat (eg **champignons vénéneux**)	**venimeux*** capable of injecting poison (also fig)	
vers* (m) line of poetry	**verset** (m) verse in Bible	
veste* (f) jacket	**veston** (m) jacket (but becoming out- of-date)	
vigne (f) vine (plant)	**vignoble** (m) vineyard	
vitrail (m) (see **2.4** *glass*)	**vitre** (f)	
vomissement (m) action of vomitting	**vomissure** (f) R3 what is vomitted (usu pl)	

2.4   Synonyms and words with related meanings

Every word in a language is connected to other words by a series of relationships, based particularly upon similarities of meaning and oppositeness of meaning. In this section attention is focussed upon synonyms – words which are more or less equivalent to each other in meaning – and words which, while not being exact synonyms, are nonetheless linked to each other by a similarity of meaning. In order to present this aspect of the vocabulary as simply and clearly as possible, a series of circles, representing broad concepts or groups of closely-related objects, are used. These circles, or 'semantic cells', are divided into segments encapsulating the French way of viewing these concepts and objects. It should be stressed that because the semantic cells are divided up according to a French perspective, the divisions frequently do not coincide exactly with the way an equivalent cell would have been divided up from an English point of view. An attempt has been made, therefore, to provide as accurately as possible corresponding words or definitions in English. The French words are always at the centre of the circles while the English translations or explanations are near the edge. Introducing each cell is a 'lead-in' word in English which indicates the concept or group of objects analysed in the cell itself. Words accompanied by an asterisk are also deceptive cognates (see **2.1**).

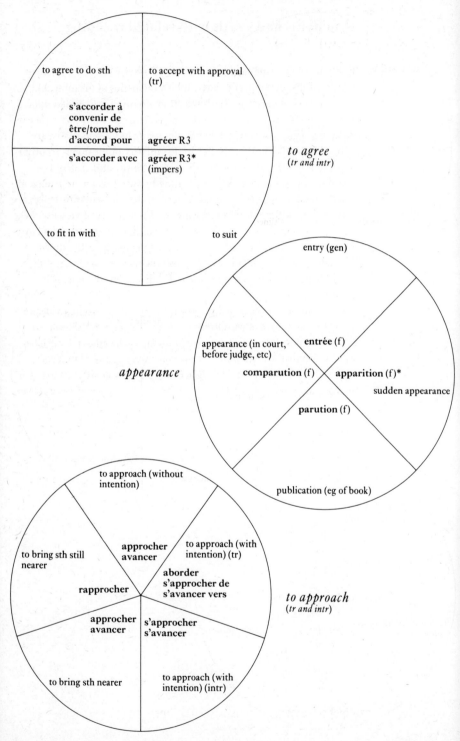

70

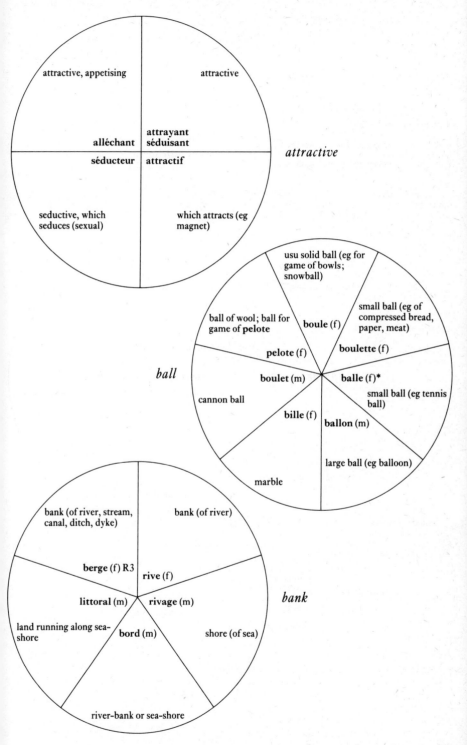

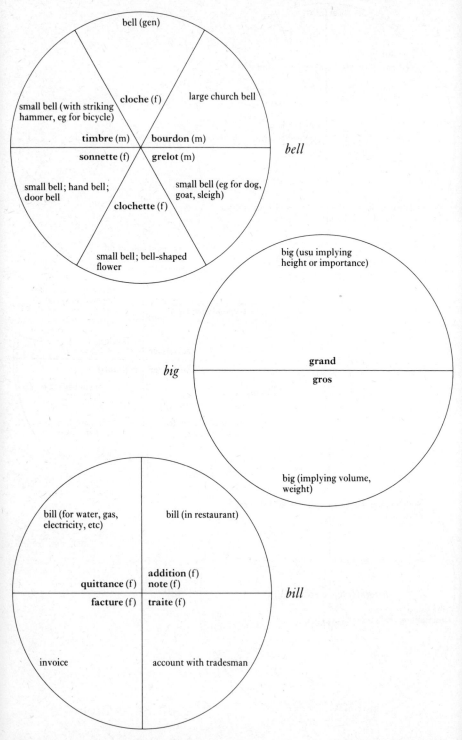

bell

bell (gen)

cloche (f)

large church bell

small bell (with striking hammer, eg for bicycle)

timbre (m)   **bourdon** (m)

sonnette (f)   **grelot** (m)

small bell; hand bell; door bell

small bell (eg for dog, goat, sleigh)

clochette (f)

small bell; bell-shaped flower

big

big (usu implying height or importance)

grand

gros

big (implying volume, weight)

bill

bill (for water, gas, electricity, etc)

bill (in restaurant)

addition (f)
note (f)

quittance (f)

facture (f)   **traite** (f)

invoice

account with tradesman

72

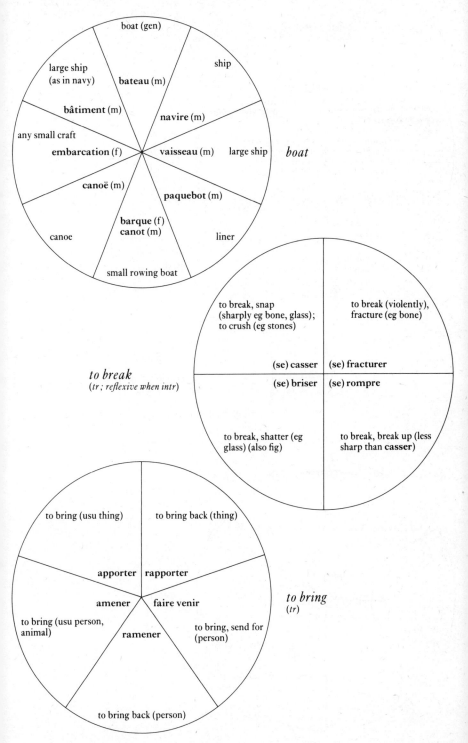

boat

- boat (gen) — **bateau** (m)
- ship — **navire** (m)
- large ship (as in navy) — **bâtiment** (m)
- any small craft — **embarcation** (f)
- large ship — **vaisseau** (m)
- canoe — **canoë** (m)
- liner — **paquebot** (m)
- small rowing boat — **barque** (f) / **canot** (m)

to break
(*tr ; reflexive when intr*)

- to break, snap (sharply eg bone, glass); to crush (eg stones) — **(se) casser**
- to break (violently), fracture (eg bone) — **(se) fracturer**
- to break, shatter (eg glass) (also fig) — **(se) briser**
- to break, break up (less sharp than **casser**) — **(se) rompre**

to bring
(*tr*)

- to bring (usu thing) — **apporter**
- to bring back (thing) — **rapporter**
- to bring (usu person, animal) — **amener**
- to bring, send for (person) — **faire venir**
- to bring back (person) — **ramener**

73

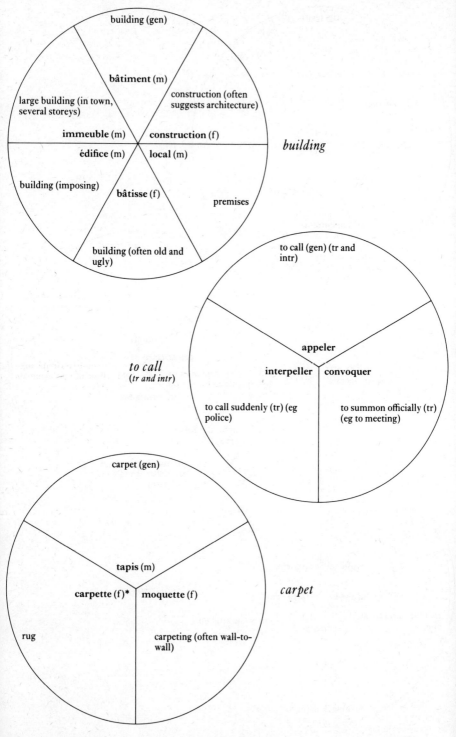

building

- building (gen) — **bâtiment** (m)
- large building (in town, several storeys) — **immeuble** (m)
- construction (often suggests architecture) — **construction** (f)
- building (imposing) — **édifice** (m)
- premises — **local** (m)
- building (often old and ugly) — **bâtisse** (f)

building

to call
(*tr and intr*)

- to call (gen) (tr and intr) — **appeler**
- to call suddenly (tr) (eg police) — **interpeller**
- to summon officially (tr) (eg to meeting) — **convoquer**

to call
(*tr and intr*)

carpet

- carpet (gen) — **tapis** (m)
- rug — **carpette** (f)*
- carpeting (often wall-to-wall) — **moquette** (f)

carpet

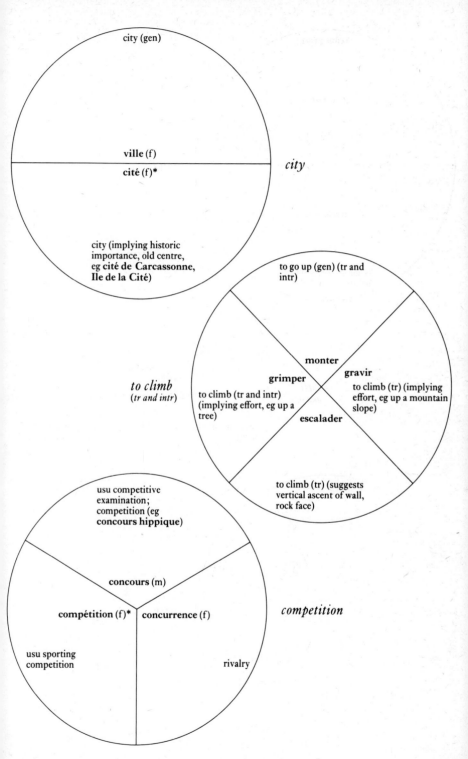

city

city (gen)

ville (f)
cité (f)*

city (implying historic importance, old centre, eg **cité de Carcassonne, Ile de la Cité**)

to climb
(*tr and intr*)

to go up (gen) (tr and intr)

monter

grimper

gravir

to climb (tr and intr) (implying effort, eg up a tree)

to climb (tr) (implying effort, eg up a mountain slope)

escalader

to climb (tr) (suggests vertical ascent of wall, rock face)

competition

usu competitive examination; competition (eg **concours hippique**)

concours (m)

compétition (f)* concurrence (f)

usu sporting competition

rivalry

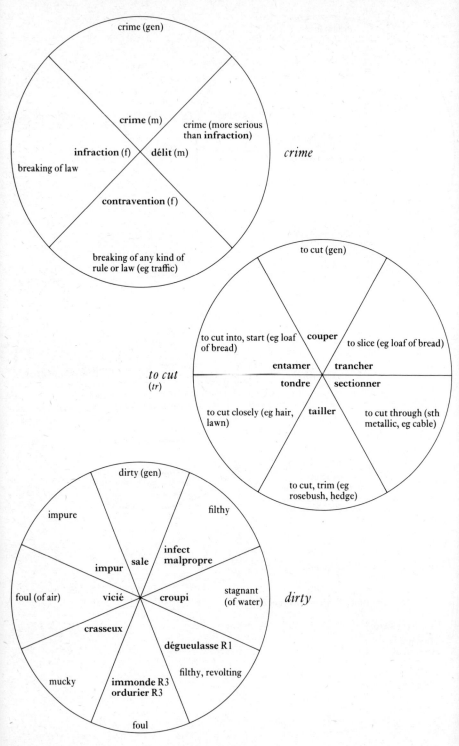

crime

crime (gen)

crime (m)
crime (more serious than infraction)

infraction (f) · délit (m)

breaking of law

contravention (f)

breaking of any kind of rule or law (eg traffic)

to cut (tr)

to cut (gen)

to cut into, start (eg loaf of bread) · couper

to slice (eg loaf of bread)

entamer · trancher

tondre · sectionner

to cut closely (eg hair, lawn) · tailler

to cut through (sth metallic, eg cable)

to cut, trim (eg rosebush, hedge)

dirty

dirty (gen)

filthy

impure

infect malpropre

impur · sale

foul (of air) · vicié · croupi

stagnant (of water)

crasseux

dégueulasse R1

mucky

immonde R3 ordurier R3

filthy, revolting

foul

76

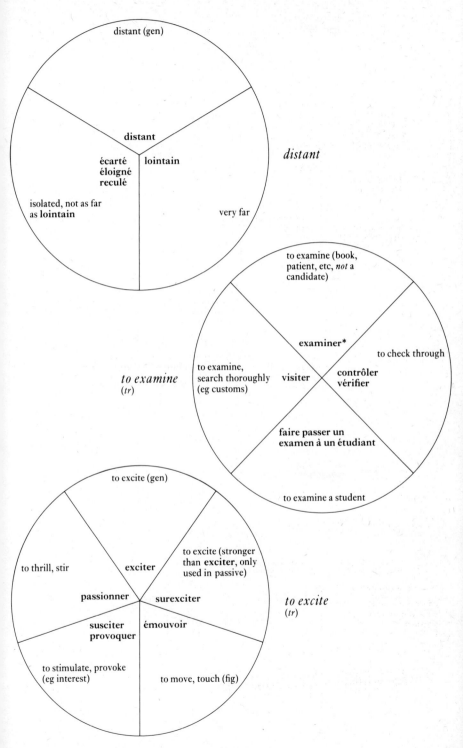

distant

distant (gen)

distant

écarté | lointain
éloigné
reculé

isolated, not as far
as **lointain**

very far

distant

---

to examine
(*tr*)

to examine (book,
patient, etc, *not* a
candidate)

examiner*

to check through

to examine,
search thoroughly
(eg customs)

visiter | contrôler
vérifier

faire passer un
examen à un étudiant

to examine a student

---

to excite (gen)

to thrill, stir | exciter

to excite (stronger
than **exciter**, only
used in passive)

passionner | surexciter

susciter | émouvoir
provoquer

to stimulate, provoke
(eg interest)

to move, touch (fig)

to excite
(*tr*)

77

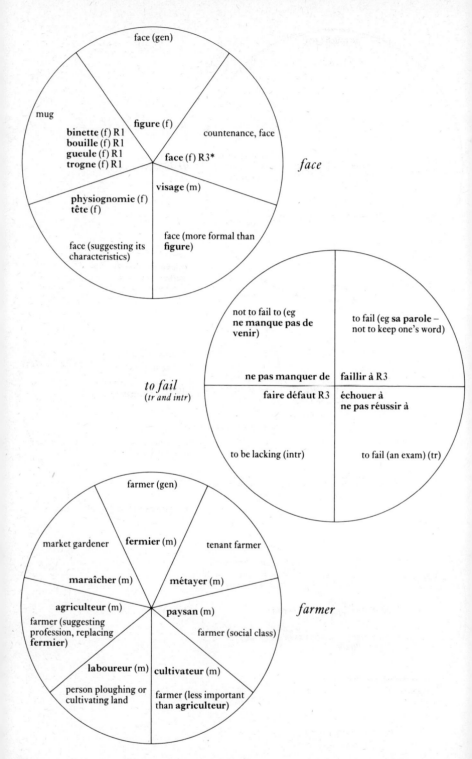

face

- face (gen)
- mug
- **figure** (f)
- **binette** (f) R1
- **bouille** (f) R1
- **gueule** (f) R1
- **trogne** (f) R1
- countenance, face
- **face** (f) R3*
- **physiognomie** (f)
- **tête** (f)
- **visage** (m)
- face (suggesting its characteristics)
- face (more formal than **figure**)

to fail
(*tr and intr*)

- not to fail to (eg **ne manque pas de venir**)
- to fail (eg **sa parole** – not to keep one's word)
- **ne pas manquer de**
- **faillir à** R3
- **faire défaut** R3
- **échouer à**
- **ne pas réussir à**
- to be lacking (intr)
- to fail (an exam) (tr)

farmer

- farmer (gen)
- market gardener
- **fermier** (m)
- tenant farmer
- **maraîcher** (m)
- **métayer** (m)
- **agriculteur** (m)
- **paysan** (m)
- farmer (suggesting profession, replacing **fermier**)
- farmer (social class)
- **laboureur** (m)
- **cultivateur** (m)
- person ploughing or cultivating land
- farmer (less important than **agriculteur**)

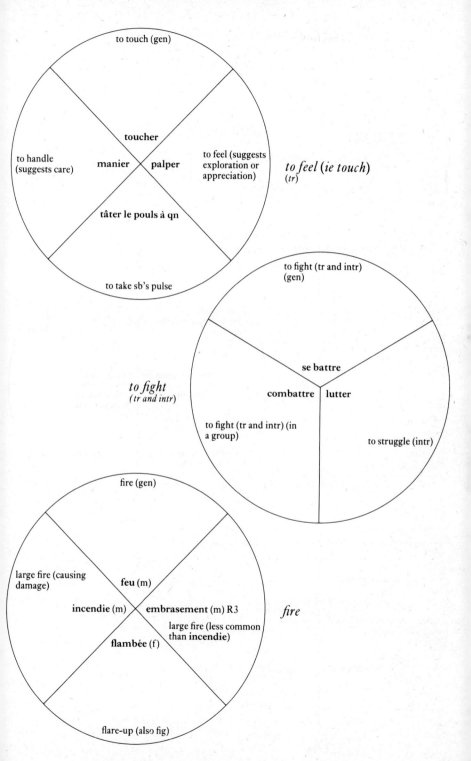

to touch (gen)

toucher

to handle (suggests care)

manier | **palper**

to feel (suggests exploration or appreciation)

to feel (ie touch)
(tr)

tâter le pouls à qn

to take sb's pulse

to fight (tr and intr) (gen)

se battre

to fight
(tr and intr)

combattre | **lutter**

to fight (tr and intr) (in a group)

to struggle (intr)

fire (gen)

feu (m)

large fire (causing damage)

incendie (m) | **embrasement** (m) R3

fire

large fire (less common than **incendie**)

flambée (f)

flare-up (also fig)

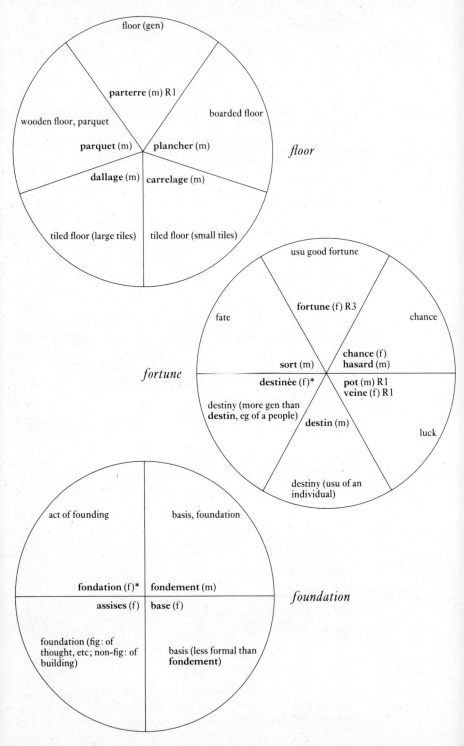

floor

- floor (gen)
- **parterre** (m) R1
- boarded floor
- wooden floor, parquet
- **parquet** (m) **plancher** (m)
- **dallage** (m) **carrelage** (m)
- tiled floor (large tiles)
- tiled floor (small tiles)

fortune

- usu good fortune
- **fortune** (f) R3
- fate
- chance
- **chance** (f) **hasard** (m)
- **sort** (m)
- **destinée** (f)*
- **pot** (m) R1 **veine** (f) R1
- destiny (more gen than **destin**, eg of a people)
- **destin** (m)
- luck
- destiny (usu of an individual)

foundation

- act of founding
- basis, foundation
- **fondation** (f)* **fondement** (m)
- **assises** (f) **base** (f)
- foundation (fig: of thought, etc; non-fig: of building)
- basis (less formal than **fondement**)

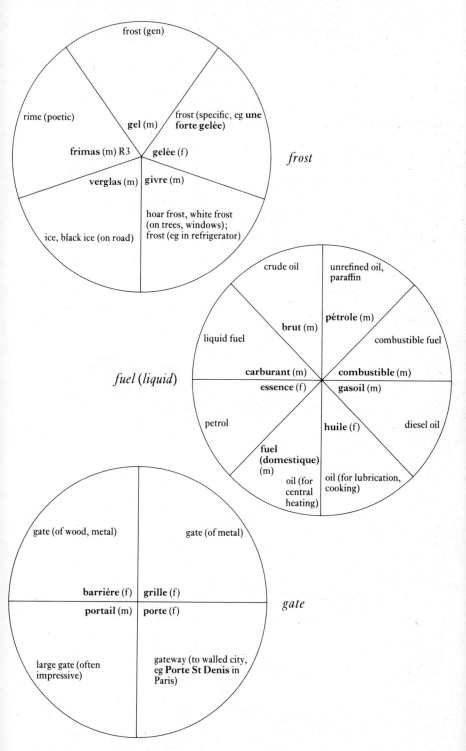

frost

- frost (gen)
- rime (poetic)
- frost (specific, eg **une forte gelée**)
- **gel** (m)
- **frimas** (m) R3
- **gelée** (f)
- **verglas** (m)
- **givre** (m)
- ice, black ice (on road)
- hoar frost, white frost (on trees, windows); frost (eg in refrigerator)

fuel (*liquid*)

- crude oil
- unrefined oil, paraffin
- **brut** (m)
- **pétrole** (m)
- liquid fuel
- combustible fuel
- **carburant** (m)
- **combustible** (m)
- **essence** (f)
- **gasoil** (m)
- petrol
- **huile** (f)
- diesel oil
- **fuel (domestique)** (m)
- oil (for central heating)
- oil (for lubrication, cooking)

gate

- gate (of wood, metal)
- gate (of metal)
- **barrière** (f)
- **grille** (f)
- **portail** (m)
- **porte** (f)
- large gate (often impressive)
- gateway (to walled city, eg **Porte St Denis** in Paris)

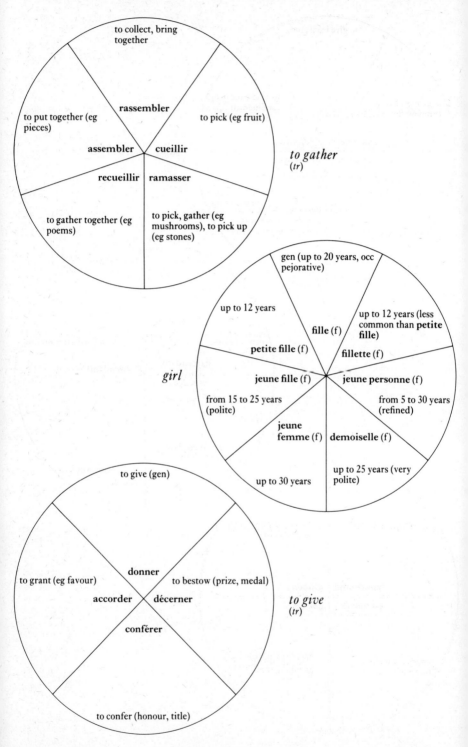

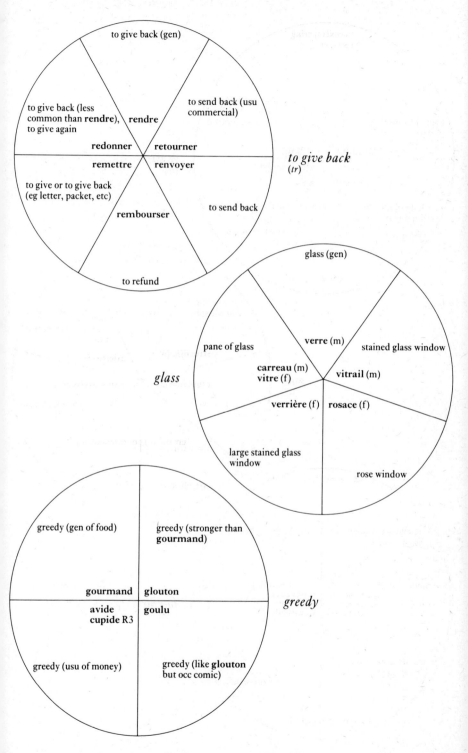

to give back (gen)

to give back (less common than **rendre**), to give again

to send back (usu commercial)

rendre

redonner **retourner**

remettre **renvoyer**

to give back (tr)

to give or to give back (eg letter, packet, etc)

rembourser

to send back

to refund

glass (gen)

pane of glass

verre (m)

stained glass window

glass

carreau (m) **vitre** (f)

vitrail (m)

verrière (f) **rosace** (f)

large stained glass window

rose window

greedy (gen of food)

greedy (stronger than **gourmand**)

gourmand **glouton**

avide **goulu**
cupide R3

greedy

greedy (usu of money)

greedy (like **glouton** but occ comic)

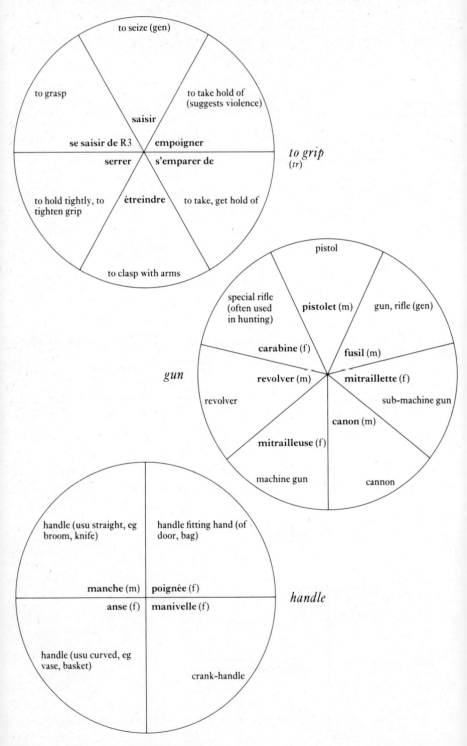

to grip *(tr)*

- to seize (gen)
- to grasp
- to take hold of (suggests violence)
- **saisir**
- **se saisir de** R3   **empoigner**
- **serrer**   **s'emparer de**
- to hold tightly, to tighten grip
- **étreindre**
- to take, get hold of
- to clasp with arms

gun

- pistol
- special rifle (often used in hunting)
- gun, rifle (gen)
- **pistolet** (m)
- **carabine** (f)   **fusil** (m)
- **revolver** (m)   **mitraillette** (f)
- revolver
- sub-machine gun
- **canon** (m)
- **mitrailleuse** (f)
- machine gun
- cannon

handle

- handle (usu straight, eg broom, knife)
- handle fitting hand (of door, bag)
- **manche** (m) | **poignée** (f)
- **anse** (f) | **manivelle** (f)
- handle (usu curved, eg vase, basket)
- crank-handle

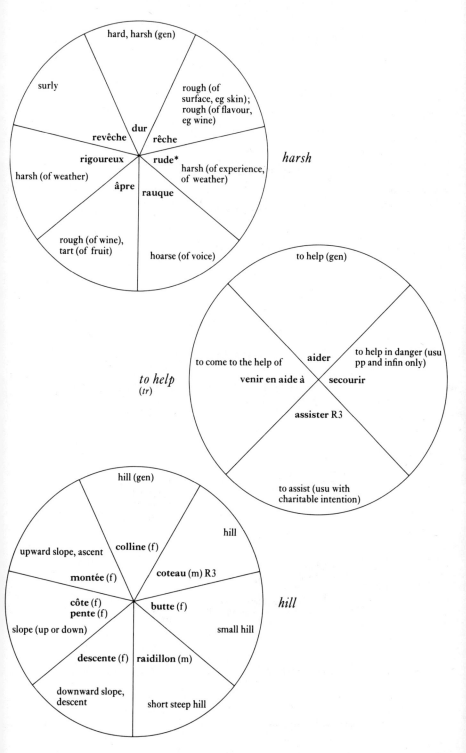

harsh

- hard, harsh (gen) — **dur**
- surly — **revêche**
- rough (of surface, eg skin); rough (of flavour, eg wine) — **rêche**
- harsh (of experience, of weather) — **rude***
- harsh (of weather) — **rigoureux**
- rough (of wine), tart (of fruit) — **âpre**
- hoarse (of voice) — **rauque**

to help (tr)

- to help (gen) — **aider**
- to help in danger (usu pp and infin only) — **secourir**
- to come to the help of — **venir en aide à**
- to assist (usu with charitable intention) — **assister** R3

hill

- hill (gen) — **colline (f)**
- hill — **coteau (m)** R3
- upward slope, ascent — **montée (f)**
- small hill — **butte (f)**
- slope (up or down) — **côte (f) pente (f)**
- downward slope, descent — **descente (f)**
- short steep hill — **raidillon (m)**

85

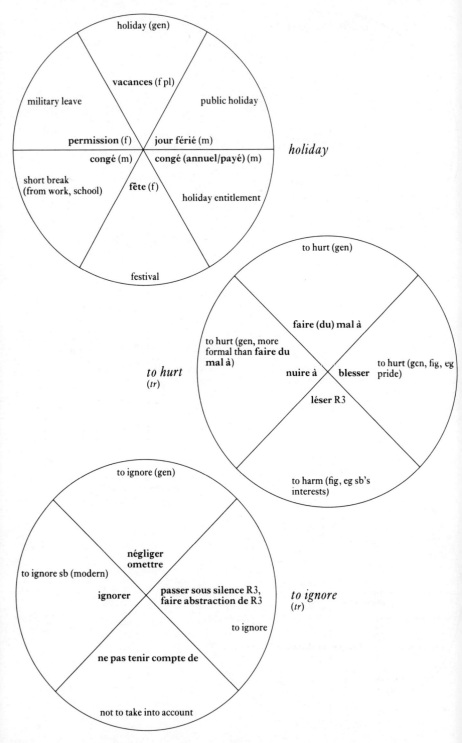

holiday

- holiday (gen)
- **vacances** (f pl)
- military leave
- public holiday
- **permission** (f)
- **jour férié** (m)
- **congé** (m)
- **congé** (annuel/payé) (m)
- short break (from work, school)
- **fête** (f)
- holiday entitlement
- festival

to hurt (*tr*)

- to hurt (gen)
- **faire (du) mal à**
- to hurt (gen, more formal than **faire du mal à**)
- **nuire à** **blesser**
- to hurt (gen, fig, eg pride)
- **léser** R3
- to harm (fig, eg sb's interests)

to ignore (*tr*)

- to ignore (gen)
- **négliger** **omettre**
- to ignore sb (modern)
- **ignorer**
- **passer sous silence** R3, **faire abstraction de** R3
- to ignore
- **ne pas tenir compte de**
- not to take into account

86

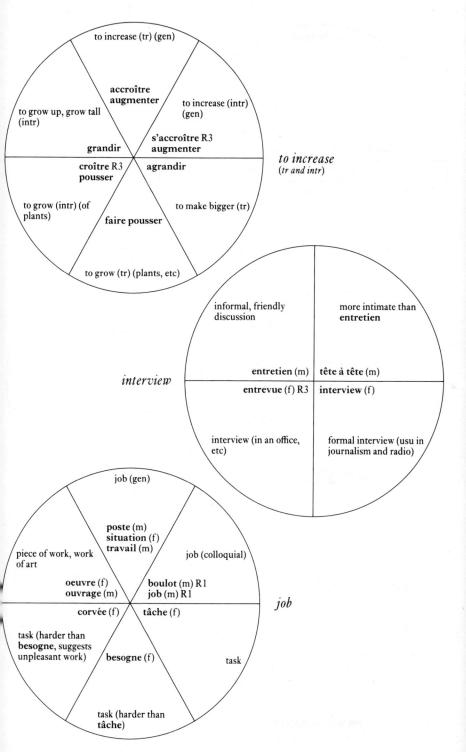

to increase
(tr and intr)

- to increase (tr) (gen)
- **accroître**
  augmenter
- to increase (intr) (gen)
- to grow up, grow tall (intr)
- **s'accroître** R3
  augmenter
- **grandir**
- **croître** R3
  pousser
- **agrandir**
- to grow (intr) (of plants)
- to make bigger (tr)
- **faire pousser**
- to grow (tr) (plants, etc)

interview

- informal, friendly discussion
- more intimate than **entretien**
- **entretien** (m)
- **tête à tête** (m)
- **entrevue** (f) R3
- **interview** (f)
- interview (in an office, etc)
- formal interview (usu in journalism and radio)

job

- job (gen)
- **poste** (m)
  situation (f)
  travail (m)
- job (colloquial)
- piece of work, work of art
- **boulot** (m) R1
  job (m) R1
- **oeuvre** (f)
  ouvrage (m)
- **corvée** (f)
- **tâche** (f)
- task (harder than **besogne**, suggests unpleasant work)
- **besogne** (f)
- task
- task (harder than **tâche**)

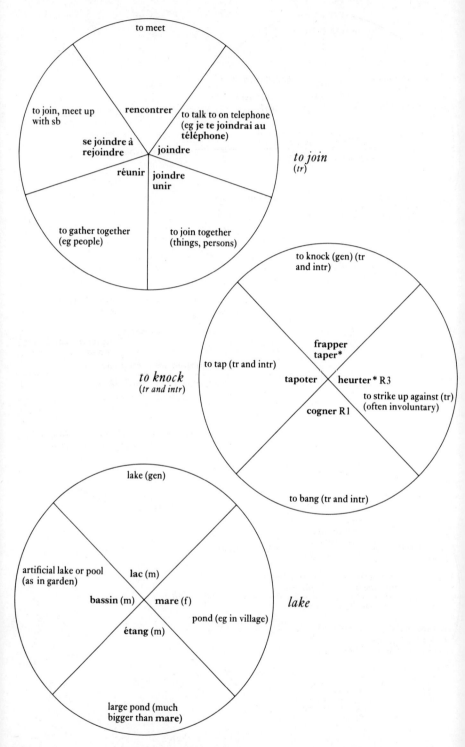

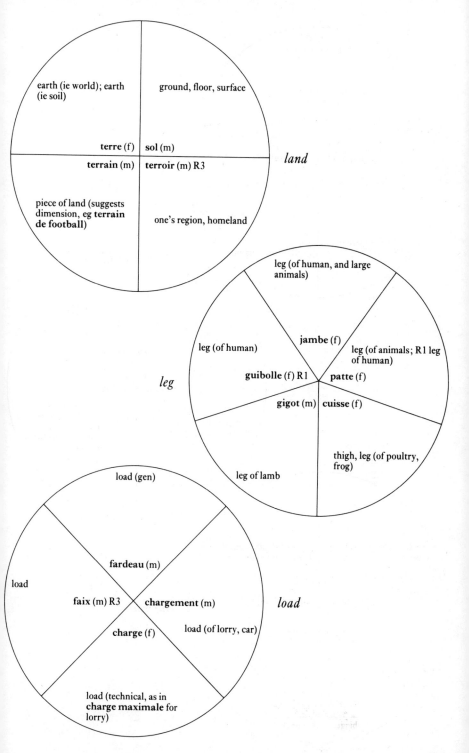

land

earth (ie world); earth (ie soil)

ground, floor, surface

terre (f) | **sol** (m)
terrain (m) | **terroir** (m) R3

piece of land (suggests dimension, eg **terrain de football**)

one's region, homeland

leg

leg (of human, and large animals)

leg (of human)

jambe (f)

leg (of animals; R1 leg of human)

guibolle (f) R1 | **patte** (f)

gigot (m) | **cuisse** (f)

leg of lamb

thigh, leg (of poultry, frog)

load

load (gen)

load

fardeau (m)

faix (m) R3 | **chargement** (m)

charge (f)

load (of lorry, car)

load (technical, as in **charge maximale** for lorry)

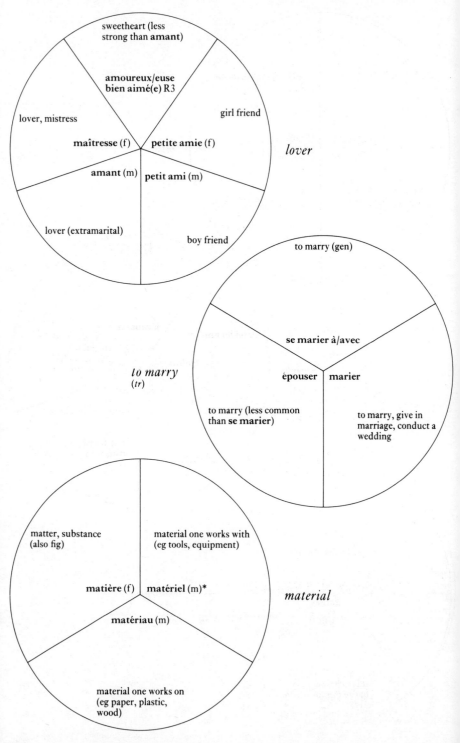

lover

- sweetheart (less strong than **amant**)
  - **amoureux/euse bien aimé(e) R3**
- girl friend
  - **petite amie** (f)
- lover, mistress
  - **maîtresse** (f)
- **amant** (m) **petit ami** (m)
- lover (extramarital)
- boy friend

to marry (*tr*)

- to marry (gen)
  - **se marier à/avec**
- **épouser** **marier**
- to marry (less common than **se marier**)
- to marry, give in marriage, conduct a wedding

material

- matter, substance (also fig)
  - **matière** (f)
- material one works with (eg tools, equipment)
  - **matériel** (m)*
- **matériau** (m)
- material one works on (eg paper, plastic, wood)

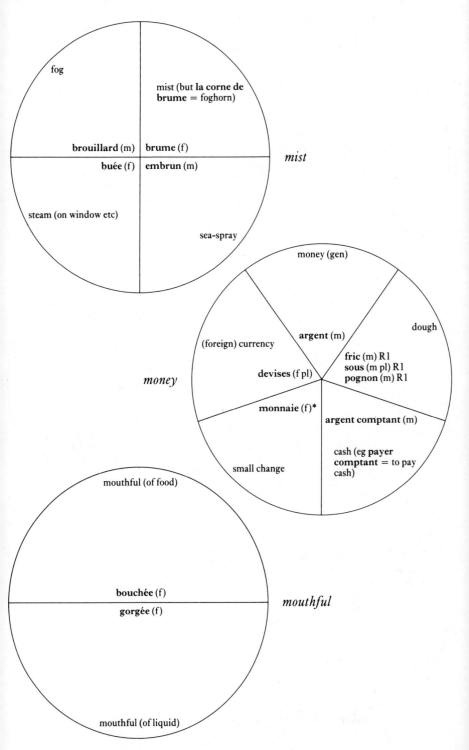

mist

fog

mist (but **la corne de brume** = foghorn)

brouillard (m) | **brume** (f)
buée (f) | **embrun** (m)

steam (on window etc)

sea-spray

money

money (gen)

(foreign) currency

argent (m)

dough

fric (m) R1
sous (m pl) R1
pognon (m) R1

devises (f pl)

monnaie (f)*

argent comptant (m)

small change

cash (eg payer **comptant** = to pay cash)

mouthful

mouthful (of food)

bouchée (f)
gorgée (f)

mouthful (of liquid)

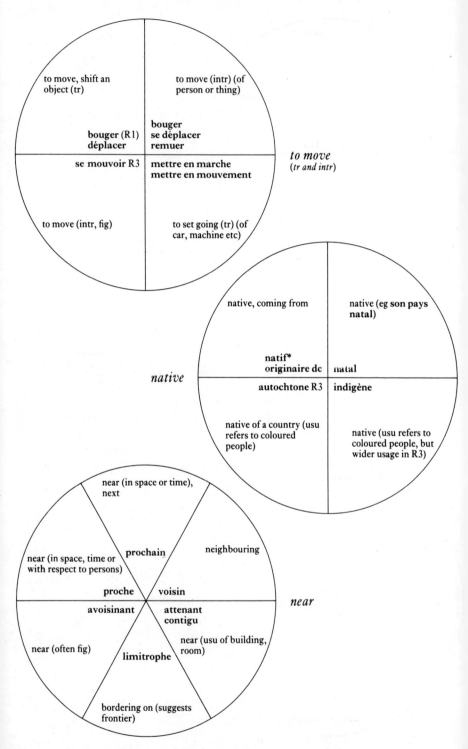

to move
(tr and intr)

- to move, shift an object (tr)
- to move (intr) (of person or thing)
- to move (intr, fig)
- to set going (tr) (of car, machine etc)

bouger (R1)
déplacer
se mouvoir R3

bouger
se déplacer
remuer
mettre en marche
mettre en mouvement

native

- native, coming from
- native (eg **son pays natal**)
- native of a country (usu refers to coloured people)
- native (usu refers to coloured people, but wider usage in R3)

natif*
originaire de
autochtone R3

natal
indigène

near

- near (in space or time), next
- neighbouring
- near (in space, time or with respect to persons)
- near (usu of building, room)
- near (often fig)
- bordering on (suggests frontier)

prochain
proche
avoisinant
voisin
attenant
contigu
limitrophe

92

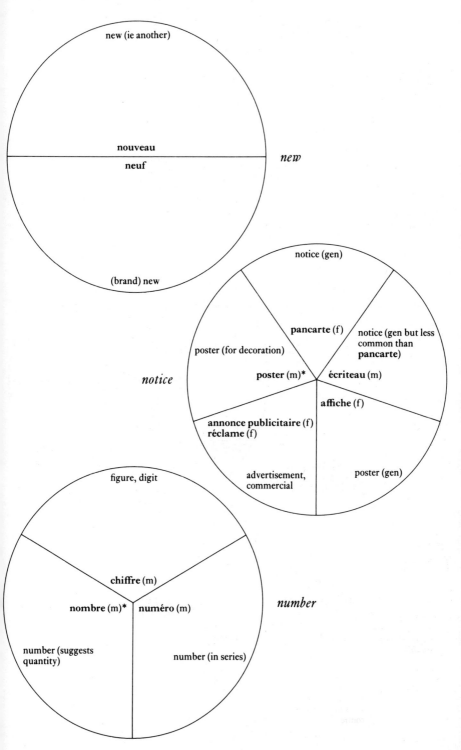

new (ie another)

nouveau
neuf

new

(brand) new

notice (gen)

pancarte (f)

poster (for decoration)

notice (gen but less
common than
pancarte)

poster (m)*   écriteau (m)

affiche (f)

notice

annonce publicitaire (f)
réclame (f)

advertisement,
commercial

poster (gen)

figure, digit

chiffre (m)

nombre (m)*   **numéro** (m)

number

number (suggests
quantity)

number (in series)

93

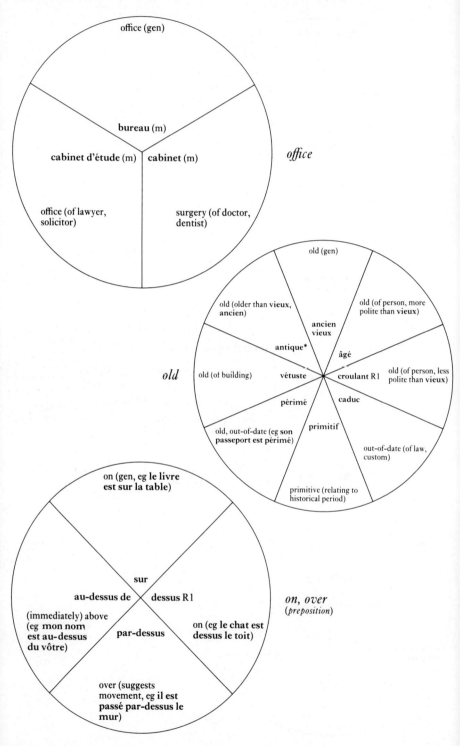

office

bureau (m)
office (gen)
cabinet d'étude (m)
office (of lawyer, solicitor)
cabinet (m)
surgery (of doctor, dentist)

old

ancien
vieux
old (gen)
old (older than vieux, ancien)
old (of person, more polite than vieux)
antique*
âgé
vétuste
croulant R1
old (of building)
old (of person, less polite than vieux)
périmé
caduc
old, out-of-date (eg son passeport est périmé)
primitif
out-of-date (of law, custom)
primitive (relating to historical period)

on, over
(preposition)

sur
au-dessus de
dessus R1
(immediately) above (eg mon nom est au-dessus du vôtre)
par-dessus
on (eg le chat est dessus le toit)
over (suggests movement, eg il est passé par-dessus le mur)

94

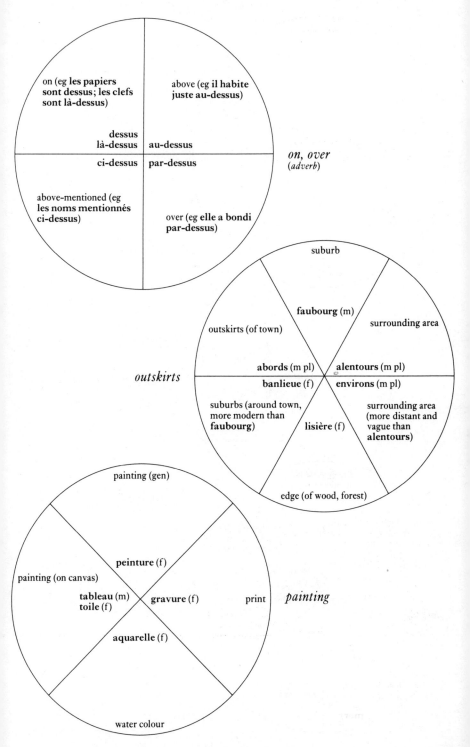

on, over *(adverb)*

on (eg **les papiers sont dessus; les clefs sont là-dessus**)

above (eg **il habite juste au-dessus**)

dessus
là-dessus au-dessus

ci-dessus par-dessus

above-mentioned (eg **les noms mentionnés ci-dessus**)

over (eg **elle a bondi par-dessus**)

outskirts

suburb

faubourg (m)

outskirts (of town)

surrounding area

abords (m pl) **alentours** (m pl)
banlieue (f) **environs** (m pl)

suburbs (around town, more modern than **faubourg**)

lisière (f)

surrounding area (more distant and vague than **alentours**)

edge (of wood, forest)

painting

painting (gen)

peinture (f)

painting (on canvas)

tableau (m) **toile** (f) **gravure** (f) print

aquarelle (f)

water colour

95

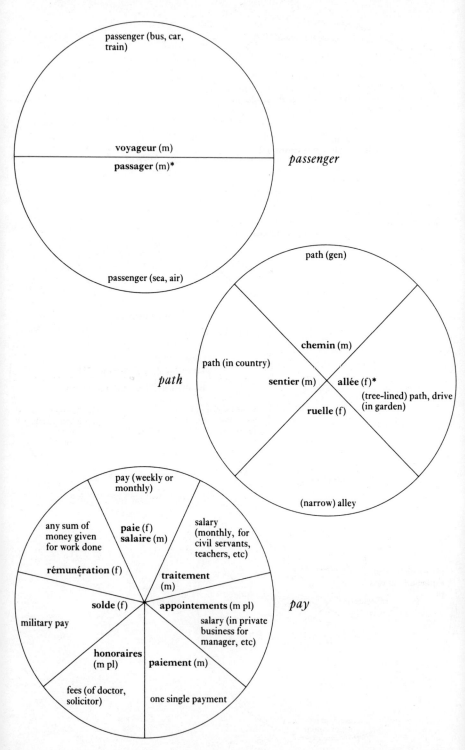

passenger

- passenger (bus, car, train)
- voyageur (m)
- passager (m)*
- passenger (sea, air)

path

- path (gen)
- chemin (m)
- path (in country)
- sentier (m)
- allée (f)*
- (tree-lined) path, drive (in garden)
- ruelle (f)
- (narrow) alley

pay

- pay (weekly or monthly)
- paie (f)
- salaire (m)
- any sum of money given for work done
- rémunération (f)
- salary (monthly, for civil servants, teachers, etc)
- traitement (m)
- solde (f)
- appointements (m pl)
- military pay
- salary (in private business for manager, etc)
- honoraires (m pl)
- paiement (m)
- fees (of doctor, solicitor)
- one single payment

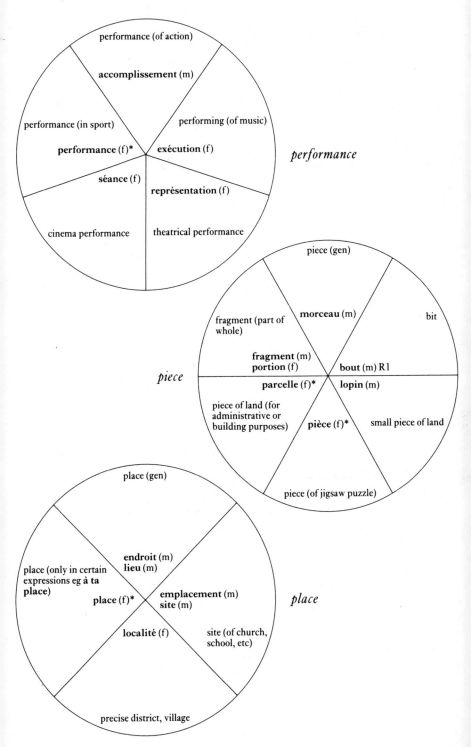

performance

- performance (of action) — **accomplissement** (m)
- performing (of music) — **exécution** (f)
- performance (in sport) — **performance** (f)*
- — **séance** (f)
- — **représentation** (f)
- cinema performance
- theatrical performance

pièce

- piece (gen) — **morceau** (m)
- bit
- fragment (part of whole) — **fragment** (m) / **portion** (f)
- **bout** (m) R1
- **parcelle** (f)* / **lopin** (m)
- piece of land (for administrative or building purposes)
- **pièce** (f)*
- small piece of land
- piece (of jigsaw puzzle)

place

- place (gen) — **endroit** (m) / **lieu** (m)
- place (only in certain expressions eg **à ta place**) — **place** (f)*
- **emplacement** (m) / **site** (m)
- **localité** (f)
- site (of church, school, etc)
- precise district, village

97

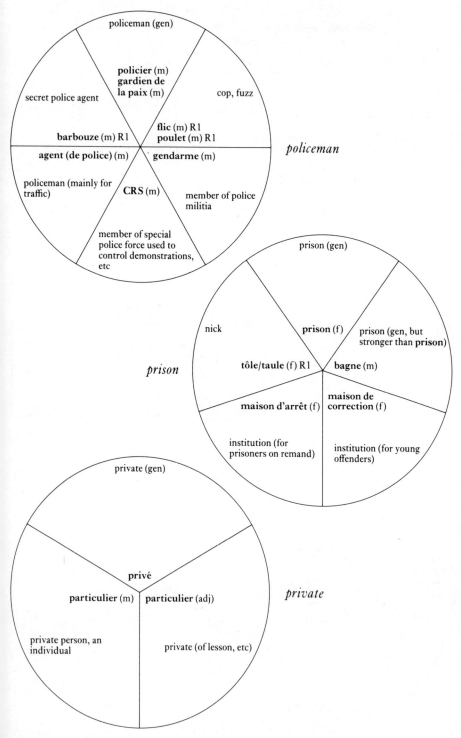

policeman

policeman (gen)

policier (m)
**gardien de
la paix** (m)

cop, fuzz

secret police agent

flic (m) R1
poulet (m) R1

barbouze (m) R1

agent (de police) (m)   **gendarme** (m)

policeman (mainly for
traffic)

CRS (m)

member of police
militia

member of special
police force used to
control demonstrations,
etc

prison

prison (gen)

prison (f)

nick

prison (gen, but
stronger than **prison**)

tôle/taule (f) R1   **bagne** (m)

maison d'arrêt (f)   **maison de
correction** (f)

institution (for
prisoners on remand)

institution (for young
offenders)

private

private (gen)

privé

particulier (m)   **particulier** (adj)

private person, an
individual

private (of lesson, etc)

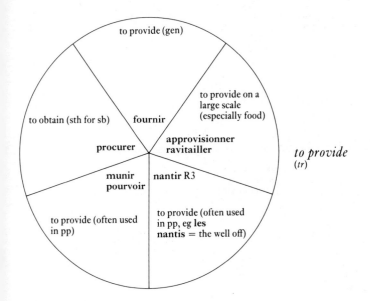

to provide
(tr)

purple/scarlet

mauve, light purple	violet, purple	purplish red	crimson	maroon, carmine	scarlet	light red, vermilion
mauve	violet	pourpre	cramoisi	carmin	écarlate	vermeil

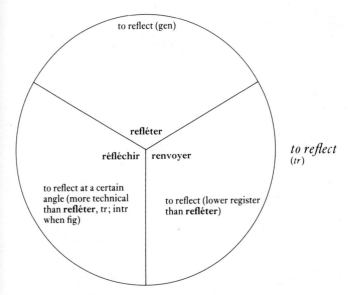

to reflect
(tr)

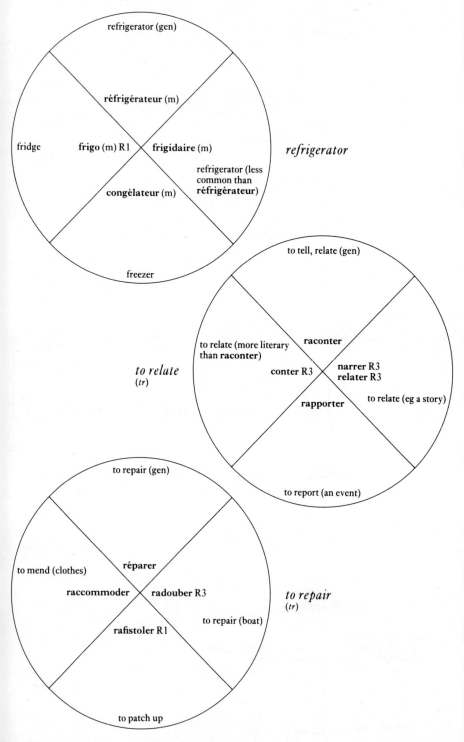

refrigerator

- refrigerator (gen)
- réfrigérateur (m)
- fridge
- frigo (m) R1
- frigidaire (m)
- refrigerator (less common than réfrigérateur)
- congélateur (m)
- freezer

to relate (*tr*)

- to tell, relate (gen)
- raconter
- to relate (more literary than raconter)
- conter R3
- narrer R3
- relater R3
- to relate (eg a story)
- rapporter
- to report (an event)

to repair (*tr*)

- to repair (gen)
- réparer
- to mend (clothes)
- raccommoder
- radouber R3
- to repair (boat)
- rafistoler R1
- to patch up

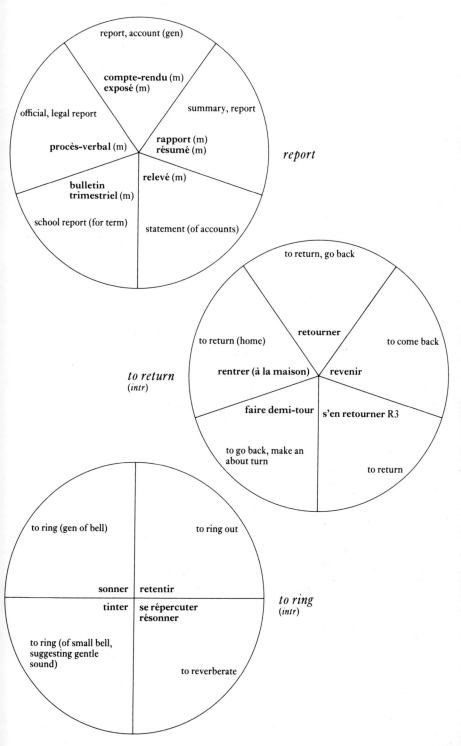

101

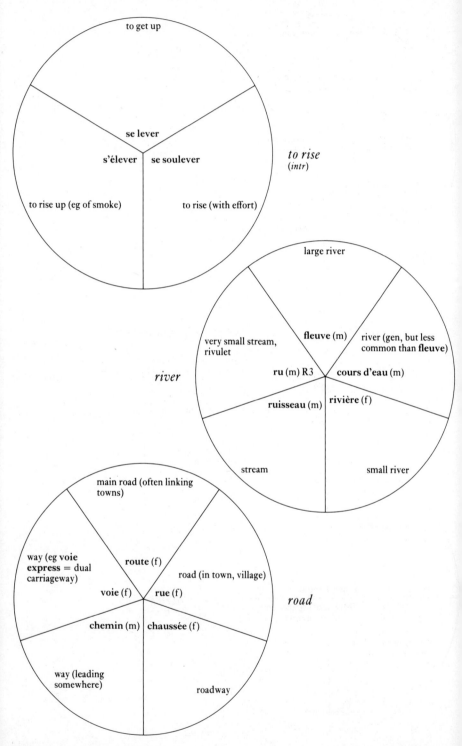

to get up

se lever

s'élever se soulever

to rise
(*intr*)

to rise up (eg of smoke) to rise (with effort)

large river

very small stream, **fleuve** (m) river (gen, but less
rivulet common than **fleuve**)

river **ru** (m) R3 **cours d'eau** (m)

ruisseau (m) **rivière** (f)

stream small river

main road (often linking
towns)

way (eg **voie** **route** (f)
express = dual
carriageway) road (in town, village)

voie (f) **rue** (f) *road*

chemin (m) **chaussée** (f)

way (leading
somewhere) roadway

102

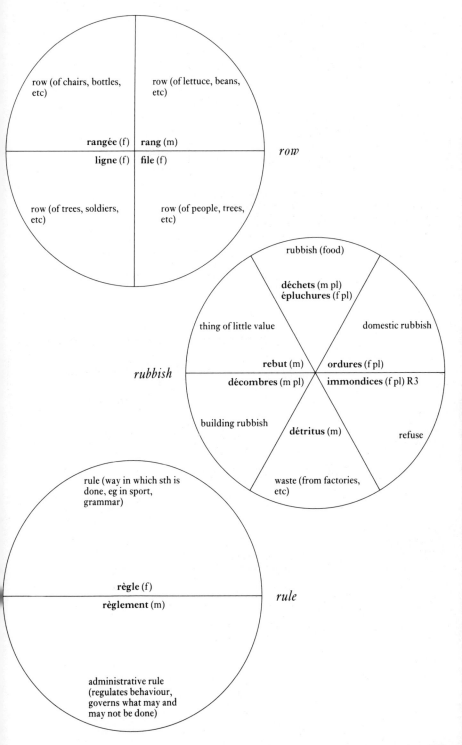

row

row (of chairs, bottles, etc)

row (of lettuce, beans, etc)

rangée (f)   **rang** (m)

ligne (f)   **file** (f)

row (of trees, soldiers, etc)

row (of people, trees, etc)

rubbish

rubbish (food)

déchets (m pl)
épluchures (f pl)

thing of little value

domestic rubbish

rebut (m)   **ordures** (f pl)

décombres (m pl)   **immondices** (f pl) R3

building rubbish

détritus (m)

refuse

waste (from factories, etc)

rule

rule (way in which sth is done, eg in sport, grammar)

règle (f)

règlement (m)

administrative rule (regulates behaviour, governs what may and may not be done)

103

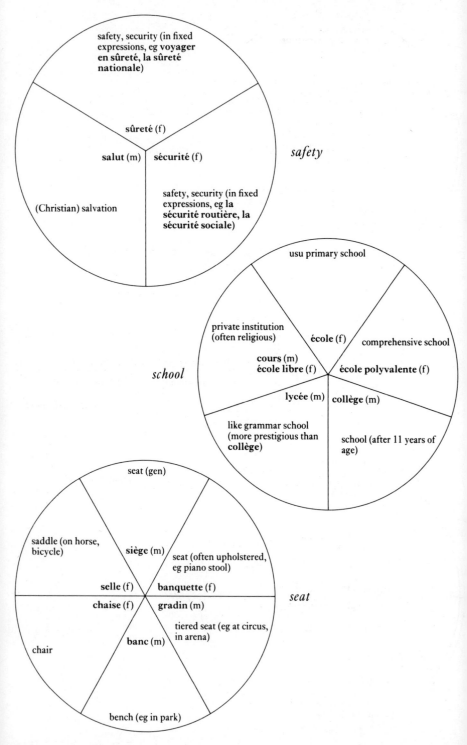

safety, security (in fixed expressions, eg **voyager en sûreté, la sûreté nationale**)

sûreté (f)

salut (m) | **sécurité** (f)

(Christian) salvation

safety, security (in fixed expressions, eg **la sécurité routière, la sécurité sociale**)

safety

usu primary school

private institution (often religious) | **école** (f)

comprehensive school

cours (m)
école libre (f) | **école polyvalente** (f)

school

lycée (m) | **collège** (m)

like grammar school (more prestigious than **collège**)

school (after 11 years of age)

seat (gen)

saddle (on horse, bicycle) | **siège** (m)

seat (often upholstered, eg piano stool)

selle (f) | **banquette** (f)

chaise (f) | **gradin** (m)

seat

tiered seat (eg at circus, in arena)

chair

banc (m)

bench (eg in park)

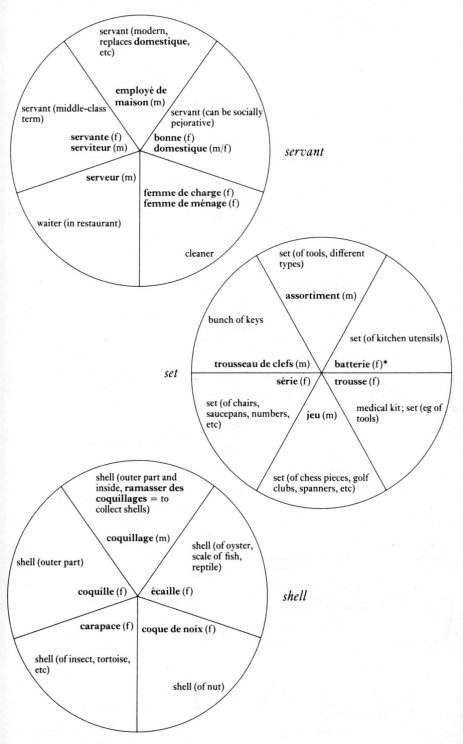

servant

- servant (modern, replaces **domestique**, etc)
- **employé de maison** (m)
- servant (can be socially pejorative)
- servant (middle-class term)
- **servante** (f) **serviteur** (m)
- **bonne** (f) **domestique** (m/f)
- **serveur** (m)
- **femme de charge** (f) **femme de ménage** (f)
- waiter (in restaurant)
- cleaner

set

- set (of tools, different types)
- **assortiment** (m)
- set (of kitchen utensils)
- bunch of keys
- **trousseau de clefs** (m)
- **batterie** (f)*
- **série** (f)
- **trousse** (f)
- set (of chairs, saucepans, numbers, etc)
- **jeu** (m)
- medical kit; set (eg of tools)
- set (of chess pieces, golf clubs, spanners, etc)

shell

- shell (outer part and inside, **ramasser des coquillages** = to collect shells)
- **coquillage** (m)
- shell (of oyster, scale of fish, reptile)
- shell (outer part)
- **coquille** (f)
- **écaille** (f)
- **carapace** (f)
- **coque de noix** (f)
- shell (of insect, tortoise, etc)
- shell (of nut)

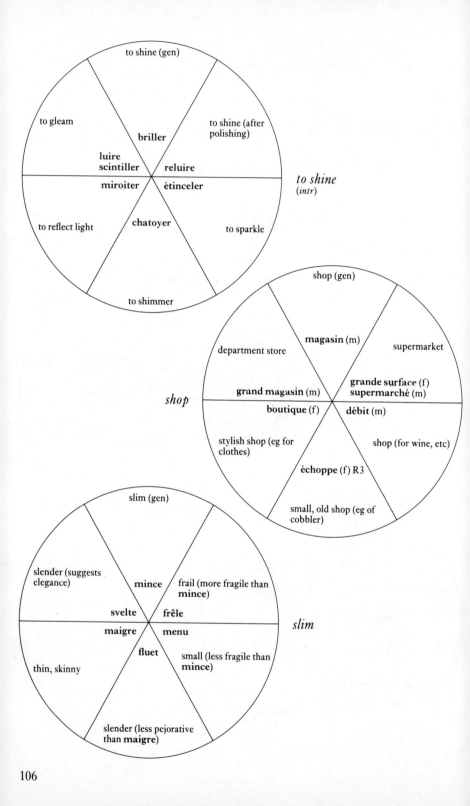

to shine (gen)

to gleam

to shine (after polishing)

briller

luire
scintiller **reluire**
miroiter **étinceler**

to shine
(*intr*)

chatoyer

to reflect light

to sparkle

to shimmer

---

shop (gen)

department store

supermarket

magasin (m)

grand magasin (m)

grande surface (f)
supermarché (m)

shop

boutique (f) **débit** (m)

stylish shop (eg for clothes)

shop (for wine, etc)

échoppe (f) R3

small, old shop (eg of cobbler)

---

slim (gen)

slender (suggests elegance)

frail (more fragile than **mince**)

mince

svelte **frêle**
maigre **menu**

slim

fluet

thin, skinny

small (less fragile than **mince**)

slender (less pejorative than **maigre**)

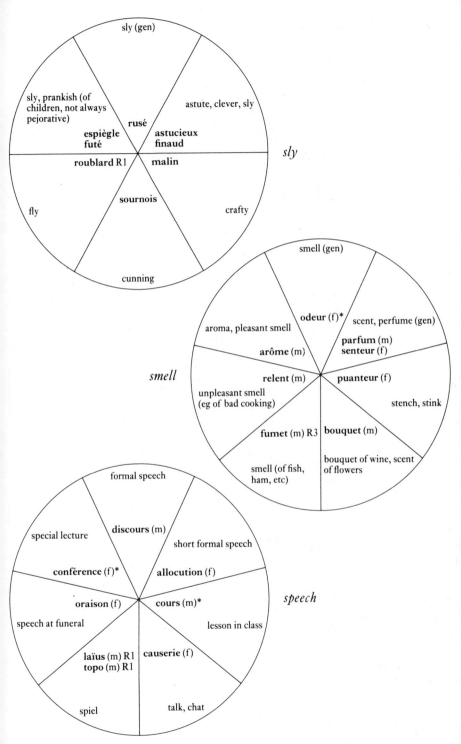

sly

- sly (gen) — **rusé**
- astute, clever, sly — **astucieux** / **finaud**
- **malin**
- crafty
- cunning
- **sournois**
- fly
- **roublard** R1
- sly, prankish (of children, not always pejorative) — **espiègle** / **futé**

smell

- smell (gen) — **odeur** (f)*
- scent, perfume (gen) — **parfum** (m) / **senteur** (f)
- **puanteur** (f)
- stench, stink
- bouquet of wine, scent of flowers — **bouquet** (m)
- smell (of fish, ham, etc) — **fumet** (m) R3
- unpleasant smell (eg of bad cooking) — **relent** (m)
- aroma, pleasant smell — **arôme** (m)

speech

- formal speech — **discours** (m)
- short formal speech — **allocution** (f)
- lesson in class — **cours** (m)*
- talk, chat — **causerie** (f)
- spiel — **laïus** (m) R1 / **topo** (m) R1
- speech at funeral — **oraison** (f)
- special lecture — **conférence** (f)*

107

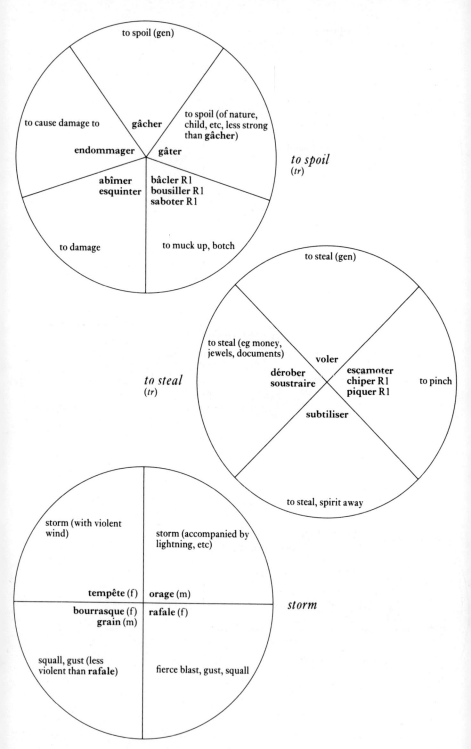

to spoil (gen)

to cause damage to

gâcher

to spoil (of nature, child, etc, less strong than **gâcher**)

endommager

gâter

abîmer
esquinter

bâcler R1
bousiller R1
saboter R1

to damage

to muck up, botch

to spoil
(tr)

to steal (gen)

to steal (eg money, jewels, documents)

voler

dérober
soustraire

escamoter
chiper R1
piquer R1

to pinch

subtiliser

to steal
(tr)

to steal, spirit away

storm (with violent wind)

storm (accompanied by lightning, etc)

tempête (f)

orage (m)

bourrasque (f)
grain (m)

rafale (f)

squall, gust (less violent than **rafale**)

fierce blast, gust, squall

storm

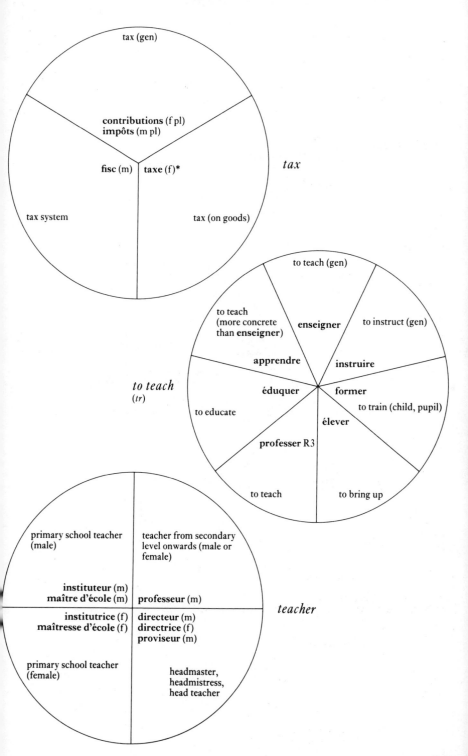

tax

- tax (gen)
- **contributions** (f pl)
  impôts (m pl)
- **fisc** (m) | **taxe** (f)*
- tax system
- tax (on goods)

to teach
(*tr*)

- to teach (gen)
- **enseigner**
- to instruct (gen)
- to teach (more concrete than **enseigner**)
- **apprendre**
- **instruire**
- **éduquer**
- **former**
- to educate
- to train (child, pupil)
- **élever**
- **professer** R3
- to teach
- to bring up

teacher

- primary school teacher (male)
- teacher from secondary level onwards (male or female)
- **instituteur** (m)
  maître d'école (m) | **professeur** (m)
- **institutrice** (f)
  maîtresse d'école (f) | **directeur** (m)
  directrice (f)
  proviseur (m)
- primary school teacher (female)
- headmaster, headmistress, head teacher

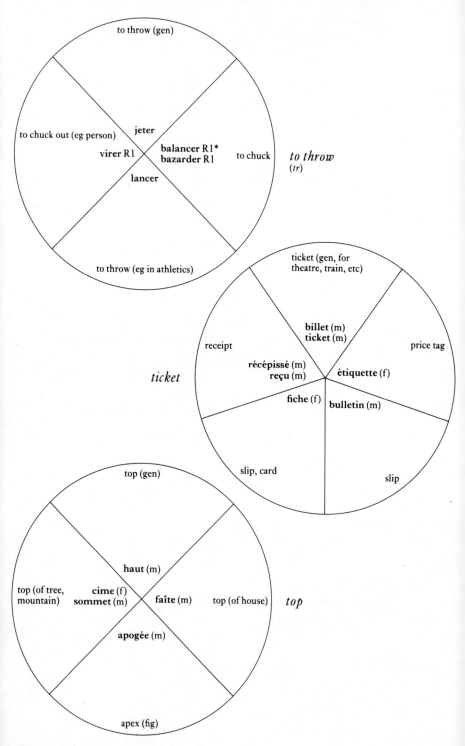

to throw (gen)

jeter

to chuck out (eg person)

virer R1 | balancer R1* | to chuck
bazarder R1

lancer

to throw
(*tr*)

to throw (eg in athletics)

ticket (gen, for theatre, train, etc)

billet (m)
ticket (m)

receipt | price tag

récépissé (m) | étiquette (f)
reçu (m)

fiche (f) | bulletin (m)

ticket

slip, card | slip

top (gen)

haut (m)

top (of tree, mountain)

cime (f) | faîte (m) | top (of house)
sommet (m)

apogée (m)

top

apex (fig)

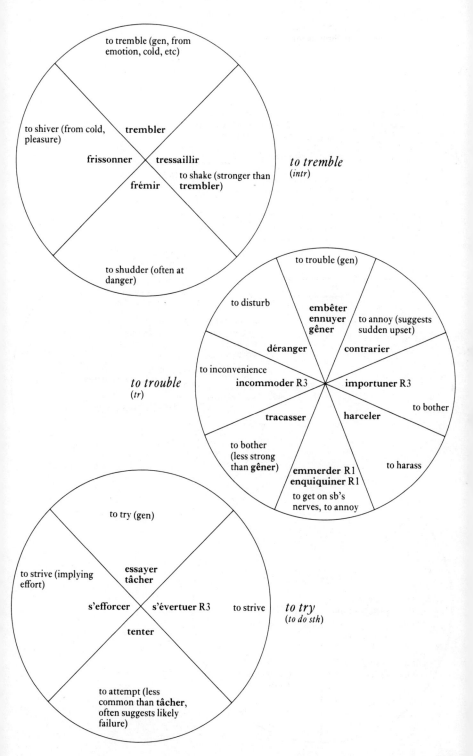

to tremble circle:

to tremble (gen, from emotion, cold, etc)

to shiver (from cold, pleasure)

trembler

frissonner **tressaillir**

frémir

to shake (stronger than **trembler**)

to shudder (often at danger)

to tremble
(intr)

to trouble circle:

to trouble (gen)

to disturb

embêter
ennuyer
gêner

to annoy (suggests sudden upset)

déranger **contrarier**

to inconvenience
incommoder R3 **importuner** R3

to bother

tracasser **harceler**

to bother
(less strong
than **gêner**)

emmerder R1
enquiquiner R1

to harass

to get on sb's
nerves, to annoy

to trouble
(tr)

to try circle:

to try (gen)

to strive (implying
effort)

essayer
tâcher

s'efforcer **s'évertuer** R3 to strive

tenter

to attempt (less
common than **tâcher**,
often suggests likely
failure)

to try
(to do sth)

111

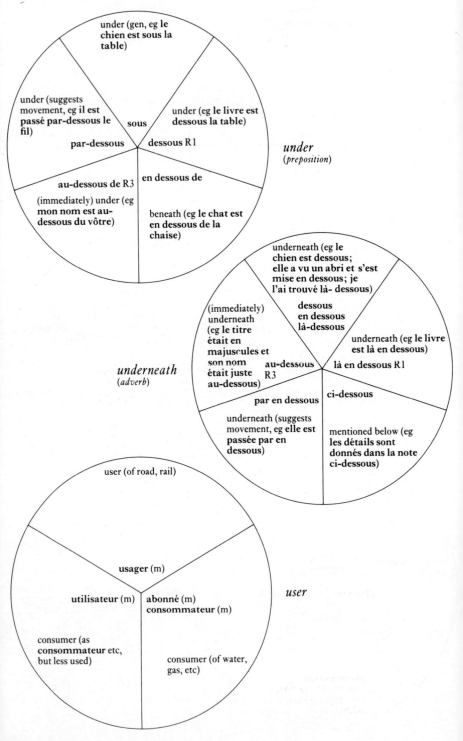

under (*preposition*)

- under (gen, eg le chien est sous la table) — **sous**
- under (eg le livre est dessous la table) — **dessous** R1
- beneath (eg le chat est en dessous de la chaise) — **en dessous de**
- (immediately) under (eg mon nom est au-dessous du vôtre) — **au-dessous de** R3
- under (suggests movement, eg il est passé par-dessous le fil) — **par-dessous**

underneath (*adverb*)

- underneath (eg le chien est dessous; elle a vu un abri et s'est mise en dessous; je l'ai trouvé là-dessous) — **dessous / en dessous / là-dessous**
- underneath (eg le livre est là en dessous) — **là en dessous** R1
- mentioned below (eg les détails sont donnés dans la note ci-dessous) — **ci-dessous**
- underneath (suggests movement, eg elle est passée par en dessous) — **par en dessous**
- (immediately) underneath (eg le titre était en majuscules et son nom était juste au-dessous) — **au-dessous** R3

user

- user (of road, rail) — **usager** (m)
- consumer (of water, gas, etc) — **abonné** (m) / **consommateur** (m)
- consumer (as **consommateur** etc, but less used) — **utilisateur** (m)

112

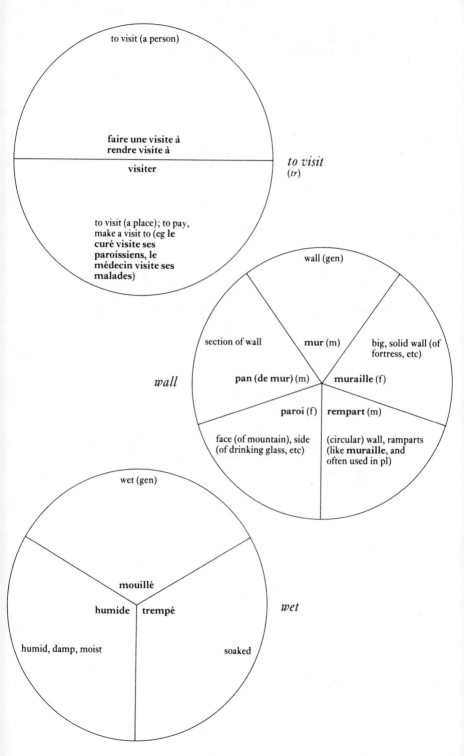

to visit (a person)

faire une visite à
rendre visite à

visiter

to visit
(*tr*)

to visit (a place); to pay,
make a visit to (eg **le
curé visite ses
paroissiens, le
médecin visite ses
malades**)

wall (gen)

wall

section of wall   **mur** (m)

big, solid wall (of
fortress, etc)

pan (de mur) (m)   **muraille** (f)

paroi (f)   **rempart** (m)

face (of mountain), side
(of drinking glass, etc)

(circular) wall, ramparts
(like **muraille**, and
often used in pl)

wet (gen)

wet

mouillé

humide | **trempé**

humid, damp, moist   soaked

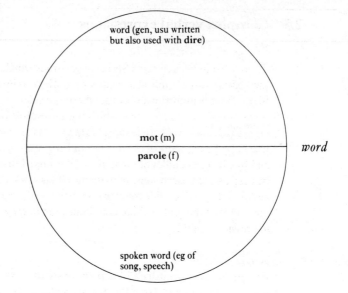

word (gen, usu written but also used with **dire**)

mot (m)

parole (f)

word

spoken word (eg of song, speech)

2.5   Complex verbal expressions

There exist in French many verbal expressions which, as a result of their apparently complicated structure, students tend to be reluctant to use. This is unfortunate because these expressions often convey important shades of meaning, which it is impossible to express otherwise, and also because some of them are very common in current usage. By listing some of the most frequently employed expressions and by giving examples of them in use, it is hoped that students will be prepared to absorb some of them into their workaday vocabulary, and that they will be able to recognise the others. Again, it should be remembered that unless there is an indication to the contrary, all these expressions are R2.

il s'agit de   = it is a question of
il s'agit de comprendre l'idée principale du texte
it is a question of understanding the main idea in the text
il s'agissait de le faire correctement
it was a question of doing it correctly
il s'agira de récrire la lettre
it will be a question of rewriting the letter

NOTE: this is an impersonal expression, and the subject can only ever be **il**, never a noun

s'attendre à ce que + subj = to expect
je m'attends à ce qu'elle revienne sous peu
I expect she will return soon

NOTE: **attendre** can also mean 'to expect':
il est attendu dans la soirée
he is expected this evening

avoir beau faire qch = to do sth in vain
elle a beau faire, elle n'aura pas ses examens
whatever she does she will not pass her examinations

avoir l'interdiction/la défense de faire qch (R3) = to be forbidden to do sth
ils ont eu l'interdiction de fumer en cours
they were forbidden to smoke in class

avoir à cœur de faire qch = to be anxious to do sth
j'ai à cœur d'accomplir cette tâche
I am anxious to complete this task

se défendre d'être (R3) = to refuse to admit, to deny being

il se défend d'être anti-européen
he refuses to admit that he is anti-European

elle s'est toujours défendue de vouloir créer un nouveau parti politique
she has always refused to admit that she wanted to create a new political party

je ne m'en défends pas
I do not deny it

se disputer le droit/privilège de faire qch = to argue over the right/privilege to do sth

les deux frères se disputaient le droit de conduire la voiture
the two brothers argued over who would drive the car

(il) n'empêche que + indicative = nevertheless

on avait une bonne défense; (il) n'empêche qu'ils ont marqué trois buts
we had a good defence but they still scored three goals

NOTE: the expression is more familiar if the impersonal il is omitted

comme si de rien n'était = as if nothing had happened

après notre querelle elle est revenue comme si de rien n'était
after our quarrel she came back as if nothing had happened

s'ennuyer de qn (R1) = to miss sb

je m'ennuyais de mes amis que j'avais laissés au village
I missed my friends whom I left behind in the village

s'entretenir avec qn de qch = to hold discussions with sb about sth

le ministre s'est entretenu avec le président de la politique agricole
the minister discussed the agricultural policy with the president

se faire faute de (R3) = to feel guilty or responsible

après cet accident, je me ferai toujours faute de ne pas avoir été plus prudent
after this accident I shall always feel guilty over not having been more cautious

en faire autant = to do the same thing

elle a fait de belles études; j'aimerais en faire autant
she has done very well in her studies; I should like to do the same

avoir vite fait de faire qch = to be quick in doing sth (suggesting 'too quickly')
on a vite fait de juger cette personne
this person was judged (too) quickly

faire fi de qch (R3) = to scorn sth
il fait fi de mon autorité
he defies/scorns my authority

faire peu de cas de qch = to ignore sth
il fait peu de cas de ce qu'on lui dit
he ignores what is said to him

faire honte à qn = to make sb feel ashamed
par son impolitesse à table il fait honte à son père
his poor table manners make his father feel ashamed

faire défaut = to be lacking
l'argent me fait défaut
I need money

peu s'en faut que (R3) + subj. : suggests the idea of 'almost'
il est venu s'excuser; mais peu s'en faut que le directeur aille le dire à son père
he came to apologise; but the headmaster almost feels like going to tell father

il s'en faut de beaucoup que + subj = to be far from
il s'en fallait de beaucoup qu'il soit heureux
he was far from being happy

se féliciter de qch = to express satisfaction over sth
je me félicite de vous voir venir
I am happy to see you come

se garder de = to take care *not* to
j'ai mes propres opinions mais je me garderai de les exprimer
I have my own opinions but I shall be careful not to express them

en imposer à qn = to fill sb with respect
avec sa carrure le boxeur en a imposé à son adversaire
with his enormous build the boxer made his opponent feel inferior

intenter un procès à qn (R3) = to take sb to court
elle a intenté un procès à son voisin
she took her neighbour to court

manquer à qn = to be lacking to sb
>le soleil me manque en Angleterre
>I miss the sun in England

>NOTE: **manquer de** contains the idea of 'almost' doing sth
>**dans sa précipitation il a manqué de renverser le vase**
>in his hurry he almost knocked over the vase

>NOTE: **ne pas manquer de** = not to fail to
>**ne manque pas de venir** = don't fail to come
>**manquer de**, however, in the positive form does not mean 'to fail to'
>(3.4.3)

se passer de qch = to do without sth
>tu te passeras de ton livre pour faire ton examen
>you will do without your book when you take your examination

passer en revue = to review or go through
>la reine a passé les troupes en revue
>the queen reviewed the troops
>elle a passé en revue sa garde-robe avant de partir en vacances
>she went through her wardrobe before going on holiday

porter atteinte à qch (R3) = to damage sth, to affect sth adversely
>cet acte a porté atteinte à l'honneur du roi
>this act cast a slur on the king's honour

s'en prendre à qn = to criticise sb
>les journalistes s'en sont pris au gouvernement
>the journalists criticised the government

s'en rapporter à qch = to rely on sth
>il s'en est rapporté à son jugement
>he put faith in his judgement

se réclamer de qch/qn (R 3) = to cite the authority of sth/sb
>il se réclame du marxisme pour défendre sa cause
>he appeals to Marxism to defend his cause

s'en remettre à qn = to rely on sb
>je m'en remets à vous
>I rely on you

se répercuter sur = to have repercussions upon
>les hausses de salaire se sont répercutées sur les prix
>the increases in wages had an effect upon prices

se ressentir de qch = to feel the effects of sth

>> **il se ressent toujours de l'accident**
>> he still feels the effects of his accident

ne pas savoir à quoi s'en tenir (R1) = not to know what to believe

>> **puisqu'il blague toujours, je ne sais pas à quoi m'en tenir**
>> since he is always joking I never know what to believe

savoir gré à qn (R3) = to be grateful to sb

>> **je lui sais gré de m'avoir averti**
>> I am thankful to him for warning me

>> NOTE: **je lui *suis* gré** R1

souhaiter la bienvenue à qn = to welcome sb

>> **je lui ai souhaité la bienvenue**
>> I welcomed him

>> NOTE: **vous êtes le (la) bienvenu(e)** = you are welcome

tenir à = to be anxious to

>> **je tiens à le faire**
>> I am anxious to do it

tenir rigueur à qn de qch = to hold it against sb for sth

>> **je tiendrai toujours rigueur à cet étudiant de ne pas avoir fait son travail**
>> I shall always hold it against this student for not doing his work

traiter qn de qch = to call sb sth (pejorative)

>> **il a traité son père de tyran**
>> he called his father a tyrant

trouver à redire à qch (R1 *de/sur*) = to criticise sth

>> **elle trouve toujours à redire sur ce que je fais**
>> she always finds fault with what I say

veiller à ce que + subj = to see to it that

>> **veillez à ce que le travail soit fait en temps voulu**
>> see to it that the work is done in the agreed time

venir en aide à qn = to come to sb's aid

>> **il nous est venu en aide lors de notre accident**
>> he came to our aid when we had the accident

en vouloir à qn = to hold it against sb

>> **il m'en veut de ne pas lui avoir écrit**
>> he is angry because I did not write to him

2.6 Idioms, similes and proverbs

'Honestly, I can't make head nor tail of it.' – 'What d'you mean? It's as easy as ABC.'

Idioms, similes and to a lesser extent proverbs, add colour to our speech. The following is a list, in alphabetical order of the pivotal words, of some of the most common French idioms; a small number of similes and proverbs is also given.

2.6.1 Idioms

		Register	
A	être aux abois	2	to be in extreme difficulty
	abonder dans le sens de qn	3	to be entirely of sb's opinion
	battre de l'aile	2	to flounder
	prendre des airs	2	to put on airs and graces
	parler sans ambages	3	to speak without beating about the bush
	être aux anges	2	to be in seventh heaven
	filer à l'anglaise	1 + 2	to take French leave
	avoir une araignée au plafond	1	to have a screw loose
	passer l'arme à gauche	1	to die
	être un as	1	to be an ace (eg sportsman)
	ne pas être dans son assiette	1 + 2	not to be in good form
	se faire l'avocat du diable	3	to play devil's advocate
B	plier bagage	2	to set off
	renvoyer la balle	2	to put the ball in sb else's court
	faire un ballon d'essai	3	to have a trial run
	mettre des bâtons dans les roues	2	to put a spoke in the wheel
	parler à bâtons rompus	2	to talk in a disconnected way
	chercher la petite bête	1	to be over-critical
	de but en blanc	2	straightaway
	toucher du bois	1	to touch wood
	mettre les bouchées doubles	2	to work hard
	avoir sur les bras	1	to have on one's hands

Register

	battre en brèche	3	to attack violently
	colmater la brèche/les brèches	3	to fill in the gap
	revenir bredouille	2	to come home empty-handed
	à brûle-pourpoint	3	point blank
C	boire le calice jusqu'à la lie	3	to drain the cup to the dregs
	la balle est dans son camp	2	the ball is in his court
	battre la campagne	1	to be delirious
	il fait un froid de canard	1	it's freezing cold
	passer un cap difficile	2	to weather an awkward situation
	avoir carte blanche	2	to have a free hand
	donner carte blanche à qn	2	to give sb a free hand
	être assis entre deux chaises	2	to fall between two stools
	à tout bout de champ	1	all the time
	donner le change à qn	3	to deceive sb
	la foi de charbonnier	3	simple faith
	venir de Charenton	1	to be mad
	il n'y a pas un chat	1	there's not a soul about
	appeler un chat un chat	2	to call a spade a spade
	ne pas réveiller le chat qui dort	3	to let sleeping dogs lie
	avoir un chat dans la gorge	1	to have a frog in one's throat
	donner la langue au chat	1 + 2	to give in/up (eg in guessing game)
	bâtir des châteaux en Espagne	2	to build castles in Spain
	avoir d'autres chats à fouetter	1	to have other fish to fry
	prendre le chemin des écoliers	2 + 3	to take the longest way round
	ne pas y aller par quatre chemins	2	not to beat about the bush
	couper les cheveux en quatre	2	to split hairs
	tiré par les cheveux	2	far-fetched
	ménager la chèvre et le chou	2	to sit on the fence

	Register	
vivre comme chien et chat	2	to live a cat and dog's life
il fait un froid à ne pas mettre un chien dehors	1	it's freezing cold
remuer ciel et terre	2	to move heaven and earth
être au septième ciel	2	to be in seventh heaven
faire un pas de clerc	3	to make a blunder
être collet monté	3	to be prim and proper
prêcher un converti	2	to preach to the converted
il pleut des cordes	1 + 2	it's raining cats and dogs
remuer le couteau dans la plaie	2	to twist the knife in the wound
être à couteaux tirés avec qn	2 + 3	to be at daggers drawn with sb
donner le coup d'envoi	2	to set things in motion
un honnête courtier	3	an honest broker
battre qn à plate couture	2 + 3	to beat sb hollow
être un crack	1	to be an ace (eg sportsman)
pendre la crémaillère	2	to have a house-warming
faire un créneau	1	to park between two cars
verser des larmes de crocodile	1 + 2	to weep crocodile tears

D le système D — 1 — ability to get out of a difficult situation

être sur les dents	1	to be worn out
tirer le diable par la queue	1	to be in difficult financial circumstances
un conte à dormir debout	2	a very boring story, a tall story
avoir bon dos	1	to be accused instead of another
faire le gros dos	1	to get angry
être dans de beaux draps	1	to be in a sorry state

E porter de l'eau à la rivière — 3 — to carry coals to Newcastle

une douche écossaise	2	sth unpleasantly unexpected
être gêné aux encoignures	2 + 3	to feel awkward

		Register	
	être tiré à quatre épingles	2	to be elegantly, impeccably dressed
	jeter l'éponge	1	to throw in the towel, to give up
	avoir l'esprit de l'escalier	3	to be witty when the opportunity has passed
	brûler une étape/les étapes	2	to go fast
	être dans tous ses états	1	to be in a stew
F	sauver la face	2	to save face
	brûler les feux/une gare	2+3	to go through red traffic lights/a station without stopping
	donner le feu vert	1	to give the green light
	donner du fil à retordre à qn	2+3	to give sb trouble
	faire un four	1	to be a flop
	ne pas avoir froid aux yeux	1	to be brazen
	avoir la frousse	1	to have the wind up
G	en avoir gros sur le cœur	2	to be unhappy
H	il pleut des hallebardes	3	it's raining cats and dogs
	couper l'herbe sous le pied à qn	2	to cut the ground from beneath sb's feet
	jeter de l'huile sur le feu	2	to add fuel to the fire
	faire tache d'huile	2	to spread (of strike, etc)
J	être gros Jean comme devant	1+2	to be tricked
L	y perdre son latin	2	not to be able to make head nor tail of sth
	lâcher du lest	1	to become freer (with children, etc)
	tenir les leviers de commande	2	to hold the reins, to be in control
	se tailler la part du lion	2	to give oneself the lion's share
	il fait un froid de loup	1	it's freezing cold
	il y a belle lurette qu'il le fait (pres tense)	1	he's been doing it for a long time
	il y a belle lurette qu'il l'a fait (pft tense)	1	it's a long time since he did it

		Register	
M	faire machine arrière	2	to go into reverse
	avoir maille à partir avec qn	3	to have a bone to pick with sb
	avoir plus d'un tour dans la manche	2	to have a trick up one's sleeve
	une autre paire de manches	2	another kettle of fish
	par-dessus le marché	1 + 2	into the bargain
	faire la grasse matinée	2	to lie late in bed
	vendre la mèche	2	to let the cat out of the bag
	ça ne mène à rien	2	that doesn't get us anywhere
	chercher midi à quatorze heures	1	to look for difficulties where there are none
	être le point de mire de tout le monde	2 + 3	to attract attention (involuntarily)
	être monnaie courante	2 + 3	to be common knowledge
	être au point mort	2	to be at a standstill (eg in negotiations)
	manger ses mots	1	to speak indistinctly
	retournons/revenons à nos moutons	1	let's get back to the point
	employer les grands moyens	2	to take extreme measures
N	être en nage	2	to be in a sweat
	faire la navette	2	to shuttle back and forth
	trancher le nœud gordien	3	to cut the Gordian knot
	le travail noir/travailler au noir	1	extra work without paying tax, moonlighting to do such work
	une bête noire	2	a pet hate
	avoir des idées noires	2	to have the blues
	perdre le nord	1	to get confused
O	faire de l'œil à qn	1	to ogle sb
	tourner de l'œil	1	to faint
	se faire tirer l'oreille	1 + 2	to be persuaded with difficulty (to do sth)
P	avoir du pain sur la planche	1 + 2	to have a lot on one's plate
	une vérité de la Palice	2	an obvious truth, a commonplace

	Register	
être dans les bons/petits papiers de qn	1 + 2	to be in sb's good books
se sentir bien/mal dans sa peau	1	to feel at ease/not at ease with oneself
ramasser une pelle	1	to come a cropper
faire sa pelote	1	to feather one's nest
payer de sa personne	3	to sacrifice oneself
être dans le pétrin	2	to be in a mess
ne pas savoir sur quel pied danser	1 + 2	to be indecisive
faire d'une pierre deux coups	2	to kill two birds with one stone
avaler la pilule	1	to swallow the pill, to allow oneself to be tricked
dorer la pilule	1	to sugar the pill
casser sa pipe	1	to kick the bucket
battre son plein	2	to be in full swing
parler de la pluie et du beau temps	2	to talk about nothing in particular
dormir à poings fermés	2	to sleep like a log
faire le point sur qch	2	to give a report on sth
faire un poisson d'avril à qn	2	to play an April Fools' Day trick on sb
une pomme de discorde	2	a bone of contention
tomber dans les pommes	1	to faint
tourner autour du pot	1 + 2	to beat about the bush
donner un coup de pouce à qn	2	to encourage sb to complete sth (at the last moment)
jeter de la poudre aux yeux à qn	2	to amaze, dazzle sb
tuer la poule aux œufs d'or	2	to kill the goose that laid the golden egg
aux frais de la princesse	2	on the house, free
pour des prunes	1	for little
mettre la puce à l'oreille à qn	2	to hint at sth

Q	passer un mauvais quart d'heure	1	to have a bad time of it
	à la queue leu-leu	1	in single file
	faire une queue de poisson	1	to overtake a car and then pull in suddenly

		Register	
R	le quart d'heure de Rabelais	3	the hour of reckoning
	mettre au rancart	1	to cast aside
	la règle d'or	2	the golden rule
	cela n'a ni rime ni raison	2	there's neither rhyme nor reason in it
	voir tout en rose	2	to see everything through rose-coloured spectacles
	franchir le Rubicon	3	to cross the Rubicon
S	avoir plus d'un tour dans son sac	2	to have more than one trick up one's sleeve
	ne pas savoir à quel saint se vouer	2	to be at one's wits' end
	passer un savon à qn	1	to reprimand sb
	être/mettre qn sur la sellette	1 + 2	to be/put sb on the carpet
	un dialogue de sourds	2	a dialogue between two people who refuse to understand each other
T	passer qn à tabac	1	to beat sb up
	faire table rase	2 + 3	to make a clean sweep
	arriver tambour battant	2	to come bustling up
	faire qch tambour battant	2	to hustle sth along
	sans tambour ni trompette	2	quietly
	vouloir sa tartine beurrée des deux côtés	2	to want to have one's cake and eat it
	crier sur tous les toits	2	to shout from the roof tops
	avoir du toupet	2	to have cheek
	avoir le trac	2	to get the wind up
	aller son petit train-train	2	to jog along in the usual way
	servir de tremplin	2	to act as a spring-board
	se mettre sur son trente et un	1	to put on one's Sunday best
	voir trente-six chandelles	1	to see stars
	il n'y a pas trente-six façons/moyens/possibilités/solutions	1	there are no two ways about it

Register

V	brûler ses vaisseaux	3	to burn one's boats
	renverser la vapeur	2	to go into reverse
	tirer les vers du nez à qn	1	to worm secrets out of sb
	les choses tournent au vinaigre	1	things are turning sour
	un violon d'Ingres	3	a hobby
	à vol d'oiseau	2	as the crow flies
	en vrac	2	higgledy-piggledy

2.6.2 Similes

Register

A	je m'en moque comme de l'an quarante	1	I couldn't care less
	fier comme Artaban	2	as proud as a peacock
B	rire comme une baleine	1	to laugh like a drain
	c'est simple comme bonjour	1	it's as easy as ABC
	rire comme un bossu	1	to laugh like a drain
C	il s'en moque comme de sa première chemise	1	he couldn't care less
	être malade comme un chien	1	to be as sick as a dog
E	clair comme de l'eau de roche	2	as clear as crystal
F	trembler comme une feuille	2	to tremble like a leaf
	pleurer comme une fontaine	2	to cry floods of tears
	noir comme dans un four	2	as black as pitch
L	s'entendre comme larrons en foire	2	to be as thick as thieves
	parler comme un livre	2	to speak with eloquence
	dormir comme un loir	2	to sleep like a log
	être connu comme le loup blanc	2	to be known by everyone
M	être vieux comme le monde	2	to be as old as Methuselah

		Register	
P	ça se vend comme des petits pains	2	it's selling like hot cakes
	fier comme un paon	2	as proud as a peacock
	il est bête comme ses pieds	1	he's as daft as a brush
	soûl comme un Polonais	1	as drunk as a lord
	se coucher comme les poules	1	to go to bed early
S	dormir comme une souche	1	to sleep like a log
V	parler français comme une vache espagnole	1	to murder the French language

2.6.3 Proverbs

	Register	
le jeu n'en vaut pas la chandelle	3	the game is not worth the candle
mettre la charrue devant les boeufs	2	to put the cart before the horse
chat échaudé craint l'eau froide	2	once bitten twice shy
la nuit tous les chats sont gris	1 + 2	everyone looks the same in the dark
à bon chat bon rat	2 + 3	tit for tat
le chat parti, les souris dansent	2	when the cat's away, the mice will play
une fois n'est pas coutume	2	one swallow doesn't make a summer
il faut battre le fer pendant qu'il est chaud	2	you must strike while the iron's hot
la goutte d'eau qui fait déborder le vase	1	the straw that breaks the camel's back
l'habit ne fait pas le moine	2	it's not the cowl that makes the monk
une hirondelle ne fait pas le printemps	2	one swallow doesn't make a summer
à chaque jour suffit sa peine	3	sufficient unto the day is the evil thereof
on parle du loup, on en voit la queue/il sort du bois	2	speak of the devil

	Register	
ce n'est pas la mer à boire	1	it's not so very difficult to do
il ne faut pas vendre la peau de l'ours (avant de l'avoir tué)	2	don't count your chickens (before they are hatched)
il partira quand les poules auront des dents	1	he'll be here until the cows come home
mieux vaut prévenir que guérir	2	prevention is better than cure
un 'tiens' vaut mieux que deux 'tu l'auras'	2 + 3	a bird in the hand is worth two in the bush

2.7 Proper names

2.7.1 Personal names

Although there are French equivalents for a number of English personal names (Peter = *Pierre*, Stephen = *Etienne*, Joan = *Jeanne*, Mary = *Marie*) the names of individuals are not translated from one language to the other: John Smith remains John Smith in French, and Pierre Dupont likewise remains Pierre Dupont in English.

The names of famous or notorious historical personages often have a peculiar French form. Although this does not apply to English names, Latin, Greek and Italian names are particularly affected. There are also special French forms for some modern-day Russian names as well as historical ones.

Greek	Alexandre	Homère	Périclès	Pythagore
	Aristote	Léandre	Platon	Sophocle
	Euripide	Ovide		
Latin	Auguste	Cicéron	Marc-Aurèle	Scipion
	Caton	Lavinie	Néron	Tibère
	Jules César			
Biblical	Elie (*Elijah*)	Moïse	Jean-Baptiste	
	Esaïe (*Isaiah*)	Barthélemy	Lazare	
	Esdras (*Ezra*)	(*Bartholomew*)	Zachée (*Zachaeus*)	
	Jérémie	Hérode		

NOTE: *the Old Testament character 'Saul' becomes* Saül *in French, whereas the New Testament 'Saul' is* Saul

Italian   *Sometimes the names of Italian artists and writers are preceded by* le *in French, translating the Italian* 'il'.

Arioste	Machiavel	Le Tasse
Boccace	Pétrarque	Le Tintoret
Le Corrège	Michel-Ange	(Le) Titien
Léonard de Vinci		

Russian

Borodine	Soljenitsyne	*'Catherine the Great'*
Dostoïevski	Staline	*is normally*
Kossyguine	Tchaikovski	*translated as* la
Lénine	Tolstoï	Grande Catherine
Raspoutine	Tourgueniev	

The Emperor 'Charles V' is known as Charles Quint *in French.*

For matters of gender and number of proper names, see **3.1** Gender and **3.2.1.4** Proper names.

2.7.2   Names of towns

Many towns in Europe and elsewhere have a particular French form. Below is a list of the most common ones.

Europe				
	Autriche	Vienne	Grèce	Athènes
	Belgique	Anvers		Thessalonique
		(*Antwerp*)	Hollande	La Haye
		Bruxelles	Italie	Gênes (*Genoa*)
		Gand (*Ghent*)		Livourne
	Chypre	Nicosie		(*Leghorn*)
	Danemark	Copenhague		Padoue
	Espagne	Barcelone		Rome
		Cordoue		Sienne
		La Corogne		Venise
		(*Corunna*)		Vérone
		Saint-Sébastien	Malte	La Valette (il
		Salamanque		est à La
		Séville		Valette)
		Tarragone	Pologne	Cracovie
		Tolède		Varsovie
		Valence	Portugal	Lisbonne
		(*Valencia*)	Russie	Moscou
	Grande	Cantorbéry	Sicile	Palerme
	Bretagne	Douvres	Suisse	Genève
		Edimbourg		
		Londres		

Afrique	Afrique du Sud	Le Cap (il est au Cap)	Ethiopie	Addis-Abéba
			Ghana	Khoumassi
	Algérie	Alger (un Algérois = *inhabitant of Algiers*)	Maroc	Marrakech
				Tanger
	Egypte	Alexandrie	Tunisie	Bizerte
		Le Caire (il est au Caire; un Cairote = *inhabitant of Cairo*)		
Asie	Afghanistan	Kaboul/Kabul	Malaisie	Singapour
	Chine	Chang-hai	Népal	Katmandou
		Pékin	Philippines	Manille
	Corée	Séoul	Tibet	Lhassa
Moyen Orient	Arabie Séoudite	La Mecque (il est à La Mecque)	Iran	Téhéran
			Liban	Beyrouth
		Médine	Syrie	Alep
				Damas
Amérique du Nord	Canada	Montréal /mɔ̃real/		
	Etats-Unis	La Nouvelle-Orléans (il est à la Nouvelle Orléans)		
		Philadelphie		
Amérique Centrale	Cuba	La Havane (il est à La Havane)		
	Mexique	Mexico (*Mexico City*)		
Amérique du Sud	Argentine	Buenos Aires /bɥenɔs ɛr/		

2.7.3 Pronunciation

Personal names

Generally speaking personal names are pronounced in an orthodox French manner, and even if the spelling of foreign names remains the same, their pronunciation conforms to French principles, eg Dante /dɑ̃t/, Samson /sɑ̃sɔ̃/, Romulus /rɔmylys/. There are however, a few peculiarities of pronunciation which should be noted:

Jesus-Christ /ʒesykri/, but le Christ /lə krist/

Pierre Boulez (*composer and conductor*) /pjɛr bule/ *or* /bulɛz/

les Broglie (*an eminent French family*) /le brœj/

131

Albert Camus (*French author*) /albɛr kamy/
Machiavel (*Italian politician*) /makjavɛl/
Michel-Ange (*Italian painter and sculptor*) /mikɛlɑ̃ʒ/
Robespierre (*French politician*) /rɔbɛspjɛr/
George Sand (*French author*) /ʒɔrʒ sɑ̃d/

Place names   Here is a sample of some French and Belgian place names whose pronunciation gives difficulty:
Auxerre /ɔksɛr/ *or* /ɔsɛr/
Bruxelles /bryksɛl/ *or* /brysɛl/
Chamonix /ʃamɔni/ *or* /ʃamɔniks/
Le Doubs /lə du/
Laon /lɑ̃/
Lot /lɔt/
Metz /mɛs/
Rodez /rɔdɛz/
Saint-Gaudens /sɛ̃ godɛ̃s/
Saint-Jorioz (*Alpine village*) /sɛ̃ ʒɔrio/ *or* /sɛ̃ ʒɔriɔz/
Saint-Tropez /sɛ̃ trope/ *or* /sɛ̃ tropɛz/

2.8   Abbreviations

2.8.1   General

With the proliferation of numerous types of organisations – international, political, scientific, economic and so on – it has become necessary to distinguish between them by the use of precise, but often long, titles. Inevitably, in an age when speed and efficiency are at a premium, these long titles become truncated or, more often, reduced to their initial letters. Abbreviations are now so widespread in French that they have become, to quote one French person, a *maladie*!

The desire for conciseness leads in a number of cases to the initial letters themselves forming a word in its own right: in the following list such words are indicated by a *. The other abbreviations are pronounced as a series of individual letters except for those marked ˆ, which need to be pronounced in their full form. The list contains the most widely used French abbreviations.

The gender of the abbreviation is determined by the first word: eg *le CAPES, le CES, les USA, aux USA, à la BNP.*

Abbreviation	Full form	English equivalent (or explanation)
AF	allocation familiale	*family allowance*
arr^	arrondissement	*district (of large town)*
bac*	baccalauréat	*GCE 'A' levels or school leaving certificate*
bd^	boulevard	*boulevard*
BD	bande dessinée	*comic strip*
BNP	Banque nationale de Paris	*(French bank)*
CAPES* /kapɛs/	certificat d'aptitude au professorat de l'enseignement secondaire	*Diploma of Education*
CCP	compte chèque postal	*Giro account*
CEE	Communauté économique européenne	*EEC, Common Market*
CEEA	Communauté européenne de l'énergie atomique	*Euratom*
CEG	collège d'enseignement général	*secondary school (up to 16 years*
CES	collège d'enseignement secondaire	*secondary school (up to 18 years*
CET	collège d'enseignement technique	*technical secondary school*
CFDT	Confédération française et démocratique du travail	*(French trades union)*
CGT	Confédération générale du travail	*(French trades union)*
CIDEX*	Courrier individuel exceptionnel	*(special state postal system)*
Cie^	compagnie	*Co, company*
CL	Crédit Lyonnais	*(French bank)*
CNPF	Conseil national du patronat français	*CBI, Confederation of British Industry*
CRS	Compagnies républicaines de sécurité	*riot police*
un CRS	membre des Compagnies	*riot policeman*
CV	curriculum vitae	*curriculum vitae*
le système D (R1)	le système débrouillard	*(one's ability to get out of a difficult situation)*
DCA	Défense contre avions	*anti-aircraft defences*
dép^	département	*department*
DES	diplôme d'études supérieures	*M.Phil.*
DEUG*	diplôme d'études universitaires générales	*(university diploma after two years' study)*
DOM*- TOM*	départements d'outre-mer et territoires d'outre-mer	*(French overseas possessions)*
Dr^	docteur	*doctor*
EDF	Electricité de France	*Electricity Board*

Abbreviation	Full form	English equivalent (or explanation)
E-M G	état-major général	*GHQ, general headquarters*
ENA*	Ecole nationale d'administration	*(a Grande Ecole producing France's administrative élite)*
exp^	expéditeur	*sender*
F^	franc(s)	*franc*
FEN*	Fédération de l'éducation nationale	*(trades union grouping all teachers)*
FMI	Fonds monétaire international	*IMF, International Monetary Fund*
FO	Force Ouvrière	*(trades union)*
GDB (R1)	'gueule de bois'	*hangover*
GDF	Gaz de France	*Gas Board*
la bombe H		*H-bomb*
l'heure H		*zero hour*
HLM	habitation à loyer modéré	*Council house estate/flats/low c accommodation*
IFOP*	Institut français d'opinion publique	*(opinion research organisation*
INSEE*	Institut national de la statistique et des études économiques	*(centre for study of statistics a economics)*
le jour J		*D-Day*
JO	les Jeux Olympiques	*Olympic Games*
kg^	kilogramme	*kilogram*
km^	kilomètre	*kilometre*
KO	knock out	*knock out*
M.^	monsieur	*Mr, sir*
Me^	maître (avocat)	*(title for lawyer)*
ME	moyennes entreprises	*(middle-size businesses)*
MF/FM	modulation de fréquence	*high frequency*
Mgr^	monseigneur	*monseigneur (title for cardinal*
MLF	Mouvement de libération de la femme	*Women's Liberation*
Mlle(s)^	mademoiselle, mesdemoiselles	*Miss, misses*
MM^	messieurs	*gentlemen*
Mme(s)^	madame, mesdames	*Mrs, ladies*
M-P	mandat-poste	*postal order*
OLP	Organisation de la libération de la Palestine	*PLO, Palestine Liberation Organisation*
ONU*	Organisation des Nations Unies	*UNO, United Nations Organisation*
OPEP*	Organisation des pays exportateurs de pétrole	*OPEC, Oil Producing and Exporting Countries*

Abbreviation	Full form	English equivalent (or explanation)
ORSEC*	Organisation des secours, *usually* le plan ORSEC	*(national accident service, operating in summer)*
ORTF	Office de la radiodiffusion et télévision françaises	*BBC*
OS	ouvrier spécialisé	*skilled worker*
OTAN*	Organisation du traité de l'Atlantique du Nord	*NATO, North Atlantic Treaty Organisation*
OUA	Organisation de l'unité africaine	*OAU, Organisation of African Unity*
OVNI*	objet volant non-identifié	*UFO, unidentified flying object*
PC	parti communiste	*Communist party*
PC	poste de commandement	*(military base, any centre for an official organisation)*
PDG	président-directeur général	*managing director*
PE	petites entreprises	*(small businesses)*
PME	petites et moyennes entreprises	*(small and middle-size businesses*
PNB	produit national brut	*gross national product*
PS	parti socialiste	*French socialist party*
PTT	Postes, Télégraphes, Téléphones	*Post Office*
PV	procès-verbal	*(booking, by policeman)*
PVD	pays en voie de développement	*developing countries*
QI*/kЧi/	quotient intellectuel	*IQ, intelligence quotient*
RATP	Régie autonome de transports parisiens	*(Parisian transport system)*
RER	Réseau express régional	*(Parisian surburban rail service connecting with the underground*
RF	République française	*French Republic*
RFA	République Fédérale allemande	*West Germany*
RPF	Rassemblement du peuple français	*(French political party)*
RPR	Rassemblement pour la République	*(French political party)*
RSVP	répondez, s'il vous plaît	*RSVP*
RTF	Radiodiffusion et télévision françaises	*BBC*
RU*	restaurant universitaire	*University dining-hall/canteen*
SARL*	Société anonyme à responsabilité limitée	*limited company*
SFIO	Société française de l'Internationale ouvrière	*(French political party)*
SMIC smic*	salaire minimum interprofessionnel de croissance	*guaranteed minimum income*

Abbreviation	Full form	English equivalent (or explanation)
SMIG smig*	salaire minimum interprofessionnel garanti (*same as* SMIC *but less common*)	*guaranteed minimum income*
SN	Service national	*National Service*
SNCF	Société nationale des chemins de fer français	*British Rail*
SNE sup* /snesyp/	Syndicat national de l'enseignement supérieur	*Association of University Teachers, AUT*
SNI	Syndicat national des instituteturs	*(Primary school-teachers' trad union)*
SOFRES* /sɔfrɛs/	Société française d'enquêtes pour sondages	*(opinion research organisation,*
SVPˆ	s'il vous plaît	*please*
TGV	train à grande vitesse	*high speed train*
TNP	Théâtre national populaire	*(French national theatre)*
TSF	télégraphie sans fil	*radio*
TSVP	tournez, s'il vous plaît	*PTO, please turn over*
TVA	taxe à la valeur ajoutée	*VAT, value added tax*
UDF	Union pour la démocratie française	*(French political party)*
UNEF*	Union nationale des étudiants de France	*National union of students*
URSS	Union des Républiques Socialistes Soviétiques	*USSR, Union of Soviet Socia Republics*
USA	Etats Unis	*USA*
WC (pl)	water closet, les double VC, les VC (R1)	*WC*
ZUP	zone à urbaniser en priorité/zone d'urbanisation prioritaire	*(new suburb, comprising mainl low-cost housing)*

The French mania for abbreviations is well illustrated by the terse article appearing below, first published in *Le Monde*, 26 September 1981.

Au jour le jour
T.S.M.[1]

On a eu le SAC[2] pour l'été. On allait se faire au T.G.V.[3] pour l'automne quand la D.S.T.[4] a fait irruption, lui soufflant la place au dernier moment. Pour l'hiver, on se serait contenté d'un simple R.A.S.[5]

[1] tunnel sous la Manche

[2] Service d'action civique = *special branch of the French police*

Mais M. Mitterand a compris qu'à chaque saison
son sigle : on aurait fini par se lasser. Il en a proposé
un qui dure : le T.S.M. Bravo! Car on en a pour au
moins sept ans avec le tunnel sous la Manche!
Claude-H Buffard.

[3] train à grande
vitesse = *high
speed train*

[4] Direction de la
surveillance du
territoire = *MI5*

[5] rien à
signaler = *nothing
to report*

2.8.2 Petites annonces

Penetrating the language of *les petites annonces* in newspapers and
magazines may be a bewildering task. The most esoteric examples
seem to be those relating to accommodation, *immobilier*, and it is also
in this area that the grammar appears at its most 'strangled'. The
following is a short glossary of the most frequently encountered
abbreviations and more obscure expressions.

	Abbreviation	Full form	English equivalent
position of accommodation:	2 arrdt	dans le deuxième arrondissement	*in the 2nd postal district*
	banl	en banlieue	*in the suburbs*
	ttes banl	toutes les banlieues	*easy access to the suburbs*
	camp	à la/de campagne	*in the country*
	M° Gare du Nord	Métro Gare du Nord	*nearest Métro station Gare du Nord*
accommodation:	asc./ascens.	ascenseur	*lift*
	bains/bns/s.d. bns	salle de bains	*bathroom*
	balc	balcon	*balcony*
	ch	chambre	*bedroom*
	chauf. centr.	chauffage central	*central heating*
	tt/tout cft	tout confort	*all mod cons*
	pte cour	petite cour	*small backyard*
	cuis.	cuisine	*kitchen*
	cuis. amén.	cuisine aménagée	*well-equipped kitchen*
	dche	douche	*shower*
	2e	au deuxième étage	*on the second floor*
	s. d'eau	salle d'eau	*bathroom/shower room*
	entrée	salle d'entrée	*entrance hall*
	gar.	garage	*garage*
	habit. + dép.	habitations et dépendances	*tenant houses and outhouses (eg of farm)*
	imm.	immeuble	*building*
	moq.	moquette	*with fitted carpets*
	1 p.	une pièce	*one-roomed flat (excluding kitchen and bathroom)*

	Abbreviation	Full form	English equivalent
	3+4 ps.	trois et quatre pièces	*flats with three and four rooms (excluding kitchen and bathroom)*
	park.	parking	*space for car*
	s/rue	donnant sur la rue	*overlooking the road*
	s-sol	sous-sol	*basement*
	vue dég.	vue dégagée	*uninterrupted view*
condition of accommodation:	eau EGDF	eau, électricité et gaz de France	*water, gas and electricity*
	ensol.	ensoleillé	*sunny*
	imm. ravalé	immeuble ravalé	*(exteriorly) modernised building*
	imm. réc.	immeuble récent	*new building*
	m. à rén.	maison à rénover	*house in need of renovation*
	poss.	possibilités	*with possibilities*
	tr. b. rénovat. en cours	très belle rénovation en cours	*outstanding renovation in progress*
	terrain 1.000 m² entièrement viab.	terrain de 1.000 m² entièrement viabilisé	*1,000 m² plot with all services laid on*
selling/buying process	ach.	achète	*wishes to purchase*
	apr. 18h	après 18 heures	*(viewing) after 6 pm*
	cpt	comptant	*cash sale*
	libre de ste	libre de suite	*immediate occupation*
	p. à p./part. à part.	particulier à particulier	*private sale*
	pptaire	propriétaire	*house-owner*
	px 530 000 F à débattre	prix de 530 000 F à débattre	*price 530,000 F or nearest offer*
	vd	vend	*wishes to sell*
	vend.-sam. 15-18h	vendredi à samedi entre 15 et 18 heures	*(viewing) Friday and Saturday between 3 and 6 pm*
	vis.	visiter	*viewing (recommended)*

2.9   Latin expressions

Educated French people will occasionally use Latin expressions in their fairly formal R3 speech. They may also, but less frequently, introduce certain ones into more relaxed R2 speech. However, *etc* (*et cetera*, *et caetera*), *illico*, *ex aequo*, *grosso modo* and *quidam* are probably the only Latin expressions that find their way into the most informal register. There follows a list of the more common expressions, with their meanings and where they exist, their French-language counterparts. Expressions marked with an asterisk are also used in English.

	Latin	French	Meaning
R3	a fortiori*	à plus forte raison	*with stronger reason*
	a posteriori*		*after the event*
	a priori*		*before the event*
	cum grano salis		*with a pinch of salt*
	ex cathedra*		*with the highest authority*
	ipso facto*	par le fait même	*by the very fact*
	modus vivendi*		*working agreement*
	persona non grata*		*unwelcome person*
	une condition sine qua non	indispensable	*indispensable*
R2 and R3	de visu		*as an eye witness, at first hand*
	ex-voto*		*ex voto, offering made in pursuit of a vow*
	in extremis*	à l'extrême limite	*at the last extremity*
	manu militari		*by force of arms*
	primo, secundo, tertio	premièrement, deuxièmement, troisièmement	*in the first, second, third place*

NOTE: **primo** *and* **secundo** *are used in a familiar way but* not **tertio**

	Latin	French	Meaning
	quiproquo	erreur	*mistake (English* **quidproquo** *is a deceptive cognate = sth done in return for sth else)*
	statu quo* (*note spelling*)		*unchanged position, (English:* status quo*)*
	les ultras	les extrémistes	*extremists*
	vice versa*		*conversely*

	Latin	French	Meaning
R1 and R2	ex aequo (eg il était deuxième ex aequo)	à égalité	*equal, level* *pegging (as in a race)*
	grosso modo	en gros	*in broad detail*
	illico	immédiatement	*immediately*
	quidam	un (certain) individu	*person*

NOTE: *in the following combinations* **ès** *is a survival from Old French* (**ès** = **en les**), eg docteur ès lettres, licencié ès sciences

2.10 Interjections, fillers, transition words and forms of address

2.10.1 Interjections

In the measured, self-conscious speech of R3, interjections are by definition rare. On the other hand, at the other end of the formality–informality scale, in the more spontaneous speech of R1, interjections (like slang expressions and colloquialisms) are very common indeed, occurring frequently as involuntary, emotional reflexes. R2 speech, lying between R1 and R3, also contains a certain number of interjections, but is more selective in its usage of them. In the following table an attempt has been made to grade the interjections according to intensity and decency, that is to say, the interjections are placed on a continuum, one end of which is termed 'respectable usage', and covers the expressions in the R2 column and to a lesser extent the first two of the R1 columns, and the other end of which is termed 'indecent usage' and covers the expressions in the last column.

It is accepted that 'respectable' and 'indecent' are relative terms; attitudes towards indecency and swearing are naturally highly subjective. It should be stressed that the use of interjections by non-native speakers needs to be exercised with extreme caution, as an inappropriate usage may lead to deep offence at the worst, or at the very least to embarrassment. In fact, it may be wiser for such speakers to avoid many R1 interjections altogether. It is sufficient to appreciate their force without necessarily using them oneself. Interjections of surprise and annoyance are quite often interchangeable, the emotion expressed depending entirely upon intonation and the attitude of the speaker. Popular speech and slang, including interjections, are often subject to the whims of fashion, and there is a constant gain and loss of expressions. However, the expressions in the table are all in contemporary use.

Respectable usage			**Indecent usage**
	R2	R1	R1	R1
Admiration	formidable parfait parfaitement			
Agreement	entendu d'accord	d'acc et comment	ben oui ça colle, (Anatole)	
	impeccable	OK impec pourquoi pas?	ça va va (*occurs after a statement*: Je t'aime, va!)	
Annoyance	fichtre	mince (alors)	sacré nom de Dieu (*strong*)	merde (alors)

	bigre	zut (alors)
		punaise
		flûte
		la purée
		elle (*subject*)
		  m'empoisonne
			nom d'un chien
			espèce d'idiot
				putain
				salaud
				espèce de con
				  quel con/
				  connard/
				couillon
				il me fait
				  chier/caguer

Disbelief	sans blague	mais alors mon œil		mon cul
Joy	chic alors	chouette alors sensass super bath		
Objection	mais tout de même	et après?	ben quoi? na (et) toc	

Surprise	grands Dieux
	ma foi
	parbleu
	(mille)
	  tonnerre(s) de
	  Dieu
		ça alors
		ah, non alors
		pas possible
		eh ben
			ouf
			bondieu	

Warning	attention prends garde	gare/gare-gare	fais gaffe	

2.10.2 Fillers

In informal speech, where hesitation is common and the right word is slow in coming to mind, sentences are rarely completely formed and fillers, such as the following, presented in alphabetical order, are called upon to bridge the gaps:

allez	bref (passons)	eh bien	quoi
allons donc	c'est-à-dire	enfin	remarque
alors	déjà	euh	tu vois
ben	disons	ma foi	vous voyez/
bof	écoute(z)	un peu	voyez-vous
bon			

allez	Allez, tu dis ça pour me faire rire.
allons donc	Allons donc, vous plaisantez.
alors	Alors, raconte! qu'est-ce-qui s'est passé?
	Alors, tu viens?
	Il parlait tout le temps, alors je lui ai dit de se taire.
	Et alors, que veux-tu que je fasse?
ben	Ben, je sais pas.
bof	Tu penses que cette cravate va avec mon costume? Bof! Pourquoi pas?
bon	Allons bon! Il pleut.
	Vous voulez connaître la vérité? Bon, je vais tout vous dire.
	Bon! Ne te fâche pas!
bref	J'ai passé la journée à courir d'un magasin à l'autre. Bref, je suis épuisé.
c'est-à-dire	Etes-vous sûr de l'avoir vue? C'est-à-dire, tout le monde peut se tromper.
	Je ne peux pas vous aider. C'est-à-dire, je n'en ai pas le droit.
déjà	C'est combien, déjà?
disons	Disons, (que) je ne me rappelle plus.
écoute(z)	Oh, écoute, il faut pas le faire comme ça.
	Qu'est-ce que vous pensez de ce film? – Ecoutez, il n'est pas très bon.
eh bien	Comment allez-vous? – Ça va beaucoup mieux, merci. – Eh bien, c'est parfait.
enfin	Ce meuble est très cher, mais enfin je peux peut-être l'acheter.
	Je vous ai dit ce que je pensais. Enfin, c'est à vous de décider.
euh	La rue Victor Hugo? Euh . . . Je crois que c'est la première à gauche.
ma foi	Cette maison est bien située et, ma foi, je pense qu'elle vous plaira.
un peu	Tu as des nouvelles, un peu?
	Dis moi, un peu, tu as des nouvelles?
quoi	Allons, quoi, faut pas te décourager.
	Alors quoi, on joue?
remarque	Remarque, tu peux mettre le bouquin là.
tu vois	C'est quelqu'un de très bien, tu vois. Je l'aime beaucoup.
vous voyez/	Vous voyez, il ne faut jamais désespérer.
voyez-vous	C'est un monsieur très important, voyez-vous.

2.10.3 Transition words

In R3 speech and writing, where careful organisation of structure is essential, particularly when a discussion is taking place, transition words, marking the steps and points of an argument, are very common. They also occur quite frequently in R2 usage.

alors que — Il a plu tout l'été, alors que cet hiver nous n'avons pas eu une goutte d'eau.

au contraire — Elle a dit que ce problème de maths était très simple. Moi, au contraire, je l'ai trouvé très difficile.

aussi — J'ai raté mon train. Aussi il a fallu que je prenne l'autocar.

car — Il n'a pas pu se baigner car il avait trop mangé.

en conséquence /par consé- quent — Elle n'a pas gagné beaucoup d'argent. En conséquence/par conséquent elle n'a pas pu partir en vacances.

en effet — Ils ont dit que votre équipe allait gagner. En effet c'est ce qui s'est passé.

en fait/en réalité — On a cru que Delvaux était un bon sculpteur. En fait/en réalité il est plutôt un peintre.

en résumé — Les règles de la grammaire française sont très nombreuses. En résumé, ce manuel pourra vous aider.

en revanche/ par contre — Nous n'avons pas pu visiter le château. En revanche/par contre nous sommes allés au musée.

or — Les restrictions budgétaires devraient réduire l'inflation. Or, celle-ci continue à monter.

partant (R3) — Les études littéraires sur l'œuvre de Camus sont de plus en plus nombreuses. Partant, l'intérêt des lecteurs s'est accru.

voire (R3) — Nous pourrons peut-être étudier les romans de Butor, voire même ceux de Pinget.

In addition to transition words, also frequently used in discussions and debates are balancing words, which allow contrasts and comparisons to be made more effectively.

d'un côté ... de l'autre (côté) — La critique contemporaine se divise en deux clans. D'un côté les traditionnalistes, de l'autre (côté) les modernistes.

d'une part ... d'autre part — Dans un travail de rédaction, il faut faire attention d'une part au contenu et d'autre part à la forme.

In a carefully reasoned argument the following series of terms frequently occur:

premièrement ...	deuxièmement ...	troisièmement ...
en premier lieu ...	en second lieu ...	troisièmement ...

2.10.4 Forms of address

When meeting someone or when writing a letter to him/her, it is important, from the very beginning of the encounter, to strike the right chord on the register scale: first words create first impressions, and will therefore affect the subsequent attitude of the addressee. Consequently, an appropriate opening gambit should ensure a favourable hearing thereafter. The following table illustrates the various formulae that are used in contemporary French:

in speech	R1	R2	R3
on meeting	salut	bonjour, Monsieur/ Madame/ Mademoiselle/ jeune homme, etc	
	tu vas bien?	comment vas-tu?	
	vous allez bien?	comment allez-vous?	Monsieur/Madame se porte bien?
	(comment) ça va?		
	ça marche?		
	ça boum?		
	ça gaze?		
on leave-taking	salut	au revoir	adieu
		au plaisir (de vous revoir)	
		à bientôt	
		à tout de suite	
		à la semaine prochaine, etc	
		bon retour	
		bon voyage	
		bonne route	
		bonne chance	

in letter	R1	R2	R3
introduction	Cher Jean/Chère Jeanne	Cher Monsieur/Chère Madame/ Mademoiselle	Monsieur/Madame/ Mademoiselle
		Mon cher Jean/Ma chère Jeanne	Monsieur le Directeur/le Premier Ministre/le Président

in letter	R1	R2	R3

conclusion	à bientôt
	grosses bises
	
	salut
		affectueusement
		  (eg *niece to*
		  uncle)
		
		amitiés
		
		bien à toi/vous
		
		amicalement
		
		mes amitiés à
		  vos parents
		
		une bonne poignée
		  de main (eg *between*
		  male friends)
			je vous prie de/
			  veuillez agréer
			  (l'expression de)
			  mes salutations
			  distinguées/mes
			  respectueuses
			  salutations/mes
			  sentiments les
			  meilleurs/dis-
			  tingués/
			  respectueux
			
			mes hommages/
			  respects à votre
			  dame/épouse

2.11 Differences in measurements, etc

Metrication has a long history in France, its use having become legal
in 1795 and compulsory from 1840. In Britain, on the other hand, two
systems of weights and measures, metric and imperial, coexist in
certain domains, whereas in others either the metric or imperial
system has the upper hand. The result of this is not only that
hesitation occurs in the minds of English-speakers using their own
language, but also that on many occasions different standards prevail
in the two countries. In the series of tables that follow, accepted
approximations for the two systems are stated (exact equivalents are
generally not essential in speech), certain norms are mentioned and
'records' are given to ease comparison. It is, of course, important,
when translating from English to French, to change imperial to metric
measurement.

2.11.1 Distance

metric	imperial	metric	imperial
10 centimètres	4 ins	100 mètres	100 yards
50 cms	$1\frac{1}{2}$ ft	1 kilomètre	$\frac{1}{2}$ mile
1 mètre	1 yard	2 kilomètres	1 mile
		100 kilomètres	60 miles

Height   **un enfant de quatre-vingt-dix centimètres** = a child three-foot
tall

un homme d'un mètre quatre-vingts = a man six-foot tall

un homme de deux mètres = a man six-foot-six tall

France's highest mountain: **Mont Blanc: 4 807 mètres** = 15,782
feet

the world's highest mountain: Mount Everest: **8 880
mètres** = 29,002 feet

world record high jump: **2,38 mètres** = 7 feet 8 inches

Length   world record long jump: **8,90 mètres** = 29 feet $2\frac{1}{2}$ inches

the French use the term **mille** in the following expression only:

un mille marin = a nautical mile:

1 852 mètres = 2,027 yards

Speed   **100 kilomètres/heure** = 60 mph

speed of light: **300 000 kilomètres/seconde** = 186,000 miles/second

speed of gravity: **981 centimètres/seconde carrée** = 32.2
feet/second squared

world record for car: **690 kilomètres/heure** = 429 mph

world record for aeroplane: **3 529 kilomètres/heure** = 2,113 mph

2.11.2 Weight

metric	imperial
un quart de kilogramme ⎫ **un quart de kilo** ⎬ **250 grammes** ⎭	$\frac{1}{2}$ pound
un demi-kilo (gramme) ⎫ **500 grammes** ⎬	1 pound
un kilo(gramme)	2 pounds

un homme de soixante kilos = a ten-stone man

un homme de quatre-vingts kilos = a thirteen-stone man

2.11.3 Area

metric	imperial
6 centimètres carrés	1 square inch
1 mètre carré	1 square yard
1 000 mètres carrés	a quarter of an acre
1 hectare 10 000 mètres carrés }	$2\frac{1}{2}$ acres
50 hectares	125 acres
250 hectares $2\frac{1}{2}$ kilomètres carrés }	1 square mile

une ferme de 40 hectares = a 100-acre farm

2.11.4 Volume

metric	imperial
1 litre	2 pints
4 litres	1 gallon
16 litres	4 gallons
24 litres	6 gallons

ma voiture fait six litres aux cent (kilomètres) = my car does fifty (miles) to the gallon
ma voiture fait onze litres aux cent = my car does twenty-five to the gallon
un demi-litre de bière = a pint of beer

2.11.5 Temperature

Centigrade	Fahrenheit
0	32
10	50
20	68
30	86

The following formulae convert the temperature scales:
Centigrade to Fahrenheit:

$$C \times \frac{9}{5} + 32 = F$$

Fahrenheit to Centigrade:

$$F - 32 \times \frac{5}{9} = C$$

Body temperature: 37°C = 98.4°F. One should consult a doctor when one's temperature rises above 40°C or 104°F!

2.11.6 Currency

The unit of currency is the *franc* (*lourd*), frequently designated F to avoid confusion with the 'old' franc, now called *centime*. However, many French people still speak in terms of old francs, ie *centimes*: thus, *gagner dix millions* is equivalent to 100 000 F or, at an exchange rate of 10 F to £1, it represents £10,000.

NOTE: **milliardaire** = millionaire

2.11.7 Time

The twenty-four hour system is used not only for official business – time-tables, the radio, etc – but sometimes also in daily speech:

il vient à dix-sept heures/dix-sept heures trente = he's coming at 5 o'clock/half past 5

2.11.8 Telephone

The digits composing telephone numbers in France are quoted in groups in the following way:

125.34.32: cent-vingt-cinq/trente-quatre/trente-deux
025.34.32: zéro-vingt-cinq/trente-quatre/trente-deux

2.11.9 Clothing sizes

Here are some examples of equivalents:

dress sizes	France	**38**	**40**	**42**	**44**				
	UK	10	12	14	16				
shoe sizes	France	**37**	**38**	**39**	**40**	**41**	**42**	**43**	**44**	**45**
	UK	4	5	6	7	8	9	10	11	12
shirt collar sizes	France	**30**	**33**	**35**	**38**	**41**	**43**	**46**	
	UK	12	13	14	15	16	17	18	

2.11.10 Numerals

Presentation of decimals, thousands and millions is different on the continent from in Britain.

For decimals a comma, *virgule*, is used instead of the British 'point':

10,1 = dix virgule un   **29,7 = vingt-neuf virgule sept**

For thousands and millions, instead of punctuation marks, the numerals are spaced out thus:

4 321   quatre mille, trois cent vingt et un
7 654 321   sept millions, six cent cinquante-quatre mille, trois cent vingt et un

3 Grammar

3.1 Gender

Gender constitutes a basic ingredient of French grammar. It is, therefore, crucial to assign the correct gender to a particular noun.

3.1.1 Rules of gender

3.1.1.1 Simple nouns (ie non-compounds)

Masculine
gender:

Type of noun	examples	exceptions
names of days of the week	dimanche, lundi	
names of months	janvier, février	
names of seasons	hiver, printemps	
names of languages	français, swahili	
names of trees	chêne, lilas	
names of metals	cuivre, plomb	
names of human agents ending in -eur, -ien	facteur, mécanicien	
nouns ending in -acle	cénacle, obstacle	
nouns ending in -ail	détail, éventail	
nouns ending in -at	assassinat, secrétariat	
nouns ending in -eau	chapeau, seau	eau, peau
nouns ending in -ège	collège, sacrilège	
nouns ending in -eil	soleil, sommeil	
nouns ending in -ème	chrysanthème	crème
nouns ending in -er	goûter, fer	cuiller, mer
nouns ending in -ice	sacrifice, bénéfice	justice, malice, police; *for usage with* délice *see later;* immondices (pl)

Masculine gender:	Type of noun	examples	exceptions
	nouns ending in -ier	calendrier, papier	
	nouns ending in -in	poulain, requin	fin, main
	nouns ending in -isme	gaullisme, prisme	
	nouns ending in -ment	commencement, monument	jument (*mare*)
	nouns ending in -o	numéro, zéro	dynamo
	nouns ending in -oir	arrosoir, miroir	
	nouns ending in -ou	genou, hibou	
	nouns ending in -our	four, tambour	cour, tour (2.2.1)
	nouns with two or more syllables ending in -age	sondage, virage	image

Feminine gender:	Type of noun	examples	exceptions
	names of sciences	chimie, physique	droit (*law*)
	names of F agents ending in -esse, -euse, -ière, -trice	maîtresse, ouvreuse, fermière, actrice	
	nouns ending in -ade	bourgade, limonade	
	nouns ending in -aie	haie, plaie	
	nouns ending in -aille	canaille, paille	
	nouns ending in -aine	haine, plaine	
	nouns ending in -aison	raison, saison	
	nouns ending in -ance/anse	assistance, danse	
	nouns ending in -ée	gorgée, matinée	apogée, musée, scarabée, trophée
	nouns ending in -ence/ense	magnificence, défense	silence
	nouns ending in -elle	ombrelle, sauterelle	
	nouns ending in -esse	petitesse, sagesse	
	nouns ending in -ette	allumette, baguette	squelette
	abstract nouns ending in -eur	hauteur, grandeur	honneur, labeur
	nouns ending in -ie	furie, partie	génie, incendie, parapluie
	nouns ending in -ière	prière, tanière	cimetière
	nouns ending in -ille	famille, grille	*for usage with* pupille *see* 2.2.1
	nouns ending in -ine	pénicilline, quinine	
	nouns ending in -ise	expertise, mise	
	nouns ending in -sion/tion	attention, compréhension	
	nouns ending in -té	beauté, rareté	comité, comté, côté, été

Feminine gender:	Type of noun	examples	exceptions
	nouns ending in **tié**	**moitié, pitié**	
	nouns ending in **-tude**	**habitude, solitude**	
	nouns ending in **-ue**	**charue, grue, mue**	
	nouns ending in **-ure**	**bigarrure, tournure**	**murmure**
	monosyllabic nouns ending in **-age**	**cage, plage**	*nouns denoting males, eg* **mage, page** (**2.2.1**), **sage**

3.1.1.2 Compound nouns (unhyphenated and hyphenated)

type of compound	gender	examples and comments M	F
noun + noun	assigned according to gender of head-word (ie first word if both nouns are of equal importance, eg *un spectateur-auditeur*, or, if one noun qualifies the other, the noun (usually the first), which is qualified, eg *un mot-clé, une idée-choc*)	*chou-fleur* *homme-grenouille* *timbre-poste*	*loi-programme* *ville-fantôme* *porte-fenêtre* (**3.2.1.2**)
adjective + noun *or* **noun + adjective**	assigned according to gender of noun	*coffre-fort* *rond-point*	*basse-cour* *chauve-souris* exceptions: *rouge-gorge, rouge-queue* are M
verb + noun	always M	*chauffe-eau* *pare-brise* *porte-avions* *portefeuille*	
invariable word + noun	assigned according to gender of noun, but always M if noun is plural	*avant-bras* *contrepoids* *haut-parleur* *deux-pièces* *mille-pattes*	*arrière-pensée* *contre-partie*
verb + verb	always M	*laissez-passer* *savoir-vivre*	
phrase	always M	*sauve-qui-peut* *va-et-vient*	

3.1.2 Difficult cases

However even native French-speakers are not always certain about the gender of some nouns, such as the following.

M gender			
abîme	dédale	iguane	parachute
âge	delta	incendie	parapluie
amalgame	dialecte	insecte	pastiche
antidote	dilemme	intermède	pétale
apogée	disco	interrogatoire	quelque chose
artifice	échange	intervalle	reproche
astérisque	édifice	légume	rêve
atome	effluve	liquide	rire
cadavre	élastique	luxe	scrupule
calme	éloge	mannequin	service
caractère	emblème	manque	silence
carrosse	épisode	masque	sourire
casque	espace	mérite	squelette
châle	exemple	mime	suicide
charme	exode	minuit	symptôme
chaume	fleuve	monopole	thermos
choix	formulaire	moustique	tonnerre
comble	geste	nu	trophée
conciliabule	gouffre	ongle	uniforme
crible	groupe	orchestre	ustensile
crime	hémisphère	organe	vice
culte	humour	panorama	

F gender			
alcôve	dynamo	horreur	pantomime
ancre	énigme	humeur	pédale
artère	épigramme	idole	recrue
atmosphère	épitaphe	idylle	réglisse
caractéristique	épithète	liqueur	sentinelle
cible	équivoque	mimique	sphère
cime	espèce	noix	surface
circulaire	extase	oasis	toux
croix	forêt	ombre	victime
dent	fourmi	orbite	vis
dupe			

3.1.3 Doubtful and variable genders

It should be noted that a small number of nouns are of doubtful or variable gender:

amour and **délice** are M in sg but F in pl

après-midi, pamplemousse, perce-neige, sandwich, have varied in gender but are now usually M

gens	adjectives are feminine when they precede **gens**:
	certaines gens, de vieilles gens
	when they follow **gens** they are masculine:
	des gens malheureux, des gens très bavards
espèce	is F, but in R1 is M when followed by a M noun:
	eg **un espèce de bâtiment**
Pâques	is treated as M sg when it is unaccompanied by an article:
	Pâques fut célébré avec beaucoup de solennité
	when it is accompanied by an article or any other qualifier it is treated as F pl:
	toutes les Pâques précédentes ont été célébrées avec beaucoup de solennité

Certain nouns denoting persons change their gender according to the sex of the person denoted:

eg **un/une camarade, un/une complice, un/une élève, un/une enfant** (but it is always **un bébé**), **un/une esclave, un/une pensionnaire, un/une touriste**

Certain professional names are treated in the same way:

eg **un/une artiste, un/une dentiste, un/une philosophe, un/une propriétaire, un/une secrétaire**

Others are preceded by the word **femme** to denote a woman exercising the profession in question:

eg **une femme auteur, une femme ingénieur, une femme médecin, une femme professeur**

or the simple M form is used with reference to women:

eg **elle est mon professeur favori**

In colloquial French it is quite possible to say:

elle est ma prof. favorite

3.1.4   Names of boats, cars, aeroplanes and watches

Boats	Despite controversy amongst grammarians, M gender is usually assigned to the names of boats:
	eg **le France, le Normandie, le Reine Elizabeth, le Torrey Canyon**
Cars	All names of makes of cars are F;
	eg **une Renault, une deux-chevaux (Citroën), une Ford, une Jaguar**
	(However, types of cars may be M: eg **un break** = an estate car)
Aeroplanes	As with names of boats, there is also controversy here.
	Usage assigns M gender to all names of aeroplanes except for **la Caravelle**:
	eg **le Boeing, le Concorde, le Jaguar, le Mig**
Watches	All names of watches are feminine:
	eg **la Rolex, la Seiko**

3.1.5 Names of towns

Towns provide a more difficult problem. Generally, they are masculine, as in *le tout Paris*, and *Copenhague est grand*. A few are feminine as in *Rome la belle*. The gender of some varies, eg *Marseille est grand(e)*. Usage with names of countries is illustrated in **3.9**.

3.2 Number

3.2.1 Formation of plurals

3.2.1.1 Simple words (ie non-compounds)
The following table summarises the procedures for plural-formation for simple words.

words ending in	plural ending	examples and comments	exceptions and comments
-ail	+s	détails, éventails	*a certain number of exceptions have pl in* -aux: corail, émail, travail, vitrail
-al	-aux	*the majority of* -al *words*: eg fluvial, idéal, illégal, immémorial, légal, moral, rival, signal, social, spécial	
	or		
	+s	bals, banals, carnavals, fatals, festivals, navals, récitals, chacals	
-au, -eau	+x	boyaux, noyaux, beaux, eaux	*a few rare words*
-eu	+x	cheveux, feux	bleus, pneus
-ou	+s	fous, trous	*7 words take* x *in pl*: bijou, caillou, chou, genou, hibou, joujou, pou

words ending in	plural ending	examples and comments	exceptions and comments
-s, -x, -z	*none*	mois, croix, nez	*none*
all other words	+**s**	amis, langues	*none*

If a plural-form sounds awkward, as in *final*, a French person avoids the word, although the form *finals* is available. In preference use *ultime* or *définitif*.

A very small number of words have two plural forms:

aïeul	**aïeuls**	grandparents
	aïeux	ancestors
ciel	**ciels**	skies in painting (semi-technical); roof of 4-poster bed
	cieux	skies, heavens (general)
œil	**œils**	in compounds, eg **œils-de-boeuf** = small round windows
	yeux	eyes

3.2.1.2 Compound words

type of compound	plural ending	examples and comments	exceptions and comments
unhyphenated compounds	*according to criteria outlined in* **3.2.1.1**	entresols, portemanteaux	bonshommes *(but* bonhommes R1*)*, gentilshommes, mesdames, mesdemoiselles, messieurs, messeigneurs
hyphenated compounds:			
noun + noun	*both elements take ending according to criteria outlined in* **3.2.1.1**	choux-fleurs, oiseaux-mouches	*none*
noun + adjective	*as above*	coffres-forts, états-majors	*none*

type of compound	plural ending	examples and comments	exceptions and comments
adjective + noun	*as above*	basses-cours, francs-maçons	*in the case of certain* F *nouns preceded by* grand *in* M *form, the adjective is sometimes invariable in the plural and sometimes not: eg* grands-mères *or* grand-mères; grands-tantes *or* grand-tantes (grands-pères, grands-oncles *are compulsory)*
verb + noun	*noun remains invariable or noun varies according to criteria outlined in* 3.2.1.1	des garde-manger, des perce-neige	*in certain cases the singular form already involves a plural noun:* un porte-avions, un presse-papiers
invariable word + noun	*noun varies according to criteria outlined in* 3.2.1.1	haut-parleurs, sous-marins	*usage varies with* après-midi: des après-midi *or* après-midis
verb + verb	*both invariable*	des laisser-aller, des faire-valoir	*none*
phrase	*plural formation depends upon nature of elements involved*	des vêtements prêts-à-porter, des va-et-vient	*none*

The foregoing analysis accounts for the following anomalies:
des porte-parole, where **porte** is a verb, but **des portes-fenêtres**, where **porte** is a noun
des garde-manger, where **garde** is a verb, but **des gardes-malades**, where **garde** is a noun

3.2.1.3 **Foreign words**
It is possible here to suggest only the broadest categories (many foreign words being somewhat rarely used), and it should be remembered that usage is often variable:

eg **des sandwichs/sandwiches, des matchs/matches**

Usually a well-established foreign word, which may well have lost some of its foreign appearance, conforms to the French pattern by adding -*s* in the plural:

eg **des biftecks, des boléros, des panoramas, des réferendums**

Some, on the other hand, remain invariable; this applies especially to words of Latin origin:

eg **des amen, des forum, des veto**

Still others retain the plural-form of the language from which they were adopted:

eg English: **des gentlemen, des recordmen** (a 'false anglicism'), **les tories**;

Italian: **des confetti, des graffiti** (also **du graffiti**), **des macaroni, des spaghetti,**

(consequently any verb with these nouns as subject should be in the plural-form).

NOTE: **du vermicelle** (sg)

Use of a foreign plural-form, especially of Latin words, eg **des sanatoria** instead of **des sanatoriums,** is frequently a mark of R3 speech or is simply affectation.

In the case of **addendum** and **erratum**, the Latin plural-form may be used as a singular noun, with a collective value, thus producing the following distinctions of meaning:

un addendum	= a single addition to be made (to a book)
un addenda/des addenda	= a list/lists of such additions
un erratum	= a single mistake to be corrected (in a book)
un errata/des errata	= a list/lists of such mistakes

3.2.1.4 Proper names

Generally, proper names are invariable in the plural:

eg **les Dupont, les Morand**
  il a acheté deux Peugeot
  plusieurs Caravelle sont retenues au sol à Orly

With the names of certain famous families, **-s** is added in the plural (but agreement as to the degree of fame necessary before such an honour is conferred upon a proper name is far from general):

eg **les Césars, les Bourbons, les Condés, les Stuarts**
and certain geographical names also have **-s** in the plural:

eg **les deux Amériques, les Guyanes, les Flandres**; also **la Flandre**

When an artist's name is applied to his paintings, an author's to his books, or a film director's to his films, and so on, usage varies, but normally no **-s** is used:

eg **j'ai vu un grand nombre de Monet au Grand-Palais**
  j'ai acheté trois Simenon chez un bouquiniste
  deux Buñuel viennent d'être montrés pour la deuxième fois

3.2.2 Differing usages between English and French

Sometimes a singular in English is conveyed by a plural in French:

dans les airs (R3)	= in the air
les applaudissements	= applause
les blés (R3)	= (fields of) corn
à ses côtés	= by his/her side
les couverts	= cutlery
des cris	= shouting
les eaux (R3)	= water
les équipements (also sg)	= equipment
les fiançailles	= engagement
les Finances	= the Treasury
les forces	= strength
les funérailles	= funeral
les informations	= the (pieces of) information
les labours (R3)	= ploughed land
les neiges (R3)	= snow
les nuisances	= nuisance (environmental)

   eg **les nuisances de la circulation urbaine**

les obsèques	= funeral
les orges	= (fields of) barley
faire des progrès	= to make progress
les ténèbres (R3)	= darkness

Conversely, sometimes a plural in English is conveyed by a singular in French:

la bouche	= lips (sometimes)
le collant	= tights
le dimanche	= on Sundays
être dans son droit	= to be within one's rights
le pantalon	= trousers
la pince	= pincers
le pyjama	= pyjamas
rencontrer le regard de qn	= to meet sb's eyes
le short	= shorts
le slip	= (under)pants
la troupe	= troops, also **les troupes**

Many 'apparent' plurals in English have a corresponding singular term in French:

le diabète	= diabetes
la dialectique	= dialectics
l'économie	= economics
la linguistique	= linguistics
l'optique	= optics
la physique	= physics

la polémique	= polemics
la politique	= politics
la statistique	= statistics
(see below)	
la tactique	= tactics

The most important exception is: **les mathématiques/maths.**

In French certain words have a singular–plural duality unlike their English equivalents:

un fruit	a 'piece' of fruit
des fruits	fruit, stressing individual fruit
un pain	a loaf of bread
des pains	loaves
du pain	bread, general
un raisin	type of grape
des raisins	different types of grapes
du raisin	grapes, general
un grain de raisin	grape
la recherche	practice of research, research, general
les recherches	detailed research
une statistique	single set of statistics
des statistiques	series of statistics

One or two other nouns have a different meaning in the plural from in the singular:

le devoir	usu duty
les devoirs	usu homework
l'enfer	hell
les enfers	the underworld
	eg **Orphée aux enfers**

3.2.3 Use of the partitive article before an adjective preceding a plural noun

With most adjectives **de** is used, but this is tending now to be R3 usage:

eg **après de longues années; de vieux vêtements**
j'ai reçu de très bonnes notes

Thus an R2, as well as an R1, speaker would easily say:

des vieux vêtements; des très bonnes notes

Des is also used when the adjective and noun form a group which may be considered a single unit; this is perfectly normal R2 usage:

eg **des jeunes filles/gens; des petits pains/pois**

3.3 Word order

The position which a word occupies in a sentence, in French as in
English, is very often a matter of style, personal preference or register.
Speakers or writers sometimes deliberately use unconventional or
unexpected sequences of words in their speech or writing, in order to
achieve certain effects. They may carefully balance one part of a
sentence against another, striving for symmetry or asymmetry; they
may wish to introduce a certain rhythm, harmony or euphony into
what they say or write, or they may wish to underline a certain word
or phrase by placing it in a prominent position in the sentence. There
is, therefore, as far as word order is concerned, a certain degree of
flexibility but obviously only within the limits permitted by grammar
and intelligibility. On the other hand, certain word orders are fixed
and may not be altered.

In this section it is not so much style as grammatical constraints
and usages which are treated, although it has to be admitted that it is
not always possible to dissociate style and grammar.

3.3.1 Adjectives and word order

The position of an adjective in relation to the noun it qualifies is one
of the most subtle aspects of French. The following sub-sections
indicate the major considerations to be borne in mind in this
connection.

3.3.1.1 Normal usage
The following diagram illustrates 'normal' usage for the positioning of
adjectives with respect to the noun they qualify. Normal usage means
language unaffected by particular considerations of style, emphasis
and so on.

types of adjectives which normally precede the noun	types of adjectives which normally follow the noun	examples
short, very common:	colour	*un livre noir*
bon (3.3.1.2)	nationality	*une voiture française*
gentil	arts and sciences	*une étude littéraire*
grand (3.3.1.2)		*l'acide sulfurique*
gros		
jeune	religion	*un pays musulman*
long	the quality denoted by	*une maison solide*
mauvais (3.3.1.2)	the adjective is	*une serviette inutile*
méchant (3.3.1.2)	stressed	
petit		
vieux		
vilain		
adjectives forming a unit with the noun: eg *une jeune fille* *un petit pain* *un grand garçon*	long adjectives past participles used as adjectives	*un paysage pittoresque* *un homme fatigué*

3.3.1.2 Adjectives which change their meaning according to their position

The meaning of certain adjectives changes according to their position with respect to the noun they qualify, often becoming more specialised. It should also be realised that in some cases the meaning of the adjective is conditioned in part by the meaning of the noun and will only be used in a certain position with a limited number of nouns (eg *bon, faux*).

ancien

before noun	after noun
former **un ancien forçat**	old **une coutume ancienne**

brave

before noun	after noun
obliging, honest **un brave homme**	courageous **un homme brave**

bon

before noun	after noun
good, nice **un bon homme**	kind, thoughtful **un homme bon**

certain

before noun	after noun
certain (indefinite article) **un certain fait**	unquestionable **un fait certain**

161

cher

before noun	after noun
dear, beloved **mon cher Jean**	expensive **une voiture chère**

dernier

before noun	after noun
last of series **le dernier mois de l'année**	last, preceding **le mois dernier**

différent

before noun	after noun
various **différentes maisons**	different **des maisons différentes**

divers

before noun	after noun
various **diverses opinions**	diverse, distinct **des opinions diverses**

faux

before noun	after noun
false, not genuine **la fausse monnaie**	untrustworthy, hypocritical **un homme faux**

galant

before noun	after noun
well-mannered **un galant homme**	attentive to women **un homme galant**

grand

before noun	after noun
great **un grand homme**	tall **un homme grand**

haut

before noun	after noun
high, open (of sea) **la haute mer**	high (of tide) **la mer haute**

honnête

before noun	after noun
of good breeding **un honnête homme**	honest, honourable **un homme honnête**

jeune

before noun	after noun
young **un jeune homme**	youthful **un homme jeune**

mauvais

before noun	after noun
bad **une mauvaise réputation**	evil **avoir l'air mauvais** = to look evil

méchant

before noun	after noun
disagreeable **une méchante affaire**	spiteful, naughty **un enfant méchant**

même

before noun	after noun
same	very, even
le même nom	les enfants mêmes

pauvre

before noun	after noun
poor (pitiful)	poor (impecunious)
un pauvre homme	un homme pauvre

propre

before noun	after noun
own, very	clean; appropriate
ses propres paroles	le linge propre; le mot propre

pur

before noun	after noun
simple, plain	pure, free from impurity
la pure vérité	l'or pur

sacré

before noun	after noun
(intensifying adj R1)	holy, sacred
sacré nom de Dieu R1	le nom sacré de Dieu

sale

before noun	after noun
nasty	dirty
un sale chien	un chien sale

seul

before noun	after noun
only	lonely
un seul homme	un homme seul

simple

before noun	after noun
ordinary, only	simple, unsophisticated
une simple question de temps	un plaisir simple
	un billet simple = a single ticket

triste

before noun	after noun
inauspicious, dull	sad
un triste visage	un visage triste

3.3.1.3 **Adjectives which may occur either before or after a noun**
Certain adjectives may be placed before or after the noun without changing their meaning. The only difference between the values of the adjectives in the two positions is that placing the adjective after the noun gives it a more prominent position in the noun group and consequently focusses attention upon it. Considerations of register are rarely involved.

adjective	examples	preferred position, if any
bas	de bas nuages = des nuages bas	*after noun*
bref	un bref entretien = un entretien bref	
charmant	un charmant tableau = un tableau charmant	
court	une courte histoire = une histoire courte	*after noun*
double	un double programme = un programme double	
énorme	un énorme lion = un lion énorme	
excellent	une excellente machine = une machine excellente	
fort	une forte économie = une économie forte	
futur	les futures générations = les générations futures	
gros	un gros homme = un homme gros	
innombrable	d'innombrables livres = des livres innombrables	
long	il a de longs cheveux = il a les cheveux longs	
magnifique	une magnifique voiture = une voiture magnifique	
meilleur	le meilleur livre (R1 *and* R2) = le livre le meilleur (R2 *and* R3)	
modeste	une modeste somme = une somme modeste	
principal	la principale ville = la ville principale	
rapide	un rapide coup d'œil = un coup d'œil rapide	
terrible	un terrible accident = un accident terrible	

On the other hand it should be noted that usage fixes certain expressions:

bas
un bâtiment bas
une table basse
des talons bas

charmant
un livre charmant
un film charmant

double
un mot à double entente
faire coup double = *to kill two birds with one stone*
un agent double

droit
le droit chemin
(*metaphorical*)
la ligne droite
(*literal*), *but*
en ligne droite

faux
une fausse déclaration

un homme faux

fort
de fortes chances
(pour) que
un homme fort

franc
un homme franc
une franche horreur

futur
ma future épouse
ma future maison

gros
une grosse tête

léger
un livre léger
un léger rhume

libre
la libre entreprise
l'école libre

long
une longue journée
une longue rue
une jupe longue

lourd	modeste	moyen
une lourde responsabilité	une femme modeste	un cours moyen
un poids lourd		un avion moyen courrier
l'industrie lourde		le Moyen Age

saint
un saint homme

3.3.1.4 Miscellaneous matters

Word position is also sometimes dictated by considerations of what is known as 'cadence majeure', that is, in French there is a preference for phrases to be constructed with words which increase in length, and a reluctance to form phrases with a long adjective preceding a short noun:

eg **une vue magnifique** rather than: **une magnifique vue**

When two adjectives follow a noun, the adjective immediately after the noun relates to it more intimately than the second adjective (unless they are joined by *et*, in which case they both apply equally):

eg **la littérature française contemporaine**
l'opinion politique populaire
les partis communiste et socialiste

Because of the desire for 'cadence majeure', as defined above, when a series of adjectives follows a noun, it is preferable for the longer or longest to be placed last:

eg **des murs gris et délabrés** is preferred to: **des murs délabrés et gris**

When a numeral is combined with an adjective preceding the noun, the order is: numeral + adjective + noun:

eg **les six derniers livres que j'ai lus**

Usage with *demi* and *nu*: when they precede the noun there is no agreement (and the adjective and noun are hyphenated), whereas when they follow it, agreement occurs:

before the noun	after the noun
une demi-heure	une heure et demie
nu-pieds	les pieds nus

3.3.2 Adverbs and word order

In a sentence consisting of a subject, verb, object and adverb, the adverb normally precedes the object. However, when it is stressed it follows the object. The usage with adverbs of time and place is somewhat different. Adverbial phrases (rather than simple adverbs) normally follow the object, whatever the circumstances.

		examples
normal order (other than adverbs of time and space)	subject + simple tense of verb + simple adverb + object	*j'aime beaucoup le cidre* *il attend patiemment la voiture*
	subject + compound tense of verb (auxiliary verb + simple adverb + past participle) + object	*j'ai longuement regardé le paysage* *elle a soigneusement nettoyé sa chambre*
	subject + verb + object + adverbial phrase	*j'ai lu le livre encore une fois*
order with stress on adverb	subject + verb + object + adverb	*il attend la voiture patiemment* *elle a nettoyé sa chambre soigneusement*
normal order with adverbs of time and place	subject + verb + object + adverb	*je suis allé à la bibliothèque aujourd'hui* *j'ai vu un film de Barrault hier* *je ferai mon travail demain* *il achète son journal ici/là*
order with stress on adverb of time	adverb + subject + verb + object	*aujourd'hui je suis allé à la bibliothèque* *hier j'ai vu un film de Barrault* *demain je ferai mon travail*
order with stress on *là*	subject + verb + *là* + object	*elle fait là son travail*

The position of certain common short adverbs, such as *bien* and *mieux*, as well as *tout* as a direct object, is flexible in relation to an infinitive preceded by an unstressed object pronoun:

adverb and *tout*	normal order	less frequently found order
bien	pour bien me comprendre	pour me bien comprendre
		pour me comprendre bien
mieux	pour mieux le faire	pour le mieux faire
		pour le faire mieux
trop	sans trop en prendre	sans en prendre trop
tout	je vais tout vous dire	je vais vous dire tout

The addition of an adverb like *bien* to an expression like *parler français* has certain repercussions upon the form of the expression as can be seen by the following examples:

parler français   parler bien le français
parler français extrêmement bien

When *bien* is combined with *vouloir*, the varying orders sometimes reflect a contrast of register:

structure	example	register
bien+ finite form of *vouloir*	je veux bien t'aider	all registers
	il a bien voulu me prêter de l'argent	all registers
bien+ infinitive of *vouloir*	je vous demande de bien vouloir m'excuser	R1 + R2
	je vous demande de vouloir bien m'excuser	R3

The position of adverbs in conjunction with a negative expression also requires comment: certain adverbs precede the negative particle *pas* rather than follow it:

          donc   donc
eg il ne pleut même   pas   je ne l'ai même   pas fait
          toujours   toujours

With *encore* and a simple tense, the norm is:
il ne pleut pas encore
But with a compound tense there are two possibilities:
je ne l'ai encore pas fait
je ne l'ai pas encore fait (more usual)
For inversion with adverbs, see section **3.3.4**.

3.3.3 Personal pronouns and word order

The order of unstressed pronouns excluding subject pronouns with respect to the verb is as follows:

me							
te	le			le	lui		all tenses and moods
nous	la	y	en	la	leur	y en +	of the verb, except
vous	les			les			the positive imperative
se							

examples	elle me le donne	= she gives it to me
	elle te le donne	= she gives it to you
	elle le lui donne	= she gives it to him/her
	elle nous le donne	= she gives it to us
	elle vous le donne	= she gives it to you
	elle le leur donne	= she gives it to them
	il leur en donne	= he gives them some
	il y en a	= there is/are some

positive imperative +	le la lui les	moi toi lui leur	m' t' lui leur	y en	le nous vous les	y en

examples	donne-le-moi	= give it to me
	donne-m'en	= give me some
	donne-nous-en	= give us some

NOTE: it is not acceptable to combine the direct objects *me*, *te*, *nous*, *vous*, *se*, with the indirect objects *lui*, *leur*. Instead the indirect object figures after the verb:

eg il me présente à elle
    elle se fie à eux

3.3.4 Inversion

Whereas normal word order in French requires that the subject precede the verb, inversion involves the placing of the subject after the verb. Inversion, it should be noted, is frequently a mark of formal, refined language. Inversion is used in the following circumstances:

Often in the official variety of French, when a long subject, usually consisting of an enumeration of nouns, occurring in its normal position, would delay the appearance of the verb and thus impair comprehension:

eg se sont qualifiés les numéros douze, treize, quinze, etc
    ont été augmentés le pain, le lait, le beurre

With verbs of movement and *rester* to provide an intimate link with the previous sentence or to focus attention on the noun or the verb:

eg suivit un vacarme assourdissant
    voilà deux tâches bien faites; reste une troisième

In sentences in R3 usage, introduced by adverbs and adverbial phrases of time (eg *alors*, *aujourd'hui*, *bientôt*, *enfin*) and place (eg *de là*, *ici*, *là*):

eg **de là découlent grand nombre de nos problèmes actuels**
    au jardin poussait un arbre
    ensuite arrivèrent des renforts

also, occasionally, in sentences introduced by an adjective:
eg **rares sont les écrivains qui ...**
    telle est ma volonté

In R2 and R3 usage with concessive clauses of the following type:
quelles que soient les causes, cela ne changera rien au problème

With relative clauses:
eg **une charrette que tiraient deux chevaux**
    une voiture que conduisait un vieux monsieur

With *que*-clauses:
eg **ce que dit le président doit être bien noté**

With 'incises' (ie references to speakers occurring after passages of direct speech):
eg **j'ai soif, dit-il**
    je ne fais rien, a répondu mon père

In R2 and R3 usage after initial *à peine, ainsi, aussi, du moins, encore,* and in R3 usage after initial *tout au plus*:
eg **à peine semblait-il écouter ce que disait le professeur**
    à peine la nuit était-elle venue que ...

Usage with *peut-être, sans doute* demands particular comment:

R1			R3		R1–R3	
peut-être	+que+	direct	**peut-être**	+inversion	verb +	**peut-être**
sans doute		order	**sans doute**			**sans doute**
eg **peut-être/sans doute**			eg **peut-être/sans doute**		eg **il va venir peut-**	
qu'il va venir			**va-t-il venir**		**être/sans doute**	
					il va peut-être/sans	
					doute venir	

Inversion may take the following forms:

		examples
pronoun	simply placed after the verb	**dit-il**
noun	sometimes placed after the verb, for stylistic reasons such as balance	*dans le parc se dressait un monument*
	sometimes remains before the verb and a pronoun repeats it after the verb	*aussi la jeune fille s'était-elle décidée à partir*

To summarise, inversion may occur in the following circumstances:

grammatical circumstances	register
in enumerations	R3
with verbs of movement and *rester*	R3
in sentences introduced by adverbs and adverbial phrases of time and place	R3
in sentences introduced by an adjective	R3
in concessive, relative and *que*-clauses	R2 and R3
in 'incises'	R2 and R3
after initial *à peine, ainsi, aussi, du moins, peut-être, sans doute*	R2 and R3
after initial *tout au plus*	R3

3.3.5 Interrogatives and word order

French interrogative sentences may be of two types:
1 those which involve an interrogative word and which invite a detailed reply (*qui, que, quoi, comment, où*, etc)
2 those which do not involve an interrogative word and which invite a yes/no answer.

Questions may be expressed in the following ways, considerations of register being an important factor:

type of question	form of question	register	examples
questions without interrogative word (see NOTE A)	inversion of subject + verb	R2, R3	*allez-vous manger maintenant?* *mon père, vous a-t-il téléphoné?*
	use of *est-ce que* + direct order	R2	*est-ce que vous y allez maintenant?* *est-ce que mon père vous a téléphoné?*
	addition of *n'est-ce pas* at end of direct order (see NOTE B)	R2	*vous allez manger maintenant, n'est-ce pas?* *mon père vous a téléphoné, n'est-ce pas?*
	direct order + rising intonation	R1	*vous allez manger maintenant?* *mon père vous a téléphoné?*

type of question	form of question	register	examples
questions with interrogative word: *combien, comment, lequel, où, pourquoi, quand, qui/que/quoi*	interrogative word + inversion	R2, R3	*pourquoi êtes-vous sorti?* *pourquoi votre père est-il sorti?*
	interrogative word + *est-ce que* + direct order; *est-ce qui* in the case of *qui* subject (see NOTE C)	R2	*pourquoi est-ce que vous êtes sorti?* *pourquoi est-ce que votre père est sorti?* *qui est-ce qui va venir ce soir?* *qui est-ce que vous avez invité?*
	direct order with interrogative word placed at end of question	R1	*vous sortez quand?* *votre père sort quand?*
	interrogative word + direct order	R1	*où tu vas?* *comment tu fais ça?*
	interrogative word + *c'est que*	R1	*quand c'est que vous sortez?*
	highlighting by placing noun or stressed form of pronoun before interrogative word, or at end of question in direct order (3.3.7)	R1	*votre père, pourquoi il est sorti?* *lui, pourquoi il est sorti?* *pourquoi votre père il est sorti?* *pourquoi il est sorti, lui?*

NOTE A: *Si* and not *oui* is used for an affirmative reply to a negative question or suggestion:

eg **Vous n'allez pas manger maintenant, n'est-ce pas? – Si!**

NOTE B: The use of *n'est-ce pas* implies agreement with the statement contained in the question.

NOTE C: *Qui* alone is more common as subject than *qui est-ce qui*. On the other hand the long forms of the other interrogative pronouns are more frequently used than the short forms:

eg **qui est-ce que vous voyez?** rather than: **qui voyez-vous?**

   qu'est-ce que tu fais? rather than: **que fais-tu?**

3.3.6   Exclamations and word order

form of exclamation	register	examples
inversion of subject pronoun	R3	*est-elle jolie!*
inversion of noun with repetition by pronoun	R3	*est-elle jolie, cette fille!*
comme/que + direct order with pronoun and highlighting of noun (3.3.7)	R2, R3	*comme elle est jolie!* *qu'elle est jolie, cette fille!*
ce que/qu'est-ce que + direct order and highlighting (3.3.7)	R1	*ce que/qu'est-ce que c'est bête, ce film!*
intonation	R2	*elle est jolie!*

3.3.7   Highlighting

Highlighting is the means whereby a certain element of a sentence is brought into prominence and has attention focussed upon it. It is naturally a very common process in every-day speech when it is essential for the person addressed to appreciate immediately what is the most significant point in what is being said to him or her. Highlighting is achieved by adjusting 'normal' word order:

$$\text{subject} + \text{verb} + \begin{cases} \text{adjective} \\ \text{adverb} \\ \text{object} \\ \text{prepositional phrase} \\ \text{etc} \end{cases}$$

An element that is being highlighted is called a focal element; elements of a sentence may be highlighted in the following ways:

means of highlighting	examples
by isolating the focal element in front of the sentence and, if appropriate, repeating it by a pronoun	*lui, il a écrit ce livre* *ce livre, il l'a écrit* *penser aux vacances, j'ose pas/je ne l'ose pas* *Paris, j'en rêve souvent*
by isolating the focal element after the sentence, and, if appropriate, heralding it by a pronoun	*il a écrit ce livre, lui* *il l'a écrit, ce livre* *j'en rêve souvent, de Paris* *il y en a, des voitures*

by using **c'est ... qui/que**	*c'est lui qui a écrit ce livre*
	c'est ce livre-ci qu'il a écrit
	c'est à Paris que je pense souvent
	c'est demain que je dois aller chez le médecin
by using the passive voice if appropriate	*ce livre a été écrit par Camus*
double focus may be achieved by combining means of highlighting	*ce livre, c'est lui qui l'a écrit*

3.4 Prepositions

Competent and accurate handling of prepositions is as sure a mark as any of a speaker's ease in a foreign language. The main problem for an English-speaker speaking French is knowing when to use the same preposition as in English, when to use a different one, or whether to use one at all.

Reduced to its most basic function, a preposition is a linking word, which may express a relationship between what precedes and what follows it. The relationship may be one of place, time, aim, means, manner, possession, quantity, measurement, cause, purpose, accompaniment, support/opposition, concession, exception, reference. It is well known that there is not a one-to-one correspondence between relationship and preposition (see in particular **3.4.4**). Certain prepositions have a constant value in themselves, eg *avec, devant, environ, parmi* (**3.4.4.1**), whereas others in isolation have a more indeterminate value, which may become defined to a certain extent by the meaning of the construction or context in which they occur, eg *à, de, en*. This latter series of prepositions may lose their identity altogether and become fully integrated into compound words: compare, for example, *une pomme de terre* and *la pomme de Jean*, *un sac à main* and *une canne à pommeau sculpté*.

Prepositions may link different types of words:
adjective/noun to noun
verb to infinitive
verb to noun
adjective/noun to infinitive
adverb to noun

and these groups of words function in a variety of ways, principally to introduce:

an adverbial expression:	**agir par jalousie**
an indirect object:	**donner à quelqu'un**
a complement of a verb in the passive mood:	**mordu par un chien**
an adjectival expression:	**la voiture de mon père**
an infinitival expression:	**j'ai fini par me coucher**
a prepositional phrase:	**à cause de mon mal de tête**

Just as there is not a one-to-one correspondence between relationship and preposition, neither is there a one-to-one correspondence between English and French prepositions, and herein lies the major difficulty for the student of French: which preposition to use? The most obvious illustration of this is the simple problem of knowing which preposition to use to link a verb and an infinitive in French (**3.4.1**). In English the situation is straightforward: verb + *to* + infinitive (except for modal verbs), but in French the possibilities are wider:

$$\text{verb} + \begin{cases} \text{à} \\ \text{de} \\ \text{par} \\ \text{no preposition} (\ldots) \end{cases} + \text{infinitive}$$

The symbol (...) will be used to indicate that no preposition is required to link the infinitive (or noun, or pronoun) to the verb.

In the following sections an attempt is made to provide a systematic analysis of the use of prepositions in French.

NOTE: It is necessary to repeat the preposition before coordinated nouns, pronouns and verbs which are not closely related in sense:

eg **j'ai parlé *avec* sa mère et *avec* la directrice de l'école**

On the other hand, it is not normally necessary to repeat it before coordinated nouns, pronouns and verbs which are closely related in sense:

eg **j'ai parlé *avec* sa mère et (*avec*) son père**

faire part de l'événement *à* ses amis et connaissances

3.4.1   verb + preposition

3.4.1.1   verb + preposition + infinitive

$$\text{verb} + \begin{cases} \text{à} \\ \text{de} \\ \text{par} \\ \text{pour} \\ (\ldots) \end{cases} + \text{infinitive}$$

à

eg
il s'est abaissé *à* fréquenter des gens méprisables
elle s'acharne *à* le terminer ce soir
il tarde *à* venir
nous nous sommes employés *à* le mettre à son aise

s'abaisser à
aboutir à
s'accorder à (R3) (3.4.3)
s'acharner à
s'adonner à
aimer à (R3)
s'amuser à
s'animer à
s'appliquer à
apprendre à
s'apprêter à
arriver à
aspirer à
s'assujettir à (R3)
s'astreindre à
s'attacher à
s'attendre à (3.4.3)
s'avilir à (R3)
avoir à
se borner à
se buter à
chercher à
commencer à (3.4.3)
se complaire à
concourir à
se consacrer à
consentir à
consister à
conspirer à
se consumer à
continuer à (3.4.3)
contribuer à
se décider à (3.4.3)
demander à (3.4.3)
se déterminer à
se dévouer à
se disposer à
se divertir à
s'efforcer à (R3) (3.4.3)

s'employer à
s'engager à
s'ennuyer à (3.4.3)
s'enhardir à
s'entraîner à
équivaloir à
s'essayer à
s'évertuer à
exceller à (R3)
s'exposer à
se fatiguer à
s'habituer à (3.4.3)
se hasarder à
hésiter à
incliner à (R3)
s'ingénier à
insister à (3.4.3)
s'intéresser à (3.4.3)
se mettre à
s'obstiner à
s'occuper à (3.4.3)
s'offrir à
s'opiniâtrer à (R3)
parvenir à
passer son temps à
perdre son temps à
persévérer à
persister à
se plaire à
se plier à
se prendre à
prendre plaisir à
se préparer à
se refuser à (3.4.3)
renoncer à
répugner à (R3) (3.4.3)
se résigner à
se résoudre à (3.4.3)
réussir à (3.4.3)

revenir à
servir à (3.4.3)
songer à
tarder à (3.4.3)
tendre à (R3)

tenir à (3.4.3)
travailler à
venir à (R3) (3.4.3)
viser à (R3) (3.4.3)

de

eg

il s'abstient *de* commenter l'événement
il s'avise *de* partir tout de suite
l'armée menaçait *de* franchir la frontière
vous méritez *de* recevoir une médaille
vous avez raison *de* venir

s'abstenir de
accepter de
achever de (3.4.3)
s'accuser de
affecter de
s'affliger de
ambitionner de (R3)
s'applaudir de (R3)
s'arrêter de
attendre de (3.4.3)
s'aviser de
avoir peur de
brûler de
cesser de
se charger de
choisir de
commencer de (R3) (3.4.3)
comploter de
continuer de (3.4.3)
convenir de (3.4.3)
craindre de
décider de (3.4.3)
dédaigner de (cf daigner
    below)
se dépêcher de
détester de
se devoir de (R3)
discontinuer de (R3)
disconvenir de (R3)
se disculper de
s'efforcer de (3.4.3)
s'empêcher de

s'empresser de
s'ennuyer de (3.4.3)
entreprendre de
espérer de (R3) (3.4.3)
essayer de
s'étonner de
éviter de
s'excuser de
exulter de
bien faire de
faire semblant de
se féliciter de
finir de (3.4.3)
se flatter de
être forcé de (3.4.3)
se garder de
se glorifier de
haïr de (R3)
se hâter de
s'indigner de
jurer de
manquer de (3.4.3)
en avoir marre de (R1)
méditer de
se mêler de (3.4.3)
menacer de
mériter de
négliger de
être obligé de (3.4.3)
s'occuper de (3.4.3)
offrir de
omettre de

oublier de	résoudre de (3.4.3)
parler de	se retenir de
se piquer de	risquer de
prendre garde de	rougir de
se presser de	simuler de
prévoir de (3.4.3)	souhaiter de (3.4.3)
projeter de	se souvenir de
promettre de	suffire de (3.4.3)
se proposer de	supporter de
avoir raison de	tâcher de
redouter de	tenter de
refuser de (3.4.3)	avoir tort de
regretter de	se vanter de
se repentir de	venir de (3.4.3)

par achever par (3.4.3)   finir par (3.4.3)
      commencer par (3.4.3) terminer par

pour attendre pour (3.4.3) insister pour (3.4.3)
       hésiter pour (3.4.3)   suffire pour (3.4.3)

**verb +
infinitive
ie (...)**

With certain verbs no preposition is required to link the verb with the following infinitive:

eg **j'aime le faire
je peux y aller
nous pensions lui envoyer une lettre**

aimer (...)	falloir (...)
aimer mieux (...)	manquer (...) (3.4.3)
aller (...)	oser (...)
avoir beau (...)	penser (...) (3.4.3)
compter (...)	pouvoir (...)
daigner (...)	préférer (...)
devoir (...)	savoir (...)
entendre (...) R3 = *to intend*	souhaiter (...) (3.4.3)
entrer (...)	valoir mieux (...)
espérer (...) (3.4.3)	venir (...) (3.4.3)
faillir (...) (3.4.3)	vouloir (...)

Usage with *faire, entendre, laisser* and *voir* + infinitival group:
in the group, the infinitive may have a subject and an object (which may be a *que*-clause) of its own:

eg **j'ai vu *une jeune fille* sortir de la salle**
     (subject of the infinitive)
j'ai entendu *la jeune fille* chanter *des chansons* à la guitare
     (subject of the infinitive)   (object of the infinitive)

177

The following diagram illustrates the various constructions:

structure	notes	examples
faire, etc + infinitive with subject only	if the subject is a noun, it precedes the infinitive; if it is a pronoun, it precedes the finite verb	*elle a entendu son père ouvrir la porte* *elle l'a fait crier*
faire, etc + infinitive with object only	if the object is a noun, it follows the infinitive; if it is a pronoun, it precedes the finite verb	*elle a fait réparer sa voiture* *j'ai entendu dire que ...* *j'ai entendu chanter des chansons* *elle l'a fait réparer*
faire + infinitive with subject and object	the subject figures as an indirect object	*elle lui a fait lire le journal* *il a fait admettre à sa mère que ...* *je lui ai fait comprendre que ...*
entendre, laisser, voir + infinitive with subject and object	verb + subject + infinitive + object	*nous avons entendu des garçons chanter des cantiques* *j'ai vu plusieurs ouvriers construire la maison*

3.4.1.2 verb + preposition + $\genfrac{}{}{0pt}{}{\text{noun}}{\text{pronoun}}$

$$\text{verb} + \begin{matrix} \textit{à} \\ \textit{de} \\ \textit{avec} \\ \textit{dans} \\ \textit{sur} \end{matrix} + \begin{matrix} \text{noun} \\ \text{pronoun} \end{matrix}$$

à NOTE: Whereas in English it is possible for an indirect object in an active clause to become the subject of a passive voice clause (eg my father gave *me* a book = *I* was given a book by my father), in French such a transformation is not permitted and has to be avoided. (In other words, French active voice *la réception me plaît* has no passive equivalent.)

Exceptions to this general rule are specified below.

Examples of verb + à + $\genfrac{}{}{0pt}{}{\text{noun}}{\text{pronoun}}$:

je m'attends *à* son arrivée
il pare *à* tout danger
elle a survécu *à* l'explosion
il a renoncé *à* sa carrière

assister à
s'attendre à
se confier à (**3.4.3**)
être confronté à (**3.4.3**)
consentir à (**3.4.3**)
convenir à (**3.4.3**)
croire à (**3.4.3**)
déplaire à
désobéir à

NOTE: désobéir *can be used in the passive voice with persons or things*

échapper à (**3.4.3**)
faillir à (**3.4.3**)
se fier à (**3.4.3**)
insulter à (R3) (**3.4.3**)
manquer à (**3.4.3**)
se mêler à (**3.4.3**)
nuire à
obéir à

NOTE: *as with* désobéir: eg il est obéi; mon ordre sera obéi

pardonner à

NOTE: pardonner à *can be used in passive voice*

parer à
participer à (**3.4.3**)
penser à (**3.4.3**)

plaire à
prendre part à
profiter à

NOTE: *used impersonally*: eg cela profite à l'homme

remédier à
renoncer à
répondre à (**3.4.3**)
répugner à (R3) (**3.4.3**)
résister à
ressembler à
ressortir à (R3) = to be under the jurisdiction of (**3.4.3**)
réussir à (**3.4.3**)
satisfaire à (R3) (**3.4.3**)
servir à (**3.4.3**)
songer à
subvenir à (eg aux besoins de qn)
succéder à
suffire à (**3.4.3**)
surseoir à (R3)
survivre à
téléphoner à
toucher à

NOTE: *occ, as in* toucher à sa fin

vaquer à

de   eg

elle a accouché *de* trois enfants
je conviens *de* mon erreur
il se méfie même *de* ses amis

abuser de (**3.4.3**)
s'accommoder de (**3.4.3**)
s'accompagner de
accoucher de
s'aider de
s'alimenter de
s'alourdir de
s'apercevoir de
(s') approcher de
s'armer de
avoir besoin/honte/peur de

changer de
se charger de
convenir de
se défier de (cf **3.4.3** fier)
se démettre de (R3)
démissionner de
dépendre de
se dorer de (R3)
se douter de (**3.4.3**)
s'échàpper de (**3.4.3**)
écoper de

s'embellir de	s'offenser de
s'émerveiller de	s'offusquer de
s'emparer de	s'orner de
s'ennuyer de (3.4.3)	se parer de
s'enrichir de	partir de
s'entourer de	se passer de
s'envelopper de	penser de (3.4.3)
s'évader de	profiter de
s'excuser de	répondre de (3.4.3)
s'indigner de	rire de
s'inquiéter de	se saisir de
s'inspirer de	se servir de (3.4.3)
se jouer de (R3) (3.4.3)	sortir de
jouir de	se souvenir de
manquer de (3.4.3)	se targuer de
médire de	témoigner de
se méfier de	triompher de
se mêler de (3.4.3)	se tromper de (3.4.3)
mésuser de (R3)	user de (R3) (3.4.3)
se moquer de	se vanter de
s'occuper de (3.4.3)	vivre de (3.4.3)

avec	s'accorder avec	rivaliser avec (3.4.3)
	se familiariser avec	se solidariser avec
dans	s'embarquer dans	
sur	s'accorder sur	insister sur (3.4.3)
	brancher sur (3.4.3)	se renseigner sur

There is sometimes the possibility of choice of preposition with certain verbs:

eg **l'Assemblée Nationale a débattu/a discuté (*de*) la question**
   juger (*d'*) une personne
   que fait-il *avec* le/*du* livre?

anticiper + (. . .)/sur	juger + (. . .)/de = *to*
débattre + (. . .)/de	*estimate*
délibérer + (. . .)/de (R3)	juger + sur/par = *to judge by*
divorcer + avec/d'avec (3.4.3)	méditer + (. . .)/sur
discuter + (. . .)/de	se passionner de/pour (3.4.3)
faire + avec/de (3.4.3)	présider + (. . .)/à (R3)
s'identifier + à/avec (*less*	réfléchir + sur/à
common)	rêver + à/de (*more common*)
informer + sur/de	sauver la vie + de/à qn
inscrire + dans/sur	traiter + (. . .)/de
(s') intégrer + dans/à	

3.4.1.3   verb + direct object + preposition + infinitive

verb + direct object + $\begin{array}{c} à \\ de \end{array}$ + infinitive

à

eg
les autorités l'ont autorisée *à* partir
cette idée m'amène *à* dire que ...

aider ... à	encourager ... à
amener ... à	engager ... à
autoriser ... à	entraîner ... à
condamner ... à	exhorter ... à (R3)
conduire ... à (R3)	forcer ... à (**3.4.3**)
contraindre ... à (**3.4.3**)	inviter ... à
convier ... à	obliger ... à (**3.4.3**)
décider ... à (**3.4.3**)	pousser ... à
déterminer ... à	

de

eg
la police l'accuse *de* tuer un homme
je vous remercie *de* m'avoir aidée

accuser ... de	implorer ... de
avertir ... de	intéresser ... de (impers)
conjurer ... de (R3)	(**3.4.3**)
contraindre ... de (**3.4.3.**)	menacer ... de
convaincre ... de	persuader ... de (**3.4.3**)
décourager ... de	prier ... de
défier ... de	remercier ... de
dissuader ... de	sommer ... de (R3)
empêcher ... de	soupçonner ... de
féliciter ... de	supplier ... de

3.4.1.4   verb + preposition + $\begin{array}{c} noun \\ pronoun \end{array}$ + preposition + infinitive

verb + *à* + $\begin{array}{c} noun \\ pronoun \end{array}$ + *de* + infinitive

eg **je (dé)conseille *à* la femme *de* le faire**
    elle sait gré *à* son père *de* l'aider au dernier moment
    il pardonne *à* son ami *de* l'avoir omis
    il lui tarde *de* le revoir

The comment about active-passive transformation under **3.4.1.2** is
also relevant here.

à ... de

appartenir (impers) à ... de	déconseiller à ... de
arriver (impers) à ... de	défendre à ... de
commander à ... de	demander à ... de (**3.4.3**)
conseiller à ... de	dire à ... de (**3.4.3**)

imposer à ... de
être impossible/possible
   à ... de
incomber (impers) à ... de
inspirer à ... de (R3)
interdire à ... de
ordonner à ... de
pardonner à ... de
permettre à ... de
persuader à ... de (R3)
   (3.4.3)
NOTE: persuader *may be used*

passively: je suis persuadé que ...
plaire (impers) à ... de
reprocher à ... de
répugner (impers) à ... de
   (3.4.3)
savoir gré à ... de (R3)
faire signe à ... de
souhaiter à ... de (3.4.3)
suggérer à ... de
tarder (impers) à ... de
   (3.4.3)
en vouloir à ... de

$$\text{verb} + \grave{a} + \genfrac{}{}{0pt}{}{\text{noun}}{\text{pronoun}} + \grave{a} + \text{infinitive}$$

eg le professeur apprend/enseigne *à* l'élève *à* lire le français

à ... à   apprendre à ... à   enseigner à ... à

NOTE: enseigner un enfant, *but* apprendre *cannot be used in this way.*
Also, apprendre/enseigner qch à qn (**3.4.1.5**)

3.4.1.5 $\text{verb} + \text{direct object} + \text{preposition} + \genfrac{}{}{0pt}{}{\text{noun}}{\text{pronoun}}$

$$\text{verb} + \text{direct object} + \genfrac{}{}{0pt}{}{\genfrac{}{}{0pt}{}{\grave{a}}{\text{de}}}{\genfrac{}{}{0pt}{}{\text{avec}}{\genfrac{}{}{0pt}{}{\text{dans}}{\text{par}}} + \genfrac{}{}{0pt}{}{\text{noun}}{\text{pronoun}}$$

verb + direct
object + *à*
+ noun
  pronoun

eg
cette action lui aliène toutes les sympathies
la sœur a caché la lettre *à* son frère
il évite *à* son fils la tâche de le récrire
le capitaine imposa le silence *à* ses hommes
j'ai acheté des œufs *au* fermier
NOTE: acheter qch à qn *is ambiguous, as à can mean 'for' or 'from'.*
Usually à meaning 'for' is R1 while à meaning 'from' is R1 + R2.

accommoder ... à (R3)
   (3.4.3)
accorder ... à
acheter ... à
aliéner ... à
apprendre ... à
arracher ... à (3.4.3)

assigner ... à (R3)
associer ... à
cacher ... à
chercher ... à
commander ... à
communiquer ... à
comparer ... à (3.4.3)

conférer ... à (R3)

confier ... à (3.4.3)

coûter ... à

décerner ... à

défendre ... à

demander ... à (3.4.3)

dérober ... à

devoir ... à (3.4.3)

dissimuler ... à

donner ... à

emprunter ... à

enlever ... à (3.4.3)

enseigner ... à

envier ... à

envoyer ... à

épargner ... à

éviter ... à

exprimer ... à

extorquer ... à

fournir ... à

garantir ... à

imposer ... à

imprimer ... à

inspirer ... à

interdire ... à

intéresser ... à (3.4.3)

manifester ... à

montrer ... à

octroyer ... à (R3)

ôter ... à (3.4.3)

pardonner ... à

payer ... à (3.4.3 and 3.4.5)

permettre ... à

prêcher ... à

prendre ... à (3.4.3)

préparer ... à

présenter ... à

prodiguer ... à (R3)

rappeler ... à (3.4.3)

réclamer ... à

recommander ... à

refuser ... à (3.4.3)

reprocher ... à

réserver ... à

restituer ... à

retrancher ... à

souhaiter ... à (3.4.3)

soustraire ... à

substituer ... à

transmettre ... à

voler ... à

NOTE: voler qn = *to steal from sb* (3.4.5)

verb + direct object + *de* + noun + pronoun	eg
	on l'a accusée *de* vol
	assurez-le *de* mon respect

absoudre ... de (R3)

accabler ... de

accuser ... de

approcher ... de

arracher ... de (3.4.3)

assurer ... de (3.4.3)

avertir ... de

aviser ... de

bombarder ... de

charger ... de

complimenter ... de

débarrasser ... de

décharger ... de

dégoûter ... de

délivrer ... de

détourner ... de

dispenser ... de

écarter ... de

éloigner ... de

enlever ... de (3.4.3)

excuser ... de

exempter ... de

féliciter ... de

frapper ... de

informer . . . de	persuader . . . de (**3.4.3**)
libérer . . . de	prévenir . . . de
menacer . . . de	remercier . . . de
ôter . . . de (**3.4.3**)	traiter . . . de (= *to call sb sth*)

NOTE: conjurer (R3), empêcher, prier *and* supplier *may only be used in this structure with the pronoun* en:
eg **je vous en prie**

avec   comparer . . . avec (R1) (**3.4.3**)

dans   glaner . . . dans   puiser . . . dans
                        prendre . . . dans (**3.4.3**)

par   remplacer . . . par

3.4.2   noun / adjective + preposition + infinitive

3.4.2.1   noun + preposition + infinitive

noun + à / de + infinitive   eg
son acharnement *à* compléter la tâche
son habileté *à* défendre la cause

acharnement à	habileté à
aisance à	hésitation à
aptitude à	impuissance à
ardeur à	insistance à (**3.4.3**)
avidité à	intérêt à (**3.4.3**)
détermination à	persistance à
difficulté à	regret à
facilité à	répugnance à

NOTE: un homme *à* craindre
           un homme *à* tout faire

de   eg
je me trouvais dans l'impossibilité *de* partir
sa volonté *de* l'emporter m'étonna

autorisation de	obligation de
besoin de	occasion de
capacité de	nécessité de
désir de	permission de
droit de (**3.4.3**)	plaisir de
honte de	rage de
impossibilité de	volonté de
incapacité de	

NOTE: *use of* de + *infinitive with*: avoir honte, les moyens, peur, raison, le temps, tort, faire semblant. Raison *is normally followed by* de *not* pour *with a noun or pronoun*:

    eg la raison *de* son départ

however: la raison pour laquelle + *relative clause*

          la raison pourquoi = R3

merci de *is more formal than* merci pour

3.4.2.2 **adjective + preposition + infinitive**

        adjective + $\genfrac{}{}{0pt}{}{à}{de}$ **+ infinitive**

à

    eg

    il est lent *à* raisonner
    elle est prompte *à* répondre
    il était assis *à* lire son journal

apte à	long à
assis à	préparé à
décidé à	prêt à
déterminé à	prompt à
disposé à	propre à
enclin à	quitte à
fondé à (R3)	résolu à
habile à	unanime à, *also* pour
lent à	

    NOTE: c'est lourd *à* porter (**3.8.2.1**)
            c'est facile *à* faire
            c'est agréable *à* entendre
            il est le seul/premier/deuxième, etc/dernier *à* arriver

de

    eg

    je suis curieux *de* le savoir
    vous êtes libre *de* partir

avide de	libre de
capable de	mécontent de
certain de	ravi de (R3)
content de (*not* avec)	reconnaissant de (R3)
curieux de	responsable de
désireux de (R3)	satisfait de (**3.4.3**)
heureux de (*not* avec)	sûr de

    NOTE: *also the use with past participles*: aimé, estimé, apprécié, etc
    eg il est aimé *de* tout le monde
         il est estimé *de* tous les critiques
When the agent is active, however, par *is often used*:
    eg il a été mordu *par* son chien (NB 3.4.4.2 BY)
accompagné *may be followed by* de *or* par
pour *must be used after* trop *and* assez:
    eg il est trop/assez grand *pour* le faire

185

3.4.3 Varying prepositions

In certain cases, depending upon meaning, register, euphony, context or construction, the preposition following a verb or related expression varies. It is vital to fit the right preposition with the right set of circumstances. The following list is an attempt to highlight the most important verbs and expressions involved in these prepositional variations.

abuser	**il abuse (R3) le public** he deceives . . . **il abuse *de* la bonté de son ami** he takes advantage of . . .
(s')accommoder	**il accommode (R3) sa conduite *à* toutes les circonstances** he adapts his conduct . . . **je m'accommoderai *de* ce logement modeste** I shall accept as suitable . . .
s'accorder	**tout le monde s'accorde (R3) *à* reconnaître que . . .** everyone agrees in . . . **le verbe s'accorde *avec* le nom** **ils se sont accordés *sur* le traité de paix**
achever	**il acheva *de* se ruiner** he finally . . . **il commença par rire, acheva *par* pleurer:** (here one action is added to another)
aimer	**j'aime *à* (R3) croire que . . .** **elle aime jouer *de* la guitare** **j'aime mieux travailler que *de* jouer** (NOTE: *de* after second verb)
arracher	**il arracha sa chemise *à* son frère:** (*à* with persons) **il l'arracha *de* son fauteuil:** (*de* with things, although *à* is possible)
assurer	**je lui ai assuré qu'il n'y avait rien à craindre** (suggests affirmation) **assurez-le *de* mon respect** (suggests guarantee)
attendre	**il attendait *pour/de* (R3) partir** **je ne m'attendais pas *à* un pareil traitement** I did not expect . . . **je m'attends *à* ce qu'il revienne** I expect . . . **il attend le bateau** he waits for . . .

avoir	**avoir affaire *à* qn** (more common and general than **avoir affaire avec qn**) NOTE: the difference between *avoir mal à la tête* and *avoir un mal de tête*
se battre	**il s'est battu *avec* son frère** (ie on his brother's side or against his brother) **il s'est battu *contre* l'ennemi** (ie against)
changer	**il faut le changer** **je change *de* vêtements** (ie one set of clothes for another) **il a changé ses meubles *contre* des tableaux** he exchanged . . .
commencer	**il a commencé *par* dire que** . . . **il a commencé sa conférence en disant que** . . . **il commença *à / d'*avoir des regrets:** NOTE: *de* (R3) is often used instead of *à* to avoid two or more similar sounds occurring in quick succession
comparer	**il compare une chose *à / avec* (R1) une autre** NOTE: *en comparaison de*, never *avec*
compter	**il comptait partir** **je compte *avec* lui** I take him into consideration **je compte *sur* lui** I count on him NOTE: *escompter un résultat* = to count on a result
(se) confier	**elle se confie *à* lui** **j'ai confiance *en* eux**

se connaître	**il s'y connaît**
	he is an expert on the matter
	il se connaît *en* tableaux
	he is an expert . . .
	   NOTE: *j'ai fait la connaissance de Pierre l'an dernier*
	   il a fait connaissance avec elle il y à deux semaines

consentir	**consentir un traité** (ie to authorise) **je consens *à* tout ce que vous voulez** (ie to consent to)
construire	in *une maison construite de pierre* less attention is fixed on the material than in *une maison construite en pierre* (3.4.4 *de*)
continuer	*à* and *de* are equally common with *continuer* (see note to **commencer**)
contraindre	**il la contraint *à/de* partir**

convenir	cet arrangement n'a pas convenu *à* Jean
	(ie did not suit)
	elle est convenue *de* venir
	she agreed ...
	NOTE: when *convenir* means 'to suit' it is conjugated with *avoir*.
	When it means 'to agree', it is conjugated with *être*. This difference
	is not observed by many French people.
croire	il croit *à* la médecine
	he thinks medicine is a valid discipline
	il croit *en* Dieu/*en* l'avenir/*en* l'homme
	(suggests trust)
décider	cette raison m'a décidé *à* partir
	(persuaded me)
	c'est à vous de décider *de* ma fortune
	(to make a decision over)
	j'ai décidé *de* le faire
	(here, the decision is arrived at more quickly than with *se décider à*)
	elle s'est décidée *à* quitter l'école
	she made up her mind after careful consideration
	elle s'est décidée *pour* le parti socialiste
	she declared herself in favour of ...
demander	il demande *à* partir
	son ami lui demande *de* partir
devoir	il doit faire ses devoirs
	il doit dix livres *à* son père
	vous vous devez à vous-même *de* (R3) bien travailler
	you owe it to yourself ...
dire	je lui dis *de* partir
	j'ai dit avoir lu le livre
divorcer	divorcer (intr)
	to get a divorce
	ils ont divorcé
	they got a divorce
	divorcer *avec*/*d'avec* qn
	to divorce sb
	être divorcé
	to be divorced
douter	je ne doute pas *de* son honnêteté
	I do not doubt ...
	se douter *de*
	to suspect
	je m'en doutais
	I suspected it

droit	**avoir droit** *à* + noun
	avoir le droit *de* + infinitive
échapper	**il a échappé** *à* **la mort/***à* **la police**
	(ie to avoid)
	ils se sont échappés *de* **l'embuscade**
	(ie to get clear from)
	NOTE: *s'échapper de* is not normally used for prison, use *s'évader de*.
s'efforcer	usu **s'efforcer** *de*
	s'efforcer *à* (R3)
enlever	as **arracher**
ennuyer	**il s'ennuie** *à*/*d'***attendre**
	il s'ennuyait *d'***elle**
	he missed her
	(impers: **il m'ennuie** *d'***être si longtemps séparé de vous**)
entendre	**il entend le bruit**
	il s'entend *à* (R3) **la peinture/***en* **peinture**
	he is an expert on painting
	je m'entends (bien) *avec* **lui**
	I get on well . . .
	ils se sont entendus *pour* **lui tendre un piège**
entrer	**il est entré** *dans* **l'école**
	(ie he entered the school buildings)
	il est entré *à* **l'école septembre dernier**
espérer	**j'espère arriver ce soir**
	je ne puis espérer de (R3) **recevoir cette réponse**
se fâcher	**il se fâche** *avec* **son frére**
	he quarrels with . . .
	il se fâche *contre* **elle**
	he gets angry with her
faillir	**j'ai failli gagner à la loterie nationale**
	I almost won . . .
	j'ai failli *à* **mon devoir**
	I failed in . . .
faire	**qu'est-ce qu'il a fait** *de*/*avec* **son livre?**
	il le fait *de*/*par* **lui-même**
	he does it by himself
	il ne fait que jouer
	all he does is play
	il ne fait que *d'***entrer/que** *d'***arriver/que** *de* **s'éveiller**
	he has only just . . .
se familiariser/	**il se familiarise** *avec* **le français**
être familier	**il est familier** *de*/*avec* **plusieurs langues**

se fier/	je me fie *à* mon ami
confier/	elle lui a confié une lettre
défier/méfier	il faut se défier/se méfier *de* ses ennemis
finir	il a fini *par* dire ...
	il a fini sa conférence en disant ...
	(cf commencer)
	elle a fini *d'*écrire sa lettre
forcer	son père le force *à* étudier:
	(ie active voice)
	je suis forcé *de* lire toute la journée
	(ie passive voice, cf **obliger**)
habituer/	il faut s'habituer *à* parler en public
avoir	il a l'habitude *de* se coucher tôt
l'habitude	
hésiter	il n'hésite pas *à* (st *pour*) répondre
	hésiter *entre* le vice et la vertu
	elle hésite *sur* le choix d'une profession
insister	j'insiste *à*/*pour* le faire
	j'insiste *pour* qu'il le fasse
	le professeur a insisté *sur* le fait que la lecture est importante
	son insistance *à* travailler toute la journée ...
insulter	il l'a insultée
	he insulted her
	insulter *à* (R3)
	eg le luxe insulte *à* la misère publique
intéresser/	je m'intéresse *à* y aller
avoir	vous avez intérêt *à* faire des économies
intérêt/se	it is in your interest to ...
désintéresser	il y a intérêt *à* payer maintenant
	il m'y a intéressé
	he interested me in it
	je suis intéressé *par* ce que tu dis
	elle est inintéressée/peu intéressée *par* vos idées
	cela m'intéresse *d'*écrire un roman
	il cultive un intérêt *pour* l'histoire
	il est intéressant *de* ...
	je me désintéresse *de* ses propos
	I am uninterested in ...
jouer	il joue Hamlet
	elle joue un air de Mozart *au* piano
	noun jouons *du* violon
	(ie instrument)

ils jouent *au* football
(ie sport)
se jouer *de* qn (R3)
to make fun of sb
il lui a joué un mauvais tour
he played a nasty trick on him

manquer	il manque *de* pain
	he lacks bread
	le pain manque *à* la famille
	(literally) bread is lacking in the family (ie the family needs bread)
	il a manqué (*de*) tomber
	he almost fell (2.5)
	ne manque pas *de* venir
	don't fail to come
	NOTE: *manquer de* does not mean 'to fail to'
	il a manqué *à* la consigne
	he failed in/disregarded orders
	il a manqué le train
	he missed the train

mêler	il se mêla *à* la foule et disparut
	he mingled with . . .
	il se mêle *de* la politique
	he is concerned with politics
	voilà qu'elle se mêle *de* nous donner des conseils
	there she goes, giving us advice

| obliger | as with **forcer** |

occuper	la mère s'occupe *de* l'enfant
	il était occupé *à* écrire une lettre
	elle s'occupait *à*/*de* l'habiller

| ôter | as **arracher** |

participer/ participation	elle participe *à* ma joie
	she shares in . . .
	le mulet participe *de* (R3) l'âne et *du* cheval
	the mule is of the same nature as . . .
	sa participation *au*/*dans* le débat m'étonna

passionner/ passion	il se passionne *pour* le football
	(suggests passive interest)
	elle est passionnée *de* natation
	(suggests active interest)
	elle éprouvait une passion profonde *pour* lui

payer	il a payé le livre
	he paid for the book (3.4.5)
	il a payé dix francs *à* l'homme
	il a payé dix francs le livre *à* l'homme

pénétrer	il a pénétré *dans* le jardin
	in figurative usage *dans* does not occur:
	il pénétra le mystère/le marché
penser	elle pense *à* sa mère
	she thinks of her mother
	que pensez-vous *de* Giscard d'Estaing?
	what is your opinion about . . .?
	elle pense partir en vacances
	she's thinking of going . . .
persuader	persuader *à* qn *de* faire qch (R3)
	(now ousted by **persuader** qn *de* faire qch)
	(NOTE in **3.4.1.4**)
	j'ai essayé de persuader le patron de ma bonne foi
prendre	elle le prend *à* sa sœur
	she takes it from her sister
	il le prend *dans* le tiroir
	he takes it from/out of the drawer
	il le prend *sur* la table
	he takes from/off the table
prévoir	le mariage était prévu *pour* février
	je prévois *de* partir demain
rappeler	j'ai rappelé l'incident *à* mon père
	I reminded my father of . . .
	je me rappelle le livre:
	ie **rappeler** qch *à* soi-même
	NOTE: *je me rappelle du livre* is often used, on analogy with *je me souviens du livre*, but is condemned by purists
refuser	il refuse *d'*y aller
	il se refuse *à* le faire
	il refuse le droit *à* son collègue de . . .
répondre	je réponds *à* la question
	il doit répondre *de* ses actes
	he must take responsibility for his actions
répugner	je répugne *à* (R3) le faire
	I find it repugnant to do it
	cet homme répugne *à* (R3) mon père
	my father finds that man repugnant
	cela me répugne *de* lui écrire
résoudre	j'ai résolu la question
	I solved the question
	résoudre *de*/se résoudre *à*:
	as **décider**

ressortir	**il ressort *de* chez lui** he comes out again . . . **mon affaire ressortit *au* juge de paix** (R3) my case falls within the jurisdiction of . . . NOTE: in this latter meaning *ressortir* is conjugated like *finir* (cf 2.2.4). This is not observed by many French people.
réussir	**il a réussi un grand exploit** he brought off . . . **nous avons réussi *à* le terminer** **tout lui réussit** everything succeeds with him
satisfaire	**il satisfait son maître** **satisfaire *à* (R3) une promesse/un besoin/une obligation:** the use of *à* suggests fulfilment, completion. **je suis satisfaite *de* ton travail**
servir	**le moteur peut encore servir** the engine is still fit for use **la lecture sert *à* la formation des étudiants** reading helps in . . . **un moteur sert *à* faire marcher une voiture** an engine is used to . . . **il ne sert *à* rien de l'écrire ce matin** it serves no purpose to . . . **les tables servent *de* pupitres** the tables are used as desks **elle s'est servie *du* livre** she used the book **servir qn** to serve sb
souhaiter	**j'ai souhaité (*de*) le voir** usage with or without *de* is acceptable **je te souhaite *d*'être en bonne santé** I hope you are . . . **elle lui a souhaité la bienvenue**
suffire	**dix minutes ont suffi *pour* le terminer** **cinq jours ont suffi *à* l'écrivain *pour* composer son roman** **il suffit *de* peu de chose *pour* . . .** **il suffit *de* le faire tout de suite**
tarder	**il tarde *à* venir** he is slow in coming **il lui tarde *de* revoir ses parents** (impers) he is keen to see his parents again

tenir	**l'élève tient *à* ses livres** the pupil values his books **j'y tiens/je tiens à le faire** I am keen on it/to do it, etc **il tient *de* son père** he takes after his father	
se tromper	**je me suis trompé *d*'adresse** I was mistaken over ... **il m'a trompé** he deceived me	
user	**il use ses vêtements** he wears his clothes out **il use *d*'un style recherché** he uses a refined style NOTE: *user de*: R3 but common	

venir	**je viens vous dire que ...**
	 je viens *de* lui envoyer une lettre
	 I have just ... (cf **3.6.1.5**)
	     NOTE: *venir de* cannot be followed by *revenir*. Say, for example, *il est*
	     revenu à l'instant.
	 une voiture vint *à* (R3) passer
	 a car happened to pass (this expression is normally used with the ph)	

viser	**il vise un grand marché** he is aiming at ... **il vise *à* créer un nouveau système**	
vivre	**le retraité vit *de* sa pension** the pensioner lives off ...	

3.4.4 Prepositional expressions

It is in this section that the differences between patterns in English and French appear most clearly. It is absolutely impossible to legislate on the translation of prepositional expressions from one language to another: very few clear tendencies emerge. That is why it seems best to present for both languages as many examples as possible for as many prepositions as possible. An attempt has been made, where appropriate, to classify the examples according to the relationship expressed between the preposition and the noun.

3.4.4.1 French prepositions

Λ expressing position	**à l'équateur** (cf SOUS) **aux Tropiques** (cf SOUS) **au pôle nord**	*at/on* the equator *in* the Tropics *at* the north pole

à l'horizon	*on* the horizon
à Paris	*in* Paris
à la maison	*at* home
à l'hôtel	*at* the hotel
des peintures pendues *au* mur	pictures hanging *on* the wall
au tableau noir (cf SUR)	*on* the blackboard
travailler *à* la mine	to work *in* the mines

NOTE: for a discussion on the use of A rather than DANS in this and the following six examples, see **3.4.4.2 IN**

à la campagne	*in* the country
à la montagne (cf DANS and EN)	*in* the mountains
aux champs	*in* the fields
au jardin	*in* the garden
au salon	*in* the drawing room
à la cuisine	*in* the kitchen
au plafond	*on* the ceiling
à la ferme (cf DANS)	*on* the farm
travailler *à* un ranch	to work *on* a ranch
au téléphone	*on* the telephone
au paradis	*in* paradise
entrer *au* paradis	to go *to* paradise
au soleil	*in* the sun
à l'ombre (cf DANS)	*in* the shade
à terre (R3) (cf PAR)	*on* the ground
tomber *à* terre (cf PAR)	to fall *to* the ground (from a height)
tomber *à* l'eau (cf DANS)	to fall *in* the water
au contact de l'eau	*in* contact with the water
à bord d'une voiture/un avion/un train	*in* a car/plane/train
être *à* bicyclette/vélo (cf EN and SUR)	to be *on* a bicycle
blessé *au* bras, etc	wounded *in* the arm, etc
tomber *aux* mains de qn (cf ENTRE)	to fall *into* sb's hands
avoir la pipe *à* la bouche	to have a pipe *in* one's mouth
tenir un livre *à* la main	to hold a book *in* one's hand
avoir qch *aux* pieds, etc (not SUR)	to have sth *on* one's feet, etc
à la première page	*on* the first page
à la place de/*au* lieu de	*in* place of/instead of

expressing time	*à* l'heure actuelle	*at* the present time
	à notre époque	*in* our time

195

au 20e siècle	*in* the 20th century
au printemps	*in* the spring
à l'automne (cf EN)	*in* the autumn
à la mi-avril	*in* mid-April
au bout d'un mois	a month later
au début de l'après-midi (cf EN)	*at* the beginning of the afternoon/*in* the early afternoon
à la fin de la séance (cf EN)	*at* the end of the meeting
à la mi-temps (cf EN)	*at* half-time
à mon arrivée/retour	*on* my arrival/return
au temps des Pharaons (cf DE)	*in* the time of the Pharaohs
à l'avance (cf DE and PAR)	*in* advance

figurative usage		
	à ce que je vois	*from* what I can see
	à ce que je sache	*from* what I know
	à ce que j'ai entendu	*from* what I've heard
	je ne comprends rien *à* ce qu'il dit	I don't understand a thing *of* what he says
	il ne comprend rien *au* problème	he doesn't understand anything *about* the problem
	à son avis	*in* his opinion
	à mon point de vue	*from* my point of view
	à ce point de vue-là	*from* that point of view
	reconnaître qn *à* sa voix	to recognise sb *by* his voice
	rouler *à* bicyclette/vélo (cf EN and SUR)	to travel *by* bicycle
	aller *à* moto (cf EN)	to travel *by* motorbike
	à la radio (cf 3.4.4.1 ON)	*on* the radio
	à la télé (cf 3.4.4.2 ON)	*on* TV
	écrire *à* l'encre/*au* crayon	to write *in* ink/pencil
	lire *à* la lumière d'une lampe	to read *by* the light of a lamp
	à partir de cette idée	*from* this idea
	au nom du roi (cf EN)	*in* the king's name
	ce livre vient de paraître *aux* éditions Gallimard (cf CHEZ)	this book has just been published by Gallimard
	le gouvernement *au* pouvoir	the government *in* power
	il l'a abattu *à* coups de poing/bâton/hâche/revolver/couteau	he punched him until he fell to the ground, etc
	elle l'a emporté *à* coups de pédale	she pedalled off with it
	à sa manière (cf DE)	*in* his way

	à pas lents/de géant/de **loup**	slowly/*with* giant strides/ stealthily
	à reculons	backwards
	à regret	regretfully
	à la rigueur	if need be
	au secours/voleur	help/thief
	un pot *à* beurre/eau/fleurs (cf DE)	a butter dish/water jug/ flower pot

NOTE: A indicates that the two nouns together form a single entity, whereas with DE a more lax connection is marked

	un verre *à* bière/vin (cf DE)	a beer/wine glass

NOTE: see previous note

	côte *à* côte	side *by* side
	mot *à* mot	word *by* word
	pas *à* pas	step *by* step
	un *à* un	one *by* one
	travailler *aux* PTT (cf DANS)	to work *for* the Post Office
	travailler *aux* chemins de fer (cf DANS)	to work *for* the railway

expressing measurement	*à* une vitesse de 80 kms *à* l'heure	*at* a speed of 50 miles an hour
	il lit *à* raison de 10 pages *à* l'heure	he reads *at* a rate of 10 pages an hour
	louer *à* l'heure	to hire *by* the hour
	vendre *au* litre/mètre	to sell *by* the litre/metre

AU-DESSOUS DE (R3) (cf 2.4 *under*) expressing position	il jeta la balle *au-dessous de* la table (cf EN DESSOUS DE)	he threw the ball *under* the table
figurative usage	il a trouvé un poste *au-dessous de* ses compétences	he found a post *beneath* his qualifications
AU-DESSUS DE (cf 2.4, *on*, *over*) expressing position	l'église est située *au-dessus du* village	the church stands *above* the village
	il y avait une enseigne *au-dessus de* nos têtes	there was a sign *above* our heads
	l'oiseau vola *au-dessus du* mur (cf 3.4.4.1 OVER for comment)	the bird flew *over/along* the wall

figurative usage	épouser *au-dessus de* soi	to marry *above* one's station
CHEZ expressing position	*chez* nous	*in* our country
	chez nous/lui, etc	*at* home
	chez le docteur	*at* the doctor's
figurative usage	*chez* les Français il y a une coutume	*amongst* the French there is a custom
	chez lui	*in* his case
	ce livre vient de paraître *chez* Gallimard (cf A)	this book has just been published by Gallimard
CONTRE figurative usage	échanger une chose *contre* une autre (cf POUR)	to exchange one thing *for* another
	être fâché *contre* (3.4.3 se fâcher and 3.4.4.2 WITH)	to be angry *with* sb
DANS expressing position	*dans* l'air/les airs (R3) (cf 3.2.2 and EN)	*in* the air
	dans l'espace	*in* space (of astronaut)
	dans la lune (cf SUR)	*on* the moon
	aller *dans* la lune (cf SUR)	to go *to* the moon
	dans les Alpes, etc	*in* the Alps, etc
	dans la montagne (cf A and EN)	*in* the mountains
	dans la région parisienne (cf EN)	*in* the Paris area
	dans la capitale	*in* the capital (Paris)
	dans le 19e arrondissement	*in* the 19th district (of Paris)
	dans la rue	*in* the street
	dans l'avenue/le boulevard	*in* the avenue/boulevard
	dans l'allée	*on* the path
	dans le square	*in* the square (small public square with garden)
	tomber *dans* l'eau (cf A)	to fall *in* the water
	dans une tente (cf SOUS)	*in* a tent
	dans la maison	*in* (as contrasted with outside) the house

NOTE: for a discussion of the use of DANS and A in such contexts, see 3.4.4.2 IN

	dans le stade	*in* the stadium (of spectator)
	dans la ferme (cf A)	*on* the farm
	dans l'aéroport (cf SUR)	*at* the airport (in the buildings)

dans le parking (cf SUR)	*in* the carpark (enclosed or multi-storied)
travailler *dans* la mine	to work *in* a mine

NOTE: for a discussion on the use of DANS rather than A in this and the following two sets of examples, see **3.4.4.2** IN

dans la campagne/les champs/le jardin	*in* the country/fields/garden
dans le salon/la cuisine	*in* the drawing room/kitchen
dans la chambre	*in* the bedroom

NOTE: only *dans* may be used here

dans l'escalier	*on* the stairs
dans le train	*on* the train
il est *dans* la voiture de son père	he's *in* his father's car

NOTE: dans is used when **voiture** is qualified; otherwise en is used

monter *dans* un avion	to get *into* a plane
dans un carnet (cf SUR)	*in* a note-book
dans le journal (cf SUR)	*in* the paper
être assis *dans* un fauteuil	to sit *in* an armchair
mettre qch *dans* une assiette	to put sth *on* a plate
boire *dans* un verre	to drink *from* a glass
se refléter *dans* le soleil	to be reflected *in* the sunlight
dans l'ombre (cf A)	*in* the shade

expressing time	*dans* le même temps (R3) (cf EN)	*at* the same time
	dans la semaine (cf EN)	*during* the week
	dans la matinée/après-midi/ soirée	*in* (the course of) the morning/afternoon/evening
	je le ferai *dans* dix jours	I'll do it *in* ten days (in ten days' time)

figurative usage	*dans* une forme littéraire (cf SOUS)	*in* a literary form
	dans la situation actuelle	*in* the present situation
	dans le secret/privé (cf EN)	*in* secret/private
	travailler *dans* les chemins de fer (cf A)	to work *for* the railway
	travailler *dans* les PTT (cf A)	to work *for* the Post Office

DE expressing position	le chemin *de* la gare	the road *from*/*to* the station
	le train *de* Paris	the train *from*/*to* Paris
	de Londres *à* Paris (cf 3.4.4.2 FROM)	*from* London *to* Paris

de ville *en* ville	*from* town *to* town
de porte *en* porte	*from* door *to* door
une rue *de* Marseille	a street *in* Marseilles
du haut *du* balcon/des remparts	*from* the balcony/ramparts (suggesting height)
de ce côté	*on* this side
de l'autre côté	*on* the other side
du côté de la gare	*in* the direction of the station

expressing usage with materials (cf EN)	NOTE: DE is less concrete than EN in such expressions; EN stresses the material	
	un cheval *de* bois	a wooden horse
	une chemise *de* coton	a cotton shirt
	une barrière *de* métal	a metal gate

expressing time	*de* notre temps/nos jours	*in* our time
	de temps *en* temps	*from* time *to* time
	d' heure/année *en* heure/année	*from* hour/year *to* hour/year
	de 10 heures *à* midi	*from* 10 o'clock *to* midday
	du temps des Pharaons (cf A)	*in* the time of the Pharaohs
	différer/remettre/reporter *de* 10 jours	to postpone *for* 10 days
	une jeune fille *de* 15 *à* 16 ans	a girl *between* 15 and 16 years old
	*d'*avance (cf A and PAR)	*in* advance

figurative usage	*d'*une voix heureuse/triste	*in* a happy/sad voice
	*d'*un ton heureux/triste (cf SUR)	*in* a happy/sad tone
	*d'*une façon/manière étrange (cf A)	*in* a strange way
	de l'avis de Jean	*in* John's opinion
	de la part de M. Henri	*on* behalf of M. Henri
	dites-le-lui *de* ma part	tell him *on* my behalf
	connaître qn *de* vue	to know sb *by* sight
	un pot *de* beurre/eau/fleurs (cf A)	a pot *of* butter/water/flowers
	un verre *de* bière/vin (cf A)	a glass *of* beer/wine
	je suis inquiet *de* (R3) lui (cf POUR)	I'm worried *about* him
	il est *de* mon côté	he's *on* my side
	de toutes façons (cf EN)	*at* any rate
	de l'autre côté	*on* the other hand/side

	de tout mon cœur	*with* all my heart
	de toutes mes forces	*with* all my strength
	*d'*une main tremblante	*with* a trembling hand
	battre *des* mains	to clap
	frapper *du* pied	to kick
	cligner *des* yeux	to wink
expressing measurement	avancer *de* 10 jours	to bring forward *by* 10 days
	augmenter/majorer *de* 10 francs	to increase *by* 10 francs
	réduire *de* 10 francs	to reduce *by* 10 francs
	battrc qn *de* 10 mètres	to beat sb *by* 10 yards
	être plus intelligent *de* beaucoup	to be more intelligent *by* far
	la durée est *de* 7 heures	it lasts 7 hours
	le prix est *de* 3 francs	the price is 3 francs
	la distance est *de* 10 kilomètres	the distance is 10 kilometres
expressing passive agent in passive voice	être suivi *d'*un chien (cf PAR)	to be followed *by* a dog
EN expressing position	*en* l'air (cf DANS)	*in* the air
	en République Française (R3)	*in* the French Republic
	en Avignon (regional but common)	*in* Avignon
	en région parisienne (cf DANS)	*in* the Paris area
	en métropole (cf DANS)	*in* the capital (Paris), in France
	en banlieue see note to 3.4.4.2 IN	*in* the suburbs
	en montagne (cf A and DANS)	*in* the mountains
	en car	*in* a coach
	en rade	*in* the roads (of a harbour)
	en mer (cf SUR) see note to 3.4.4.2 AT	*at* sea
	en orbite basse (cf SUR)	*in* a low orbit
	aller *en* paradis (R3) (cf A)	to go *to* paradise
	aller *en* enfer/purgatoire	to go *to* hell/purgatory
	aller *en* classe	to go *to* school
	aller *en* expédition	to go *on* an expedition
	aller *en* ville	to go *to* town

en ballon	*in* a balloon
monter *en* avion	to go up *in* a plane
voyager *en* avion (cf PAR)	to travel *by* plane
être *en* vélo (R1) (cf A)	to be *on* a bicycle
rouler *en* vélo (R1) (cf A and SUR)	to travel *by* bicycle
aller *en* moto (cf A)	to travel *by* motorbike
NOTE: *en* is more common than *à*	
voyager *en* voiture/auto (cf DANS)	to travel by car
voyager *en* train (cf PAR)	to travel *by* train
voyager *en* bateau (cf PAR)	to travel *by* boat
en radeau	*on* a raft
en selle (cf SUR)	*in* the saddle (of a horse)
en première page (cf A)	*on* the first page

expressing usage with materials (cf DE)	un cheval *en* bois	a wooden horse
	une chemise *en* coton	a cotton shirt
	une barrière *en* métal	a metal gate

expressing time	*en* même temps (cf DANS)	*at* the same time
	en (l'an) 1950	*in* 1950
	en été/hiver	*in* the summer/winter
	en automne (cf A)	*in* the autumn
	en avril	*in* April
	en semaine	*during* the week
	en début d'après-midi (cf A)	*at* the beginning of the afternoon
	en fin de séance (cf A)	*at* the end of the meeting
	en l'espace de trois semaines	*in* the space of three weeks
	je l'ai fait *en* dix jours	I did it *in* ten days
	en première/deuxième mi-temps (cf A)	*in* the first/second half (of sports match)

figurative usage	se changer/se transformer *en* simple spectateur	to change/be transformed *into* a mere spectator
	se déguiser *en* prêtre	to disguise oneself *as* a priest
	une femme *en* cheveux (R3)	a woman *without* a hat
	être *en* danger	to be *in* danger
	dormir *en* paix	to sleep *in* peace
	rester assis *en* silence	to sit *in* silence
	être *en* deuil	to be *in* mourning
	en secret/privé (cf DANS)	*in* secret/private

	en état de guerre/siège/ crise, etc	*in* a state of war/siege/ crisis, etc
	partir *en* tournée	to go *on* tour
	en mission d'enquête/ information	*on* an enquiry mission
	avoir un livre *en* chantier	to have a book *in* hand (in a state of preparation)
	être *en* permission	to be *on* leave
	des valeurs cotées *en* Bourse	shares quoted *on* the Stock Exchange
	en la situation actuelle (R3) (cf DANS)	*in* the present situation
	en sa faveur	*in* his favour
	en l'honneur de	*in* honour of
	en l'occurrence	*as* it turns/turned out
	en mon nom (cf A)	*in* my name
	en l'absence de	*in* the absence of
	en présence de	*in* the presence of
	en finale	*in* the final(s) (of a sport)
	en direct	live (of transmission by radio or television, of sport etc)
	en différé	recording (of transmission by radio or television, of sport etc)
	en jeu	*at* stake
	en tout cas (cf DE)	*at* any rate
EN DESSOUS DE (cf 2.4 *under*) expressing position	il jeta la balle *en dessous de* la table (cf AU-DESSOUS DE)	he threw the ball *under* the table
ENTRE expressing position	*entre* les maisons	*between* the houses
	tomber *entre* les mains de qn (cf A)	to fall *into* sb's hands
figurative usage	*entre* parenthèses	*in* parenthesis
HORS DE expressing position	*hors de* la maison, je me sens bien	*out of* the house, I feel fine

figurative usage	*hors de* danger	*out of* danger
	hors d' haleine	*out of* breath
	c'est *hors de* doute	it is *beyond* doubt
JUSQU'A expressing time	*jusqu'à* sept heures	*until* 7 o'clock
expressing position	il m'a accompagné *jusque* chez moi	he accompanied me home
	il m'a accompagné *jusqu'au* village	he accompanied me *as far as* the village
figurative usage	ils ont incendié *jusqu'aux* voitures	they even burnt the cars
PAR expressing position	il s'est promené *par* les champs	he walked *across* the fields
	par terre (cf A)	*on* the ground
	tomber *par* terre (cf A)	to fall *to* the ground (from a standing position)
	par-ci, *par*-là	hither and thither
	par ici/là	this/that way
expressing time	*par* un temps pareil	*in* such weather
	par un jour froid d'hiver	*on* a cold winter's day
	deux fois *par* semaine	twice a week
	par avance (cf A and DE)	*in* advance
figurative usage	*par* l'intermédiaire/ entremise de	*by* means of (a person)
	par une tierce personne	*by* a third party
	voyager *par* chemin de fer	to travel *by* rail
	voyager *par* le train (cf EN)	to travel *by* train
	voyager *par* avion (cf EN)	to travel *by* plane
	voyager *par* bateau (cf EN)	to travel *by* boat
	par écrit	*in* writing
	par parenthèse (R3) (cf ENTRE)	*in* parenthesis
	par compassion/amitié/ ignorance/amour, etc	*out of* compassion/friendship/ ignorance/love, etc
expressing active agent in passive voice	être mordu *par* un chien (cf DE)	to be bitten *by* a dog

PAR-DESSUS (cf **2.4** *on*, *over*) expressing position	il regarda *par-dessus* le mur	he looked *over* the wall

NOTE: see note to **3.4.4.2** OVER for discussion on the distinction between AU-DESSUS and PAR-DESSUS

figurative usage	*par-dessus* le marché	*into* the bargain
PENDANT expressing time	*pendant* la journée il a travaillé *pendant* dix minutes	*during* the day he worked *for* ten minutes
expressing space	il était triste *pendant* bien des kilomètres	he was sad *for* many miles
POUR expressing time	elle sera à Poitiers *pour* quinze jours elles sont ici *pour* 3 jours j'en ai assez *pour* une semaine	she will be in Poitiers *for* 2 weeks they are here *for* 3 days I've got enough *for* one week
figurative usage	il est bon/gentil *pour* moi je suis inquiet *pour* lui (cf DE) échanger une chose *pour* une autre (cf CONTRE)	he is well-disposed *towards* me I'm worried *about* him to exchange one thing *for* another
PRES expressing position	*près de* l'église les villages *près du* fleuve	*near* the church the villages *near* the river
SOUS expressing position	*sous* l'équateur (cf A) *sous* les Tropiques (cf A) il est passé *sous* le balcon *sous* une tente (cf DANS) le chien est *sous* la table *sous* la pluie/neige avoir qch *sous* les yeux	*at/on* the equator *in* the Tropics he walked *beneath* the balcony *in* a tent the dog is *under* the table *in* the rain/snow to have sth *before* one's eyes
expressing time	*sous* le règne de *sous* peu	*during* the reign of presently/shortly

figurative usage	*sous* une forme littéraire (cf DANS)	*in* a literary form
	sous un jour favorable	*in* a favourable light
	sous tous les rapports	*in* all respects
	sous peine d'amende	*on* pain of a fine
	avoir qch *sous* la main	to have sth *at* hand
	sous l'emprise/empire/ influence/le coup (R1) de	*under* the influence of

SUR expressing position	*sur* la lune (cf DANS)	*on* the moon
	aller *sur* la lune (cf DANS)	to go *to* the moon
	sur une orbite basse (cf EN)	*in* a low orbit
	mettre qch *sur* orbite	to put sth *in* orbit
	sur le parking (cf DANS)	*in* the carpark (in the open air)
	sur la mer (cf EN) see note to **3.4.4.2** AT	*at* sea
	sur l'aéroport (R1) (cf DANS)	*at* the airport (on the runway/ tarmac)
	sur le chantier	*in* the workyard
	sur les docks	*at* the docks
	sur l'hippodrome (R3)/le champ de course	*at* the racecourse
	sur la place	*in* the square (market square)
	sur le stade	*in* the stadium (of competition)
	sur le ring	*in* the (boxing) ring
	sur l'avenue/le boulevard (cf DANS)	*in* the avenue/boulevard
	NOTE: *sur* indicates greater width than *dans*	
	sur la chaussée	*in* the road (ie the middle)/ *on* the roadway
	marcher *sur* la route (cf DANS)	to walk *on* the road
	donner *sur* la rue	to look *on* to the street (of building)
	sur le trottoir	*on* the pavement
	sur (la) scène	*on* the stage
	sur le tableau noir (cf A)	*on* the blackboard
	la clef est *sur* la porte	the key is *in* the door
	être assis *sur* un canapé/ divan/sofa	to sit *on* a couch/settee
	grimper *sur* le toit	to climb *onto* the roof
	être *sur* mon/un vélo (cf A and EN)	to be *on* my/a bike

	sur la selle	*in* the saddle (of a bicycle)
	un chat est assis *sur* le mur	a cat is sitting *on* the wall
	sur un carnet (cf DANS)	*in* a note-book
	sur le journal (R1) (cf DANS)	*in* a newspaper
	revenir *sur* ses pas	retrace one's steps

figurative usage		
	un livre *sur* la mode	a book *about* fashion
	je suis inquiet *sur* son sort	I'm worried *about* his fate/what becomes of him
	sur un ton heureux/triste (cf DE)	*in* a happy/sad tone
	huit *sur* dix	eight *out of* ten

VERS expressing position		
	aller *vers* la ville	to go *towards* town

figurative usage		
	je viendrai *vers* midi	I'll come *about* midday

The following prepositions have a specific and restricted value:
examples illustrating their usage may be found under the appropriate
English prepositions in **3.4.4.2**.

à cause de	= because of	environ	= about
à force de	= by	moyennant	= by
		parmi	= among(st)
à même	= from	NOTE: although ***parmi*** is usually	
à propos de	= about	used with pl nouns, it may also	
à travers	= across	accompany a sg collective noun:	
au dehors de	= outside	eg **parmi la foule**	
au moyen de	= by	près de	= near
au sujet de	= about	quant à	= as for
au travers de	= across	sans	= without
avant	= before	NOTE: ***sans*** + infinitive =	
avec	= with	present participle:	
concernant	= about	eg **elle l'a fait sans parler**	
d'après	= according to	she did it without speaking	
		selon	= according to
devant	= before		
durant	= during	suivant	= according to
en dehors de	= outside		
en raison de	= because of		
en travers de	= across		
envers	= to		

3.4.4.2   **English prepositions**

ABOUT expressing 'concerning'	a book *about* fashion	un livre *sur/au sujet de/à propos de/concernant* la mode
	he doesn't understand anything *about* the problem	il ne comprend rien *au* problème
	I'm worried *about* him	je suis inquiet *de* (R3)/*pour* lui
	I'm anxious *about* his fate/ what becomes of him	je suis inquiet *sur* son sort
expressing 'approxi- mately'	*about* 60 people were present	*environ* 60 personnes/60 personnes *environ* étaient présentes
	I'll come *about* midday	je viendrai *vers* midi
ABOVE (cf 2.4 *on, over*) expressing position	the church stands *above* the village	l'église est située *au-dessus* du village
	there was a sign *above* our heads	il y avait une enseigne *au-dessus de* nos têtes
figurative usage	to marry *above* one's station	épouser *au-dessus de* soi
ACCORDING TO	*according to* what he says	*d'après/selon/suivant* ce qu'il dit
ACROSS expressing position (3.6.6)	he ran *across* the meadow	il traversa le pré en courant
	she swam *across* the river	elle traversa la rivière à la nage
	she walked *across* the road	elle traversa la rue
	they walked *across* the bridge	ils franchirent le pont

> NOTE: verbs of motion cannot normally be used
> with *à travers* when the space crossed is
> narrow, or limited like a road, a river, a stream, a
> yard, a field. However, one can say
> **elle a couru/marché *à travers* les champs,**
> **les prés, le bois, la forêt, etc**
> where distance is implied.

	his journeys *across* the world	ses voyages *à travers* le monde here the idea is concrete

NOTE: however in
il étudia le communisme *au travers des* écrits de Marx
he studied communism through . . . *à travers* is also possible here. Although they are largely synonymous, in their abstract meaning *au travers de* is of a higher register than *à travers*.

the tree fell *across* the road	**l'arbre tomba *en travers de* la route**

NOTE: neither *à travers* nor *au travers de* is possible here

AMONG(ST) expressing position	*amongst* the French there is a custom	***chez* les Français il y a une coutume**
	amongst the débris	***parmi* les débris**
AS expressing position	*as far as* the village	***jusqu'au* village**
figurative usage	*as* for him	***quant à* lui**
	to disguise oneself *as* a priest	**se déguiser *en* prêtre**
AT expressing position	*at* the equator	***à/sous* l'équateur**
	at the north pole	***au* pôle nord**
	at sea	***sur* la/*en* mer**

NOTE: *en* is more general,
eg il y a un accident *en* mer
there is an accident *at* sea, but standing on the shore, one would more readily say:
il est là, *sur/dans* la mer
there he is, *in* the sea

at home	***à* la maison** (cf *in* the house)/***chez* nous /lui, etc**
at the doctor's	***chez* le docteur**
at the hotel	***à* l'hôtel**, but ***dans* l'hôtel** = inside the hotel
at the airport	***dans/sur* (R1) l'aéroport**

NOTE: *sur* refers to the runway or tarmac; *dans* to the buildings. Of course *à l'aéroport* may be used.

at the docks	***aux/sur* les docks**
at the racecourse	***au/sur* le champ de course**

expressing time	*at* the present time	*à* l'heure actuelle
	at the same time	*dans* le (R3)/ *en* même temps
	at the beginning of the afternoon	*en* début d'/*au* début de l'après-midi
	at the end of the meeting	*à* la fin de la/*en* fin de séance
	at half-time	*à* la mi-temps
	NOTE: **en première/deuxième mi-temps** in the first/second half	

figurative usage	*at* a speed of 50 miles an hour	*à* une vitesse de 80 kms *à* l'heure
	he reads *at* a rate of 10 pages an hour	il lit *à* raison de 10 pages *à* l'heure
	to have sth *at* hand	avoir qch *sous* la main
	at any rate	*de* toutes façons/ *en* tout cas
	at stake	*en* jeu

| **BECAUSE OF** | *because of* his age | *à cause de/en raison de* son âge |

| **BEFORE** expressing position | he stood *before* the house | il se tint *devant* la maison |
| | to have sth *before* one's eyes | avoir qch *sous* les yeux |

| expressing time | he'll come *before* 11 o'clock | il viendra *avant* 11 heures |

| **BENEATH** (cf 2.4 *under*) expressing position | *beneath* us | *au-dessous de* (R3)/ *en dessous de* nous |
| | to disappear *beneath* the waves | sombrer *sous* les vagues |

| figurative usage | *beneath* contempt | méprisable |

| **BETWEEN** expressing position | *between* the houses | *entre* les maisons |

| expressing time | a girl *between* 15 and 16 years old | une jeune fille *de* 15 *à* 16 ans |

BY expressing position	to travel *by* train	voyager *par* le/*en* train (not *par* train)
	to travel *by* rail	voyager *en* chemin de fer (not *par*)
	to travel *by* plane	voyager *par/en* avion
	to travel *by* bicycle	rouler *à* bicyclette/*à* vélo/*en* vélo (R1)

NOTE: when *bicyclette* and *vélo* are qualified in any way, *sur* is used:

eg il est *sur* la bicyclette de son frère

	to travel *by* car	voyager *en* voiture/auto

NOTE: when *voiture* and *auto* are qualified in any way, *dans* is used:

eg il est *dans* la voiture de son père

	to travel *by* motorbike	aller *à/en* (R1) moto (*en* is more common)
	to travel *by* boat	voyager *par/en* bateau
figurative usage	*by* means of	**par/moyennant/au moyen de/à force de/à l'aide de**
	by means of (a person)	**par l'intermédiaire/ entremise de**
	by a third party	**par une tierce personne**
	to recognise sb *by* his voice	**reconnaître qn *à* sa voix**
	to know sb *by* sight	**connaître qn *de* vue**
	to read *by* the light of a lamp	**lire *à* la lumière d'une lampe**
	one *by* one	**un *à* un**
	side *by* side	**côte *à* côte**
	step *by* step	**pas *à* pas**
	word *by* word	**mot *à* mot**
expressing measurement	to beat sb *by* 10 yards	**battre qn *de* 10 mètres**
	to increase *by* 10 francs	**augmenter/majorer *de* 10 francs**
	to reduce *by* 10 francs	**réduire *de* 10 francs**
	to bring forward *by* 10 days	**avancer *de* 10 jours**
	to sell *by* the litre/metre	**vendre *au* litre/mètre**
	to hire *by* the hour	**louer *à* l'heure**
	he is more intelligent *by* far	**il est plus intelligent *de* beaucoup**
expressing agent in passive voice	to be bitten *by* a dog (active agent)	**être mordu *par* un chien**
	to be followed *by* a dog (passive agent)	**être suivi *d'*un chien**

DURING expressing time	*during* the day, etc	*durant/pendant* toute la journée/toute la journée *durant* (R3), etc
	during the week *during* the reign of	*dans* la/*en* semaine *sous* le règne de (*pendant* is also possible)

FOR (3.6.1.5)
expressing
time
	I have been living in Paris
	  for 10 years
		j'habite Paris *depuis* 10 ans
		il y a/*voilà*/ 10 ans que
		  j'habite Paris

	she will be in Poitiers *for*
	  2 weeks
	they are here *for* 3 days
	I had been living in Paris
	  for 10 years
		elle sera à Poitiers *pour*
		  quinze jours
		elles sont ici *pour* 3 jours
		j'habitais Paris *depuis* 10 ans

	he was there *for* 10 years
	she was there *for* three weeks
		il y est resté 10 ans
		elle était là *pour* trois
		  semaines/elle a été là
		  pendant trois semaines

	to postpone *for* 10 days	différer/remettre/reporter *de* 10 jours
	I've got enough *for* one week	j'en ai assez *pour* une semaine
expressing 'on behalf of'	to work *for* the Post Office to work *for* the railway	travailler *dans* les/*aux* PTT travailler *dans* les/*aux* chemins de fer

figurative
usage
	to be in mourning *for* one's
	  mother
	to exchange one thing *for*
	  another
		être en deuil *de* sa mère
		
		échanger une chose
		  contre/pour une autre

FROM
expressing
position
	the train *from* Paris
	the road *from* the station
	from the balcony/ramparts
	  (suggesting height)
	from town *to* town
	from London *to* Paris
		le train *de* Paris (cf TO)
		le chemin *de* la gare (cf TO)
		du haut du balcon/des
		  remparts
		de ville *en* ville
		de Londres *à* Paris/*depuis*
		  Londres *jusqu'à* Paris
		  (more precise)

	from door *to* door to drink *from* a glass	*de* porte *en* porte boire *dans* un verre

expressing time	*from* time *to* time	*de* temps *en* temps
	from hour/year *to* hour/year	*d'* heure/année *en* heure/année
	from 10 o'clock *to* midday	*de* 10 heures *à* midi
	from dawn/6 o'clock/the beginning	*dès* l'aube/6 heures/le début
	from 1960	*à partir de* 1960
	from now on	*dès* maintenant
figurative usage	*from* what I can see	*d'après* ce que je vois
	from what I've heard	*à/d'après* ce que j'ai entendu
	from what I know	*à* ce que je sache
	from my point of view	*à* mon point de vue
	from that point of view	*à* ce point de vue-là

NOTE: *au point de vue littéraire* and *du point de vue littéraire* have the same meaning

	from this idea	*à partir de* cette idée
	to drink straight *from* a bottle	boire *à même* la bouteille
IN(TO) expressing position	*in* the Tropics	*aux/sous* (more common) les Tropiques
	in our country	*chez* nous
	in the Alps, etc	*dans* les Alpes, etc
	in Paris	*à* Paris, but *dans* Paris = right in Paris
	in the 19th district (of Paris)	*dans* le 19ᵉ arrondissement
	in the Paris area	*dans la/en* (R3) région parisienne
	in the capital (Paris)	*en* métropole/*dans* la capitale

NOTE: one says **arriver *dans* la capitale**

	in the suburbs	*en* banlieue

NOTE: *dans* la banlieue de Paris, although one hears increasingly *en* banlieue parisienne

	in the street	*dans* la rue
	a street *in* Marseilles	une rue *de* Marseille
	he lives *in* the rue Vanneau	il habite rue Vanneau
	in the road (ie the middle)	*sur* la chaussée
	in the avenue/boulevard see note for **3.4.4.1** SUR	*dans/sur* l'avenue/le boulevard
	in the square (market square)	*sur* la place
	in the square (small public square with garden)	*dans* le square

213

in the direction of the station	*du* côté de la gare
in the roads (of a harbour)	*en* rade
in the mountains	*à* la/*en* montagne/*dans* les montagnes
in paradise	*au* paradis
to go *into* paradise	entrer *au* paradis
to fall *in* the water	tomber *à*/*dans* l'eau
in contact with the water	*au* contact de l'eau
in the air	*dans*/*en* l'air/*dans* les airs (R3) (3.2.2)
in space (of astronaut)	*dans* l'espace
to put sth *into* orbit	mettre qch *sur* orbite
in a low orbit	*sur* une/*en* orbite basse
in a tent	*dans*/*sous* une tente
in (as contrasted with outside) the house	*dans* la maison
in the stadium (of spectator)	*dans* le stade
in the stadium (of competitor)	*sur* le stade
in the (boxing) ring	*sur* le ring
in the workyard	*sur* le chantier
in places	*par* endroits
in the car park	*dans*/*sur* le parking
in solitary confinement	*au* secret
in the trees	*aux* arbres (with **grimper**, **monter**) but **se cacher** *dans* **les arbres**
the key is *in* the door	la clef est *sur* la porte
in a note-book	*dans*/*sur* un carnet
in the paper	*dans*/*sur* (R1) le journal
in the saddle (of a horse)	*en* selle
in the saddle (of a bicycle)	*sur* la selle
to sit *in* an armchair	être assis *dans* un fauteuil
in a balloon	*en* ballon
in a car/plane/train	*à bord d'*une voiture/un avion/un train
to get *into* a plane	monter *dans* un avion
to go up *in* a plane	monter *en* avion
wounded *in* the arm, etc	blessé *au* bras, etc
to fall *into* sb's hands	tomber *aux*/*entre* les mains de qn
to have a pipe *in* one's mouth	avoir la pipe *à* la bouche
to have a book *in* one's hand	tenir un livre *à* la main
in the sun	*au* soleil
to be reflected *in* the sunlight	se refléter *dans* le soleil (not *au*)

in the rain	*sous* la pluie

NOTE: *dans* would indicate that the rain is very heavy

in the snow	*sous* la neige (when snow is falling)/ *dans* la neige (when snow is on the ground)
in the shade	*à* (more common)/ *dans* l'ombre
in place of	*à la place de/au lieu de*

In the following six sets of examples DANS is more specific than A:

to work *in* a mine	travailler *à/dans* la mine

NOTE: *à* is general (in the mines), *dans* implies in a particular mine

in the country	*à/dans* la campagne
in the fields	*aux/dans* les champs
in the garden	*au/dans* le jardin
in the drawing room	*au/dans* le salon
in the kitchen	*à/dans* la cuisine
in the bedroom	*dans* la chambre

NOTE: only *dans* may be used here

expressing time

In the following three examples the use of DANS implies 'in the course of':

in the morning	le matin/ *dans* la matinée (cf 2.3)
in the afternoon	l'après-midi/ *dans* l'après-midi
in the evening	le soir/ *dans* la soirée (cf 2.3)
in the early afternoon	*en* début d'après-midi/ *au* début de l'après-midi

NOTE: the latter is slightly more literary

in April	*en* avril
in mid-April	*à* la mi-avril
in the spring	*au* printemps
in summer/winter	*en* été/hiver
in the autumn	*à l'/en* automne
in 1950	*en* 1950/ *en* l'an 1950 (R3)
in the 20th century	*au* 20e siècle
in our time	*à* notre époque/ *de* notre temps/ *de* nos jours
in the time of the Pharaohs	*au/du* temps des Pharaons

I will do it *in* ten days (in ten days' time)	je le ferai *dans* dix jours
I did it *in* ten days (within a period of ten days)	je l'ai fait *en* dix jours
in the space of three weeks	*en* l'espace de trois semaines (not *dans*)
in such weather	*par* un temps pareil
in advance	*à l'/d'/par* avance

figurative usage	*in* a literary form	*dans/sous* une forme littéraire
	in writing	*par* écrit (eg **confirmez-le par écrit** confirm it in writing)
	to write *in* ink/pencil	écrire *à* l'encre/*au* crayon
	in a happy/sad voice	*d'*une voix heureuse/triste
	in a happy/sad tone	*d'/sur* un ton heureux/triste
	in a strange way	*d'*une façon/manière étrange (hence: **la façon/manière *dont* on fait qch**)
	in his way	*à* sa manière/*à* sa guise/*à* son gré
	in a favourable light	*sous* un jour favorable
	in secret/private	*dans* le/*en* secret/privé
	in his opinion	*à* son avis
	in John's opinion	*de* l'avis de Jean
	in his case	*chez* lui
	to be *in* danger	être *en* danger
	to sleep *in* peace	dormir *en* paix
	to sit *in* silence	rester assis *en* silence
	to be *in* mourning	être *en* deuil
	the government *in* power	le gouvernement *au* pouvoir
	in a state of war/siege/crisis, etc	*en* état de guerre/siège/crise, etc
	in the final(s) (of a sport)	*en* finale
	in the present situation	*dans/en* (R3) la situation actuelle
	in all respects	*sous* tous les rapports
	in parenthesis	*par* parenthèse (R3)/*entre* parenthèses

ON expressing position	*on* the plains	*dans* la plaine
	on the farm	*à/dans* la ferme

NOTE: *sur* la ferme
on top of the farmhouse

to work *on* a ranch	travailler *à/dans* un ranch
on the ground	*à* (R3)/*par* terre
on the ceiling	*au* plafond
on the telephone	*au* téléphone
pictures hanging *on* the wall	des peintures pendues *au* mur
a cat is sitting *on* the wall	un chat est assis *sur* le mur
on the stairs	*dans* l'escalier
on the blackboard	*au/sur* le tableau noir
to sit *on* a couch/settee	être assis *sur* un canapé/divan/sofa
on the stage	*sur* (la)/*en* scène
on the path	*dans* l'allée
on the pavement	*sur* le trottoir
on the roadway	*sur* la chaussée
to walk *on* the road	marcher *sur* la route/*dans* la rue
to look *on* to the street (of building)	donner *sur* la rue
on the Champs-Elysées	*sur* les Champs-Elysées
to be *on* a bicycle	être *à* bicyclette/*à*/*en* (R1) vélo
to be *on* a/my bike	être *sur* un/mon vélo
on the train	*dans* le train

NOTE: *sur* le train
on top of the train

on a raft	*en* (general)/*sur* (precise) un radeau
on the first page	*à* la/*en* première page
to put sth *on* a plate	mettre qch *dans* une assiette (not *sur*)
to have sth *on* one's feet, etc	avoir qch *aux* pieds, etc
on this side	*de* ce côté
on the other side	*de* l'autre côté

expressing time	*on* May 6th	le six mai
	on a cold winter's day	*par* un jour froid d'hiver
	on my arrival/return	*à* mon arrivée/retour

figurative usage	*on* the radio	*à* la radio, but *sur* Radio France
	on TV	*à* la télé, but *sur* la première/deuxième chaîne on the first/second channel
	on an enquiry mission	*en* mission d'enquête/ information
	to go *on* tour	partir *en* tournée
	shares quoted *on* the Stock Exchange	des valeurs cotées *en* Bourse
	on pain of a fine	*sous* peine d'amende
	to be *on* leave	être *en* permission
	on behalf of M. Henri	*de* la part de M. Henri
	tell him *on* my behalf	dites-le-lui *de* ma part
	on the other hand	*d'*autre part
	he's *on* my side	il est *de* mon côté
OUT OF expressing position	*out of* the house, I feel fine	*hors de* la maison, je me sens bien
figurative usage	it's *out of* the question	c'est *hors* sujet
	out of breath	*hors d'*haleine
	eight *out of* ten	huit *sur* dix

The following examples represent a very large
group of expressions where *out of* = *par*:

	out of compassion	*par* compassion
	out of friendship	*par* amitié
	out of ignorance	*par* ignorance
	out of love	*par* amour
OUTSIDE expressing position	the dog is *outside* the house	le chien est *au dehors de* (R3)/ *en dehors de* la maison
	outside the town	*en dehors de* la ville
figurative usage	that's *outside* my competence	cela dépasse ma compétence
OVER (cf **2.4** *on, over*)	he looked *over* the wall	il regarda *par-dessus* le mur
	the bird flew *over* the wall (ie to the other side)	l'oiseau vola *par-dessus* le mur
	the bird flew *over* the wall (ie along/above the wall)	l'oiseau vola *au-dessus du* mur

NOTE: ***par-dessus*** implies a more rapid
movement across to the other side, while ***au-
dessus de*** implies either high above or along.
Au-dessus de can involve a static idea,
eg le ballon est/vole ***au-dessus de*** la ville
(not ***par-dessus***)

TO(WARDS) expressing position	to go *to* the moon	aller ***dans/sur*** la lune (not *à*)
	to go *towards* town	aller ***vers*** la ville
	to go *to* town	aller ***en*** ville
	to go *to* school	aller ***en*** classe
	the road *to* the station	le chemin ***de la*** gare (cf FROM)
	the train *to* Paris	le train ***de*** Paris (cf FROM)
	to fall *to* the ground (from a height, suggesting a gap between feet and ground)	tomber ***à*** terre (R3)
	NOTE: *à* is being replaced by *par* in this case; see next example	
	to fall *to* the ground (from a standing/sitting position)	tomber ***par*** terre
	to go *to* paradise	aller ***au/en*** (R3) **paradis**
	to go *to* hell/purgatory	aller ***en*** enfer/purgatoire
figurative usage	to have good feelings *towards* sb	**avoir de bons sentiments *envers* qn**
	NOTE: never ***vers*** with people in this figurative sense	
	he is well-disposed *towards* me	**il est bon/gentil *pour* moi**
UNDER (cf **2.4** *under*) expressing position	the dog is *under* the table	**le chien est *sous* la table**
	he threw the ball *under* the table	**il jeta la balle *au-dessous de* (R3)/*en dessous de* la table**
figurative usage	*under* the influence of	***sous* l'emprise/empire/ influence/le coup (R1) de**
UNTIL expressing time	I waited *until* seven o'clock	**j'ai attendu *jusqu'à* sept heures**
	he won't know *until* Saturday	**il ne le saura que samedi/il ne le saura pas *avant* samedi**

WITH	come *with* me	venez *avec* moi
figurative	to be angry *with* sb	être fâché *avec* (more
usage		common)/*contre* qn
		(cf 3.4.3 se fâcher)
	with a trembling hand	*d*'une main tremblante
	with all my heart	*de* tout mon cœur
	with all my strength	*de* toutes mes forces
	with giant strides	*à* pas de géant

3.4.5 Different constructions in French and English

It occasionally happens that where English or French use a
verb + preposition + noun or pronoun construction, the other
language uses a verb + direct object construction. Such differences
between the two languages need to be noted and observed.

3.4.5.1 French verb + direct object =
English verb + preposition + noun/pronoun

approuver qch	= to approve of sth
attendre qn	= to wait for sb
commenter qch	= to comment upon sth
compenser qch	= to compensate for sth
concurrencer qn	= to compete with sb
désapprouver qch	= to disapprove of sth
écouter qch	= to listen to sth
expérimenter qch	= to experiment with sth
opérer qn	= to operate upon sb
eg se faire opérer de	= to have an appendix operation
l'appendicite	
payer qch	= to pay for sth
pleurer qn	= to weep for sb
prêcher qn	= to preach to sb
présider une réunion	= to preside over a meeting
prier Dieu/la Vierge Marie	= to pray to God/Virgin Mary
raisonner qn	= to make sb see reason
(re)chercher qch	= to look for sth
regarder qch	= to look at sth
veiller qn	= to watch over sb
voler qn (cf 3.4.1.5)	= to steal from sb
voter qch	= to vote for sth
NOTE: **voter pour qn** = to vote for sb	

3.4.5.2 French verb + preposition + $\dfrac{\text{noun}}{\text{pronoun}}$ =
English verb + direct object

hériter de qch	= to inherit sth
hériter (de) qch de qn	= to inherit sth from sb
influer sur qch	= to influence sth

(but ***influencer*** + direct object)

| verbaliser contre qn | = to book sb (of police) |

3.5   Negation

3.5.1   Negative words and expressions:

The following negative words and expressions will be examined:

not used with			
ne	non		

used with *ne*	pas	que	rien
	plus	ni ... ni	aucun
	jamais	personne	

3.5.1.1   Non
Non has the following uses:

use	examples
as a negative reply to questions	est-elle là? – Non
	– Je crois que non
	– Tu peux être sûr
	que non
	tu le feras? – Peut-être que non

to negate any part of speech except a verb	
noun	c'est sa cousine, non sa sœur
past participle/adjective	une chambre non meublée
prepositional phrase	il entra non sans hésitation
	il habite non loin de Paris

Non may be combined with other negative words:

non pas more forceful than *non* alone; also negates parts of speech like *non*:

eg **il a des flatteurs, non pas des amis**

j'ai essayé, non pas de le convaincre, mais de lui expliquer mon point de vue

non pas que (see **3.7.2.6**)

non plus meaning 'neither':

eg **je ne le savais pas non plus**

je ne le savais pas. – Ni moi non plus

NOTE: *si* is always used to contradict a negative question or suggestion:

eg **tu ne le feras pas? – Si, je le ferai**

oui may be used like *non* after *que*:

eg **je crois que oui**

peut-être que oui

3.5.1.2 **Pas**

The following usages of *pas* should be noted:

In indirect questions introduced by *si*, *ne ... pas* is sometimes used to emphasise the doubt in the speaker's mind:

compare **je lui ai demandé s'il ne voulait pas venir**
je lui ai demandé s'il voulait venir

compare **elle se demande s'il n'y a pas de solution**
elle se demande s'il y a une solution

In the following example, unlike the equivalent English sentence, *ne ... (pas)* directs the listener's attention to the period of time which has elapsed since the last sighting of the person in question:

eg **voilà/il y a deux jours que je ne l'ai pas vu (R1 + R2)**
voilà/il y a deux jours que je ne l'ai vu (R3)
$\left.\begin{array}{l}\ \\ \ \\ \ \\ \ \end{array}\right\}=$ it's two days since I saw him

NOTE: for the word order of adverbs with *ne ... pas* see **3.3.2**

There are a few alternatives to **ne ... pas**:

point *point* is little used nowadays and has no more emphasis than *pas*

mot used only with verbs of speaking in R3 usage:

eg **il ne dit mot** = he remained completely silent

goutte used only with *voir* in R1 speech:

eg **je n'y vois goutte** = I can't see a thing

que dalle a slang term, used only in R1 speech:

eg **je ne pige que dalle** = I don't understand a thing

pas de is used with nouns in a negative sentence:

eg **il n'a pas de livres**

il n'a pas d'argent

il n'y a pas de solution

pas un	is stronger than *pas de*, and is equivalent to 'not a single one':
	eg **il n'a pas un livre**
	je ne vois pas une maison
	pas un des garçons n'a répondu
pas without **ne**	is used in very similar circumstances to **non**, but in a less formal register:

use	examples
to negate any part of speech except a verb:	
noun	j'ai vu son frère mais pas sa sœur
past participle/adjective	elle est jolie, pas belle
prepositional phrase	il habite pas loin de Paris
	j'ai assez de pommes, mais pas assez de poires
in informal, often elliptical speech situations	Tu viens ce soir? – Pourquoi pas!
	Elle vient de mettre au monde des triplés. – Pas possible, je ne savais pas qu'elle était enceinte!

3.5.1.3 Plus

ne ... plus	refers both to time and quantity:
	eg **je suis retourné chercher mon parapluie; il n'y était plus**
	il n'y travaille plus
	je ne veux plus de cerises
plus	alone may have a negative value and refers only to quantity:
	eg **plus de chansons** = no more songs

3.5.1.4 Jamais

In more formal R3 speech and writing *jamais* may introduce a sentence (unlike English this does not cause inversion of the subject and verb), but normally it follows the verb:

eg **jamais il n'est venu me voir**
   il ne vient jamais

Jamais is quite frequently used without *ne*, meaning 'ever':

eg **l'avez-vous jamais fait?**
   sans jamais comprendre
   si jamais il téléphone

3.5.1.5 Que

Que must be placed immediately before the element of a sentence which is being qualified (not as in English, where 'only' may be at

some distance from the relevant element), with the result that
sometimes *que* is a long way from negative *ne*:

eg il n'est revenu qu'hier soir

ce n'était que ce matin que j'ai entendu la nouvelle

je ne voudrais lui parler aujourd'hui ou demain qu'en
présence de son père

je ne viendrai te voir dimanche ou lundi au plus tard que si
j'ai une réponse

cela ne fait que rendre le choix plus difficile

rien que   = merely:

eg **rien qu'à le lire** = merely by reading it

When *ne . . . que* is combined with *pas* it means 'not only':

eg **il n'y a pas que des tables** = there are not only tables

In speech *que* may occasionally stand by itself:

eg **ça ne m'a coûté que vingt francs. – Que vingt francs?**

3.5.1.6   Ni . . . ni

When *ni . . . ni* is used with two singular subjects the verb may be
either singular or plural:

eg **ni l'un ni l'autre ne l'a/ont fait**

ni le chauffage ni la lumière n'a/ont fonctionné

Ni . . . ni may be combined with any part of speech except finite
verbs, when only one *ni* is required:

eg **il n'a vu ni elle ni moi**

ce livre n'est ni bon ni utile

je ne peux ni ne veux y aller

Ni . . . ni is used in infinitival phrases introduced by *sans*:

eg **sans parler ni à sa mère ni à sa sœur, il partit** (ni = either)

R1 speakers generally avoid *ni . . . ni*, preferring instead a
construction with *non plus* (cf **3.5.1.1**):

eg **j'aime pas le prof., l'école non plus**

3.5.1.7   Personne, rien, aucun

Personne, *rien* and *aucun* have negative value themselves when used
without a verb.

personne   je n'ai vu personne

qui a frappé à la porte? – Personne

rien   je n'ai rien fait

qu'est-ce que tu as fait? – Rien

aucun   je n'ai aucun désir de le faire

combien de pommes vous reste-t-il? – Aucune

3.5.1.8 Combinations of negative words
When combined negative words are ordered in the following way:

1	2	3	examples
jamais	plus	personne rien que ni … ni	je n'y comprends plus rien il ne m'a jamais rien donné il n'y a plus personne il n'a jamais ni stylo ni crayon je ne pourrais jamais plus le faire

3.5.2 The negation of infinitives

The various elements are ordered in the following way:

	examples	
ne pas	il me recommande de ne pas y aller	

ne rien
        + infinitive
ne jamais
	il m'a demandé de ne
	  rien acheter	

ne plus	il s'est engagé à ne
	  plus jamais revenir
		je vous conseille
		  de ne rien dire
		  à personne

ne
ne + infinitive + **personne**
nulle
        part
	sans voir personne
	
	il m'a demandé de n'aller
	  nulle part sans lui	

The following illustrates how the position of the negation and the number of negations influence the meaning of the sentence:

je ne peux pas le faire   = I can't do it
je peux ne pas le faire   = I can not (can refuse to) do it
je ne peux pas ne pas le faire = I can't not do it

The following table shows how more complex constructions involving the negation of infinitives work and are influenced by considerations of register:

	order			examples
R2	**ne pas**	**+être/** *auxiliary* *of past* *infinitive*		je lui reproche de ne pas être honnête/de ne pas avoir été honnête
R2+R3	**ne**	**+être/** *auxiliary* *of past* *infinitive*	**+jamais/** **rien/plus**	il me reproche de ne l'avoir jamais compris il me reproche de n'avoir rien fait il me reproche de n'avoir plus rien fait
R3	**ne**	**+être/** *auxiliary* *of past* *infinitive*	**+pas**	je lui reproche de n'être pas honnête/de n'avoir pas été honnête
	ne jamais/ **rien/plus**	**+être** *auxiliary* *of past* *infinitive*		il me reproche de ne jamais l'avoir compris il me reproche de ne rien avoir fait

3.5.3 Negation and register

The impact of register considerations upon negation causes the
following adjustments to the normal *ne . . . pas* pattern:
R1 users and to a lesser extent R2 users tend to prefer *pas* without *ne*,
whereas R3 users, and very occasionally R2 users, prefer *ne* without
pas:

feature	register	examples
no *ne*	R1, sometimes R2	*(je) crois pas* *c'est pas juste/vrai* *Henri Laporte? – Connais pas* *ça fait rien*
no *pas*	R3	with *cesser, oser, pouvoir, savoir*: 　*il ne cesse de pleuvoir* 　*je n'ose le faire* 　*je ne sais le prononcer* 　*je ne saurais le faire*

feature	register	examples
		in rhetorical questions introduced by *qui* or *que* :
		qui ne l'aurait compris?
		qui ne viendrait dans de telles circonstances?
		que ne ferait-elle pour vous plaire?
		in certain set expressions :
		qu'à Dieu ne plaise
		qu'à cela ne tienne = certainly
		je n'ai que faire de vos excuses
		n'ayez crainte
	R3, sometimes R2	in certain conditional clauses :
		si je ne me trompe
		si je ne m'abuse
		s'il n'était venu à mon secours, je me noyais
		si ce n'est
		n'importe

3.5.4 Superfluous *ne*

In certain types of subordinate clauses a superfluous *ne*, usually known as expletive *ne*, occurs in R3 usage, occasionally in R2, but never in R1.

circumstance	examples
with verbs and expressions of fearing	*avoir crainte/peur, craindre, de crainte/peur*
	je crains que vous ne tombiez
with verbs expressing avoiding and preventing	*empêcher, éviter, prendre garde*
	il faut empêcher qu'il ne parte
with *s'en falloir de peu*	*il s'en faut de très peu qu'il ne comprenne*
	peu s'en est fallu qu'il ne tombe
with expressions of doubt in negative (= probably)	*ne pas douter, ne pas nier, nul doute*
	je ne doute pas qu'il n'ait raison
	nul doute qu'il n'ait raison

circumstance	examples
with *à moins que* and *avant que*	*à moins qu'il ne revienne le premier* (R2)
	avant qu'elle ne puisse sortir, il faut qu'elle prenne son dîner
in comparisons	*il est plus/moins intelligent que je ne le pensais*
	elle l'a accompli mieux que je ne le croyais
	NOTE: it is preferable to use *ne le* rather than simple *ne* in these cases

3.6 Verbs

It is impossible, given the scope of this book, to present a systematic survey of the types, forms and functions of French verbs. Instead significant differences between French and English usages will be concentrated upon and illustrated.

3.6.1 Tenses

There are many occasions where the usage of tenses in French corresponds closely to the usage of tenses in English. However, it is also the case that there are many other occasions where the usages of tenses in the two languages do not correspond. Taking the present tenses of the two languages as an example, it can be shown that an English present tense will frequently be used in exactly the same way as a French present tense, whereas at other times the French present tense will refer to future or past time in ways that are not possible in English. The same remark also applies to the other tenses. In the following discussion the three principal time-perspectives (present, future and past) will each be examined in detail, indicating the various factors which influence tense-selection in French. Such factors will include register, the attitude of the speaker towards the event, and the precise setting of the event on the time scale. At the end of the three sections on time-perspective, comments about special uses of individual tenses will be found.

3.6.1.1 Present time
From the point of view of tense usage this is the most straightforward of the three time-perspectives mentioned above, in that only the present tense is used.

aspect of present time	conveyed by	examples
present time proper		*je chante en ce moment*
habitual time	present tense	*je mange à six heures tous les jours*
universal time		*deux et deux font quatre*

Continuous tense in present time: in order to convey the English continuous present *I am doing something* (which implies, despite its name, that an activity in progress at the present time is going to stop sooner or later), French has recourse to the following constructions:

construction	register	examples
être en train de + infinitive	R1–R3	*je suis en train de prendre mon déjeuner* *elle est en train de coudre*
aller + (*en*) + present participle	R3	*l'industrie va croissant* *les couleurs vont en se dégradant*

Special points concerning the present tense: the present tense may also be used to refer to future time (**3.6.1.2**) and past time (**3.6.1.3**).

3.6.1.2 Future time
The idea of futurity may be conveyed in the following ways:

tense	comments	examples
future	normal usage	*je viendrai demain*
present	to describe an event occurring in the near future	*je descends au prochain arrêt*
conditional	normal usage to refer to future in the past	*elle savait qu'il comprendrait*
	also used to express doubt	*avez-vous entendu dire qu'il n'y aurait pas de cours demain?*
	and probability	*il pourrait arriver à temps*
aller + infinitive	to express fulfilling of intention/imminent fulfilment	*tu vas voir* *je vais te l'expliquer* *il va pleuvoir*

A continuous tense in future time may be conveyed in the following ways:

construction	register	examples
être en train de + infinitive	R1–R3	*je serai en train de faire mes devoirs quand tu arriveras à la maison ce soir*
aller + (*en*) + infinitive	R3	*il est à espérer que la production des voitures ira croissant pendant le restant de cette année*

On occasions French specifies explicitly future time when English leaves time-orientation vague:

eg **faites ce que vous voudrez**

(It is also possible to say in the same circumstances:

faites ce que vous voulez)

Special points concerning the future and conditional tenses: The future tense is sometimes used instead of an imperative to tone down an order or a request:

eg **tu le feras cet après-midi**

The future perfect and conditional tenses are sometimes used to imply conjecture or allegation:

eg **elle aura manqué le car** (R2) = she's probably missed the coach

il aura su le résultat (R3) = he probably knew the result

il y a eu un accident: il y aurait trente blessés (newspaper language) = there has been a road accident: it is reported (but is not certain) that thirty people have been injured

selon certains rapports il y aurait d'autres projets = according to certain reports other projects exist

The following typical uses of the conditional in French should be noted:

on dirait un fou = he seems mad

on aurait dit un fou = he seemed mad/you would have thought he was mad

(In R3 usage an imperfect subjunctive might be used:

on eût dit un fou)

3.6.1.3 Past time

Past time may be envisaged in several ways, as the following table demonstrates:

past time envisaged	past	present	tense generally used
as a point of time with no link with or repercussion upon the present	*elle regarda/a regardé par la fenêtre* • point in time		past historic perfect
as a point of time which relates to the present	*elle est arrivée tout à l'heure* •————————————→ point in time		perfect
as a period of time	*ils s'amusaient à écouter des disques* ———— period of time		imperfect
as a period of time interrupted by an event	*elle lisait le magazine quand sa sœur entra/est entrée* ↓ ———— time		past historic or perfect of interrupting imperfect
as a repetition of an action/event	*il prenait son repas à la même heure tous les jours* • • • repeated action/event		imperfect
from the standpoint of present time beyond a significant event in the past to another single event further back in the past	*elle m'a dit que sa mère était repartie* • • ← point in point in time time		pluperfect
from the standpoint of present time beyond a significant event in the past to an event of long duration further back in the past	*il est clair qu'avant de monter le film, il avait passé de longues heures à ramasser du matériel* ————• ← period of time		pluperfect

However, usage is not always quite as clear-cut as the table suggests: the past tenses sometimes overlap in usage. The past historic and perfect are sometimes used to record past events and repetitions of events of any duration (normally the prerogative of the imperfect tense) considered from an historical perspective as single events:

eg il vécut soixante-dix ans
la guerre dura trente ans

Conversely the imperfect tense is occasionally used, particularly in journalism, to refer to a single event in the past (normally the prerogative of the perfect or past historic tenses); in this way attention is drawn to the event evoked and a dramatic dimension is added:

eg **il y a cent ans naissait Staline**
dans son discours il évoquait la crise énergétique
hier soir M. Dupont définissait sa théorie sur
l'industrialisation

Past time may also be conveyed by the present tense, which denotes an event which has occurred in the recent past:

eg **je quitte à l'instant mon ami**
c'est la première fois que je le fais
une lettre me parvient à l'instant

There also exists in French an historic present which invests the events recounted with a particularly lively, dramatic quality, as if they were happening in the present:

eg **Après son arrivée, les choses se précipitèrent. Le voilà qui**
donne des ordres, qui fait des caprices. Tout le monde
accourt à son appel. Il distribue des tracts et ils repartent
tout de suite.

As is the case for present and future time and formed in the same way, there exists for past time a continuous tense:

construction	register	examples
être en train de + infinitive	R1–R3	*j'étais/avais été en train de regarder un film à la télévision*
aller + (*en*) + present participle	R3	*la tension entre les états allait augmentant pendant les années 70*

The following table helps distinguish between circumstances in which the past historic and perfect tenses are used. It should be noted that the perfect tense is the normal tense used in all registers when referring to a past event while the past historic is restricted to R3 usage.

past tense	circumstances of usage
perfect	principally in speech, but also in writing
examples	*j'ai déjà fait cinq années de français.*
	Le premier ministre a annoncé son intention de diminuer les impôts: il a reçu une véritable ovation dans la Chambre des Députés.
past historic	in writing, especially novels, students' essays, fairy stories, etc.;
	sometimes in newspapers; talks on radio and television dealing with historical topics; formal speeches, lectures.
examples	*Il partit, revint et finalement repartit.*
	Au bout de quelque temps elle vit la maison.
	speech given by Général de Gaulle, Edinburgh, 23 June 1942:
	Dans chacun des combats où, pendant cinq siècles le destin de la France fut en jeu, il y eut toujours des hommes d'Ecosse pour combattre côte à côte avec les hommes de France. Ce que les Français pensent de vous, c'est que jamais un peuple ne s'est montré, plus que le vôtre, généreux de son amitié. (C. de Gaulle, *Mémoires de Guerre*, I, Paris, 1954)

Special points concerning past tenses:

The past historic of *vouloir* implies 'tried':

eg **il voulut sortir mais il n'y réussit pas**

Similarly, the past historic of *pouvoir* implies 'managed to', and that of *savoir* 'learned':

eg **au bout d'une semaine difficile il put le terminer**
après trois jours d'attente il sut le résultat

The French pluperfect is occasionally equivalent to an English simple past tense or perfect tense:

eg **je vous l'avais bien dit** = I told you so
nous vous avions parlé du = we've already told you about
problème the problem

The past anterior is purely a written tense and is used only in the following situations:

tense of main/ introductory clause	subordinate clause introduced by	tense of subordinate clause
past historic	*après que* *aussitôt que* *dès que* *lorsque* *quand*	past anterior
examples	*dès que j'eus compris, il voulut partir* *quand il eut commandé son dîner, son ami arriva*	

tense of main/ introductory clause	main/introductory clause introduced by	tense of subordinate clause
past anterior	*à peine*	past historic
example	*à peine eut-il fermé la porte que sa femme éclata de rire*	

Since the past historic is not used in ordinary speech, the past anterior, being closely allied to it, does not occur there either. Its place is taken either by the pluperfect or, increasingly, by the double compound past tense (in French *le passé surcomposé*):

> eg   **aussitôt que nous eûmes fini, elle alla se promener**
> **aussitôt que nous avions fini, elle est allée se promener**
> **aussitôt que nous avons eu fini, elle est allée se promener**

3.6.1.4   **Sequence of tenses**

The main difference between English and French usages concerns the sequence of tenses in sentences containing a subordinate clause of time or a clause introduced by *quand même*, as the following table illustrates:

tense in main/ introductory clause	tense in subordinate clause	French example	English equivalent
future	future	**je le ferai quand/ lorsque j'aurai le temps**	I'll do it when I've got the time
		je t'aimerai tant que je vivrai	I'll love you for as long as I live
		quand il sera parti, je pourrai allumer la télévision	when he's gone, I can put the television on
past	conditional	**elle me demanda d'écrire la lettre dès que je serais de retour**	she asked me to write the letter as soon as I got back
conditional	conditional perfect	**je lui ai dit que je le ferais quand il m'aurait donné de l'argent**	I told her I'd do it when he had given me some money

Usage with *même si, quand même* and their variants is determined by considerations of register:

register	French example	English equivalent
R1	elle me l'aurait dit je n'aurais pas pu le faire	even if she'd told me, I couldn't have done it
R2	même si elle était venue, je ne l'aurais pas fait	even if she had come, I would not have done it
R3	quand même vous le feriez, je ne viendrais pas	even if you did it, I wouldn't come
	quand (bien) même le feriez-vous que je ne viendrais pas	were you to do it, I should not come

The sequence of tenses in sentences containing a hypothetical clause introduced by *si* is as follows:

tense in *si*-clause	tense in main clause	examples
present	present	*si tu as faim il faut manger quelque chose*
	future	*si je la vois, je te téléphonerai*
	future perfect	*si tu continues à manger comme ça, tu auras fini trop tard*
	imperative	*si tu veux du chocolat, va au magasin d'à-côté*
perfect	present	*si vous avez conduit 200 kilomètres vous devez être fatigué*
	future	*si vous avez conduit une telle distance, vous aurez besoin de sommeil*
	imperfect	*si on vous a dit ça, c'était un mauvais tour*
	perfect	*si le professeur est déjà arrivé, il a dû courir vite*
	future perfect	*s'il a lu cent pages ce matin, il aura terminé le livre ce soir*
	imperative	*si tu as fini, porte ton assiette à la cuisine*
imperfect	conditional	*si je la voyais, je te téléphonerais*
	conditional perfect	*si tu m'aimais, tu n'aurais pas dit ça*
pluperfect	conditional	*si tu avais gardé tes gants, tu n'aurais pas froid*
	conditional perfect	*si je l'avais vue, je t'aurais téléphoné*

3 *Grammar*

(For *si* + hypothetical clause + *que* + hypothetical clause, see **3.7.2.6** NOTE 2.)

The above sequences of tenses do not apply when *si* is used to introduce an indirect question; future and conditional tenses may be used in the *si*-clause:

eg **je me demande si elle viendra**
    je me demandais si elle viendrait

Usage with *c'est*: unlike the equivalent English phrase *it is/it was*, French *c'est* tends not to vary in tense and may be used to refer to past time:

eg **c'est lui qui m'a demandé d'y aller**

In the following situation involving *fois*, *c'était* is used with reference to past time, and the sequences of tenses in English and French are quite different:

c'est la première fois que je te vois ici	= it's the first time I've seen you here
c'était la première fois qu'elle le faisait	= it was the first time she had done it

3.6.1.5 **Other differences between French and English tense usages**

depuis:

je suis ici depuis dix ans	= I've been here for ten years
(but **je n'ai pas été ici depuis dix ans**	= I haven't been here for ten years)
depuis quand/combien de temps étudiez-vous le français?	= how long have you been studying French?
j'étais là depuis un an	= I had been there for a year
je n'étais pas là depuis un an	= I hadn't been there for a year
depuis quand/combien de temps habitait-il Paris?	= how long had he lived in Paris?
mille exemplaires ont été publiés depuis 1970	= a thousand copies have been published since 1970

il y a …
que/voilà
… que, etc

il y a dix ans que je suis ici	= I've been here for ten years
voilà plus de trois jours que je t'attends	= I've been waiting for you for more than three days
ça/cela fait dix jours qu'il est là	= he's been there for ten days now

venir de:	il vient d'arriver	= he's just arrived
	il venait de se baisser quand	= he had just bent down when the
	la voiture l'a heurté	car ran into him

NOTE: a French speaker would not use *venir de + venir*

3.6.2 The infinitive

In French the infinitive may be used in certain circumstances where English would use a finite verb or a participle:

circumstance	examples	
in questions:	*que faire?*	*pourquoi le dire?*
	pour quoi faire?	*comment y aller?*
	moi partir maintenant?	*à quoi bon envoyer une lettre?*
as an order:	*s'adresser à la direction*	
	rayer la mention inutile	
	ne pas se pencher au dehors	
in instructions on merchandise:	*faire chauffer à petit feu*	
	remuer la solution	
	bien nettoyer la surface à peindre avant de …	
as a narrative infinitive introduced by *et* in R3 speech or writing:	*et lui de dire qu'elle avait raison*	
	et ma sœur de partir tout de suite	
as a subject:	*tromper, c'est mentir*	
	voir, c'est croire	
	se tenir en équilibre sur une jambe n'est pas facile	
with verbs relating to the senses:	*je l'ai vu sortir*	
	il m'a entendu entrer	
	elle sentit son cœur s'arrêter de battre	

In the following example French, unlike English, does not require a direct object:

j'entendais marcher dans le	= I heard someone walking along
couloir	the corridor

A choice between the infinitive and a *que*-clause is affected by considerations of register. In the first two cases, in the following table, both parts of the sentence have the same subject; in the third case different subjects are involved:

structure	R1	R2+R3
present infinitive versus *que*-clause	il a cru qu'il a vu une lumière	il a cru voir une lumière
(same subject in both parts of the sentence)	je pense que je peux vous aider	je pense pouvoir vous aider
past infinitive versus *que*-clause	je croyais que je l'avais lu	je croyais l'avoir lu
(same subject in both parts of the sentence)	il dit qu'il l'a pris	il prétend/nie l'avoir pris
	elle dit qu'elle ne l'a pas fait	elle déclare ne pas l'avoir fait (see note below)

	R2	R3
infinitive versus *que*-clause	demandez à M. Dupont de me donner un coup de téléphone	demandez à M. Dupont qu'il me téléphone
(different subjects in the two parts of the sentence)	dites à votre fils de venir me voir	dites à votre fils qu'il vienne me voir

NOTE: for a discussion of the position of *ne pas* in relation to a past infinitive, see **Negation 3.5.2**

3.6.3 Participles

3.6.3.1 Present participles
The following table illustrates the various ways in which present participles are used in French:

adjectival usage	**agreement between participle and noun qualified** elle semblait très belle ce matin-là avec ses yeux brillants et ses dents éclatantes nous avons des histoires effrayantes à raconter
verbal usage	**no agreement**
	a present participle alone is equivalent to a relative or causal clause les automobilistes venant de Cannes ont trouvé des embouteillages affreux ne sachant que faire, elle a commencé à lire un roman
	***en* + present participle acts as an adverbial phrase of time or manner** vous ne réussirez pas en agissant ainsi je l'ai vu en passant
	***tout en* + present participle expresses simultaneous actions** j'ai continué de travailler tout en prenant mon déjeuner

3.6.3.2 Past participles

When past participles are used as adjectives they agree with the nouns they qualify:

eg   **arrivée au coin de la rue, elle a jeté un coup d'œil en arrière**

    surprise par le mauvais temps, elle a couru s'abriter sous un arbre

    des bruits venus de je ne sais où m'ont beaucoup effrayé

Certain past participles and *étant donné* function as prepositions. Normally they precede the noun and are invariable; however, a few may also follow the noun and agree in number and gender with it.

	examples
past participle as preposition preceding the noun	vu les conséquences de ses actions, elle a décidé de quitter sa maison
	étant donné la situation actuelle la guerre semble inévitable
	y compris ma tante nous serons cinq
	excepté une petite minorité tous les spectateurs se sont bien conduits au match
	vous trouverez ci-joint quittance
past participle as preposition following the noun	une petite minorité exceptée tous les spectateurs se sont bien conduits au match
	j'ai vendu toutes mes affaires, ma voiture comprise (NOTE: *no* y)
	les pièces ci-jointes

3.6.3.3 A difference between French and English usages

Many past participles in French correspond to present participles in English:

accoudé	assis	pendu
accroupi	blotti	perché
adossé	couché	tapi
agenouillé	juché	
appuyé	penché	

eg   **je l'ai trouvé agenouillé devant le corps de son fils**

    elle restait assise pendant longtemps

    la lampe était pendue au plafond

3.6.4 Formation of compound tenses

3.6.4.1 Use of *avoir* and *être* to form compound tenses

Most verbs form their compound tenses by combining the auxiliary *avoir* with the past participle. A much smaller number use *être* to form their compound tenses: this group includes:

all reflexive verbs and certain intransitive verbs:

aller	naître	retomber
arriver	partir	retourner
décéder	parvenir	revenir
demeurer	rentrer	sortir
devenir	repartir	survenir
entrer	ressortir (2.2.4)	tomber
mourir	rester	venir

When *monter* and *descendre* are used literally they are conjugated with *être*:

eg   **elle est descendue**

When they are used figuratively, they are conjugated with *avoir*:

eg   **les prix ont monté**

However, when *descendre, monter, rentrer, retourner, sortir* are used transitively, they form their compound tenses with *avoir*:

eg   **le porteur a déjà monté vos bagages, monsieur**
     il a sorti son revolver

Convenir may be used with either *avoir* or *être* depending upon the meaning intended, although the distinction is being lost. *Avoir* has almost entirely replaced *être*.

convenir = to suit: ***avoir***

eg   **l'hôtel m'a convenu**

convenir = to be in agreement with: ***être***

eg   **nous sommes convenus de son départ**

Certain other verbs use either *avoir* or *être* when no distinction of transitivity or meaning is involved: in such cases it appears that when *avoir* is used an action is implied, and when *être* is used a state is implied:

eg   **ce livre a paru avant hier**
     ce livre est paru depuis longtemps

   also: *accourir, apparaître, disparaître*.

With *passer* both *avoir* and *être* may be used without distinction, but it is clear that here and in the previous cases, *être* is being used with increasing frequency:

eg   **il est passé ce matin**   is more likely than
     il a passé ce matin

3.6.4.2   **Agreement of past participles in compound tenses**
Agreement of *être* + past participle: the following table illustrates
usage:

non-reflexive
  verbs as in
  3.6.4.1
verbs in passive
  mood
	agreement is always with the subject

examples	**elle est arrivée ce matin**
	nous sommes entrés dans la salle de
	  conférence
	elle a été obligée de quitter le
	  magasin
	nous avons été payés d'avance

reflexive verbs	agreement is with the reflexive pronoun provided it is a direct object
examples	**elle s'est assise à côté de son ami** **hier nous nous sommes couchés à** **neuf heures**

The following examples illustrate the contrast between those reflexive
verbs whose reflexive pronoun is a direct object and those whose
pronoun is an indirect object:

pronoun as direct object	pronoun as indirect object
mes deux fils se sont giflés	**mes deux fils se sont donné des** **gifles**
elle s'est lavée à l'eau chaude	**elle s'est lavé les mains avec de** **l'eau chaude**

Agreement of *avoir* + past participle with preceding direct object.

  Agreement occurs between the past participle conjugated with
avoir and the preceding direct object:
eg   **la voiture que j'ai achetée**
      ces filles? je les ai vues tout à l'heure
      les bruits qu'elle a entendus

Difficulty arises when the past participle is followed by an infinitive: agreement occurs when the direct object relates to the past participle, but not when it relates to the infinitive:

eg   *les personnes* que j'ai entendu*es* parler
              object of past participle
      les vers que j'ai entendu *réciter*
              object of infinitive
      la maison que j'ai fait *construire*
              object of infinitive

However, there is a tendency not to make the agreement.

3.6.5   Reflexive versus non-reflexive forms of the same verb

A number of verbs have both a reflexive and non-reflexive form (eg *approcher – s'approcher*). In a small number of cases the two forms may be used interchangeably, but on other occasions there is an important distinction between the values of the two forms, as is illustrated in the following tables:

verbs with no distinction between the values of reflexive and non-reflexive forms	examples
(se) reculer	il s'est/a reculé de dix mètres
(se) terminer	les cours (se) terminent à cinq heures
	le livre (se) termine par un meurtre
(s') imaginer: *the non-reflexive form is more common*	je (m') imagine qu'il a fini le livre

verbs with a distinction between the values of the two forms		examples
unintentional	approcher	il approche la quarantaine
		l'heure approche
deliberate	s'approcher	l'ennemi s'approche de la ville
habitual	fermer	les portes du magasin ferment tous les jours à six heures
specific	se fermer	la porte se ferme lentement
	also (s') ouvrir	
state	coucher	je couche à l'hôtel/sous la tente
action	se coucher	je me couche à six heures
state	arrêter	il a arrêté de fumer = *for good*
	s'arrêter	il s'est arrêté de fumer = *for the moment, but also for good*
action	s'arrêter	NOTE: *in the imperative, the non-reflexive* arrête! *is used; but* arrête-toi (R1)
state	loger	je loge en ville
action	se loger	il est arrivé en ville et s'est logé à l'hôtel
abstract	incliner	j'incline à penser que tout ira bien

verbs with a distinction between the values of the two forms		examples
concrete	s'incliner	il s'incline devant l'autel
	also (se) figurer	
less strong	attaquer	il a attaqué le gouvernement
more strong	s'attaquer	il s'est attaqué au gouvernement
	also décider de/se décider à	
	refuser de/se refuser à	
	résoudre de/se résoudre à	

3.6.6 Verbs of movement in French and English

An important difference between the French and English verbal systems concerns the way in which expressions of movement are analysed and treated in the two languages. In French the direction of movement is often indicated by the verb itself and the manner of movement by a phrase, either *en* + present participle or an adverbial expression, whereas in English the verb conveys the manner of the movement and an adverb or prepositional expression the direction.

French: *direction indicated by verb*	**English:** *direction indicated by adverb/prepositional expression*
manner indicated by phrase	*manner indicated by verb*
elle a monté l'escalier en courant	she ran up the stairs
il gagna en rampant le mur de la prison	he crawled towards the prison wall
elle revint en boitant de la cuisine	she hobbled back from the kitchen
il entra en coup de vent	he burst in
elle a traversé la rivière à la nage	she swam across the river
elle a descendu l'escalier sur la pointe des pieds	she tiptoed downstairs
elle est revenue à vélo	she cycled back

However, with certain compound prepositions, French follows the English pattern:

French	English
direction indicated by prepositional expression/adverb	*direction indicated by adverb/prepositional expression*
manner indicated by verb	*manner indicated by verb*
elle est passée par-dessus le mur	she climbed over the wall
ils se sont promenés le long de la rivière	they walked alongside the river
ils ont marché à travers les champs	they walked across the fields
NOTE: **traverser** would be used with **champ** in the singular (3.4.4 ACROSS)	
il a bondi par-dessus	he jumped over

Often where the manner of movement is specified in English, it is left vague or is ignored completely in French: a general verb is used in French where English uses an explicit verb, although English may also use a general verb like French:

eg **il a traversé la rue** = he walked across the road/he crossed the road

Implicit within *traverser*, for example, is the idea of walking; if the person had run across the road, the phrase *en courant* would have been added.

3.7 Subjunctive Mood

Whereas the subjunctive is extremely rare in English and is by and large restricted to R3 usage, verging in fact on the positively archaic, in French the subjunctive is still a mood to be reckoned with.

What is often disconcerting to the student about the French subjunctive is that in some cases its use seems to conform to clearly defined rules, whereas in others it seems to be a matter of choice. In the following discussion the term 'black and white' subjunctive will be applied to those circumstances where the use of the subjunctive is obligatory, and the term 'grey' subjunctive to those where a degree of choice is permissible. It should be noted with respect to the 'grey' subjunctive that its use is often determined by instinct, particularly on the part of someone who is very conscious of the way he or she uses language. Consequently, the subjunctive appears more frequently and regularly in R3 usage than in R1 usage. Although an R2 user will attempt to use the 'grey' subjunctive in accordance with traditional prescriptions, the 'grey' subjunctive and even the 'black and white' subjunctive may disappear in speech through inadvertence and because of the frequent breaks in continuity of structure which are characteristic in particular of R1 speech, but also of R2 speech. It is considered a sign of ignorance when a person omits the subjunctive incorrectly. (It is comforting to realise that the French themselves experience difficulty with certain forms of the subjunctive, using for example *veuillons* for the correct *voulions*, and *aie* for *ait*.) It is interesting to speculate that the decline of the subjunctive in French is parallel to, but lags a long way behind, the subjunctive in English.

3.7.1 Sequence of tenses with subjunctive in subordinate clause

As far as the sequence of tenses with the subjunctive in a subordinate clause is concerned, it is important to understand that R3 practice often differs from that of the other two register divisions. In broad terms the practices may be characterised as follows:

	R3, R2+R1			R3	R2+R1
il faut	qu'il vienne		il fallait	qu'il vînt	. . . qu'il vienne
il faudra	qu'il vienne		il fallut	qu'il vînt	. . . (qu'il vienne)
il a fallu	qu'il vienne		il faudrait	qu'il vînt	. . . qu'il vienne

	R3	R2+R1
je dois m'en aller	avant qu'il (n') arrive	. . . avant qu'il arrive
je suis allé me coucher	avant qu'il (ne) soit arrivé	. . . avant qu'il arrive
le policier était parti	avant qu'il (n') arrivât	. . . avant qu'il soit arrivé
nous avions décidé de partir	avant qu'il (ne) fût arrivé	. . . avant qu'il soit arrivé

From this it appears that the imperfect subjunctive is to all intents and purposes unknown in R1 and R2 speech – if it does occur it is usually for jocular purposes or as a parody of more elevated usage. It survives in refined R3 usage, in speeches and stories, but even in these cases it is the third person singular which is generally met; the other forms are avoided and are replaced by the present subjunctive and occasionally the perfect subjunctive. It is, in fact, in prose writing that the imperfect subjunctive most frequently occurs. It is quite legitimate therefore for foreign language learners of French not to use the imperfect subjunctive in speech, although they should be aware of its appropriateness in formal writing. It may be that there is a tendency for the subjunctive to be particularly preserved with those common verbs where the indicative and subjunctive tenses are widely divergent in form:

eg *aller:* va - aille
être: est - soit
faire: fait - fasse

3.7.2 'Black and white' subjunctive

The subjunctive occurs regularly in the following circumstances:

3.7.2.1 in certain archaic set expressions:

advienne que pourra
vive le roi
puissé-je trouver le bonheur!

3.7.2.2 at the beginning of a sentence to indicate surprise, an order or a desire:

que j'aille trouver le garçon? Certainement pas!
qu'il le fasse maintenant
que Monsieur nous écrive à ce sujet

3.7.2.3 to mark hypothesis/conditional value:

qu'il reste ou qu'il parte, cela m'est égal
ne fût-ce que pour ...

3.7.2.4 when a noun clause introduced by *que* precedes the main clause: this usage is limited to R3 speech:

qu'il fasse beau demain est certain
qu'il y eût beaucoup de spectateurs tout le monde en est convenu

3.7.2.5 to express 'whoever, whatever, wherever', etc:

whoever:	qui que vous soyez
whatever: (*pronoun*)	quoi qui arrive quoi qu'il fasse
wherever:	où que vous alliez
whatever: (*adj*)	quel que soit votre problème à quelque distance que cela paraisse

however:	quelque difficile que cela paraisse
	si grand soit-il/qu'il soit
	pour grand qu'il soit
	aussi longtemps que vous travailliez

NOTE: the use of *si* for however + adjective is more common than that of *quelque/pour* + adjective

3.7.2.6 after the following conjunctive expressions:

conjunctive expression	comments
à condition que	
afin que	R2 and R3
à moins que	in R3 usage *ne* is often inserted before the verb (**3.4.5**): eg *à moins qu'il ne vienne aujourd'hui*
après que	Logic and tradition require an indicative tense after *après que* when referring to a past event. However, prevailing usage (R1 and R2) prefers the subjunctive when *après que* refers to the past, but not to the future: eg *après qu'il soit arrivé, je lui ai dit . . .*
à supposer que	
avant que	in R3 usage *ne* is often inserted before the verb (*à moins que* above)
bien que	
de crainte que	in R3 usage *ne* is often inserted before the verb (*à moins que* above)
de façon que/à ce que	it is only when *de façon que/à ce que* expresses intention that it is followed by the subjunctive mood: *il faut revenir de façon qu'il te voie* when it expresses result an indicative tense is required: eg *il est revenu de façon que je l'ai vu* the newer form *de façon à ce que* is superseding the older expression *de façon que*
de manière que/à ce que	see comments for *de façon que/à ce que*
de peur que	in R3 usage *ne* is often inserted before the verb (*à moins que* above)
de sorte que	see first two comments for *de façon que/à ce que*
en attendant que	
encore que	R3
jusqu'à ce que	
malgré que	

conjunctive expression	comments
non (pas) que	R3
(pour) autant que	
pour peu que	
pour que	
pourvu que	
quoique	
sans que	
soit que . . . soit que	
sous réserve que	

NOTE A: when the following conjunctive expressions refer to a future or conditional idea, a future or conditional indicative is used:

eg   **bien que**   **malgré que**
        encore que   **quoique**

eg   **bien que je ne pourrai pas venir, ma sœur le fera**

NOTE B: the subjunctive is used in R3 usage in the second of a set of coordinated conditional clauses when *que* is used instead of *si*:

eg   **si la pluie cesse et qu'il fasse beau demain, nous sortirons**

but not when it is introduced by *si*:

eg   **si la pluie cesse et s'il fait beau demain, nous sortirons**

3.7.2.7   **in clauses dependent upon verbs and expressions indicating desiring, wishing, begging, ordering, forbidding, preventing** (this list and those in subsequent sections are not exhaustive, but include the most frequently encountered verbs and expressions):

verbs and expressions of desiring, wishing, etc	comments
aimer mieux	
attendre	
s'attendre	$+$ *à ce que*
commander	R3
décréter	
défendre	
demander	R3
désirer	
dire	R3

verbs and expressions of desiring, wishing, etc	comments
empêcher	with *empêcher ne* is sometimes inserted before the verb in the subjunctive in R3 usage (**3.5.4**)
éviter	with *éviter ne* is sometimes inserted before the verb in the subjunctive in R3 usage (**3.5.4**)
exiger	
implorer	
insister	+ *pour que*
interdire	
s'opposer	+ *à ce que*
ordonner	
préférer	
prier	R3
proposer	
souhaiter	
supplier	R3
tenir	+ *à ce que*
veiller	+ *à ce que*
vouloir	

3.7.2.8 **in clauses dependent upon verbs and expressions indicating a feeling (eg joy, fear, regret):**

verbs and expressions of feeling	
avoir peur	in R3 usage *ne* is sometimes inserted before the verb in the subjunctive (**3.5.4**)
craindre	in R3 usage *ne* is sometimes inserted before the verb in the subjunctive (**3.5.4**)
s'étonner	
se féliciter	
s'indigner redouter	
regretter	

---

verbs and
expressions of
feeling

être	affligé	honteux
	content	mécontent
	désolé	ravi
	étonné	satisfait
	fâché	surpris
	heureux	triste

3.7.2.9 **in clauses dependent upon verbs and expressions indicating denial, doubt, evaluation, impossibility, necessity, possibility:**

---

verbs and expressions of denial, doubt, etc

---

démentir	il est	bon
douter		curieux
nier		douteux
il/c'est dommage		essentiel
il faut		exclu
il importe		important
peu importe		impossible
il s'en faut de peu		improbable
il se peut		inévitable
ce n'est pas la peine		légitime
il semble		naturel

NOTE: *il me/lui semble que* (ie *sembler* + indirect object) is always followed by the indicative. However, in such expressions as *il me semble important que* the subjunctive is used.

nécessaire

normal

opportun

peu probable

NOTE: *il est probable que* is followed by the indicative (but cf 3.7.3.3)

possible

préférable

rare

temps

3.7.2.10   **in clauses dependent upon a superlative formed with *plus*** (but cf **3.7.3.1**):

     eg   c'est le livre le plus comique que j'aie jamais lu
           c'est le garçon le plus amusant que je connaisse

3.7.2.11   **in clauses dependent upon verbs and expressions indicating chance:**

verbs and expressions of chance	comments
risquer	
il arrive que	
il n'y a aucune chance que/pour que	there is a tendency for *pour que* to be preferred to *que*
il y a de grandes chances que/pour que	there is a tendency for *pour que* to be preferred to *que*
il y le danger que	
le hasard a voulu que	
c'est un hasard que	

3.7.3   'Grey' subjunctive

As stated earlier (**3.7**), use of the subjunctive frequently corresponds to a high register of language. An R3 user may introduce subtle shades of meaning into his French by a discreet balancing and contrasting of indicatives and subjunctives, the latter being used to imply a subjective attitude to what is being said, the former to convey a concrete fact:

     eg   c'est la dernière partie de football que j'ai vue
           c'est la dernière pièce de Molière que j'aie à étudier

Such distinctions are systematically ignored by R1 users and frequently, but not always, ignored by R2 users.

     The grey subjunctive occurs in the following circumstances:

3.7.3.1   **in clauses dependent upon a superlative** (but not formed with *plus*, **3.7.2.10**) **and similar expressions** (such as *dernier, premier, seul, ne . . . que*):

meilleur, pire, dernier, etc

R1+R2	R2+R3
c'est le meilleur/pire élève que je connais	que je connaisse
il n'y a que le professeur qui le fait	qui le fasse
c'est le seul de mes collègues avec qui je me suis vraiment lié d'amitié	je me sois vraiment lié d'amitié

NOTE: after expressions involving *fois*, such as *la dernière/seule fois que*, the indicative mood is always used.

3.7.3.2 **in clauses dependent upon a negative or indefinite antecedent:**

negative or indefinite antecedent

il n'y a personne qui	il faut quelqu'un qui
il n'y a rien qui	je préfère/préférais quelque chose qui
il n'y a pas de sujet qui	j'ai besoin d'un homme qui
ce ne sont pas des gens qui	indiquez-moi un médecin qui
il n'y a aucun pays qui	je désire une situation qui

3.7.3.3 **in clauses dependent upon expressions denying and questioning certainty, probability:**

expressions denying and questioning certainty and probability

il n'est pas/est-il   certain
      clair
      probable
      sûr
      vraisemblable

Under this heading are included certain expressions associated with doubt which were excluded from **3.7.2.9**: verbs and expressions indicating denial, doubt, etc:
il n'y a pas de doute
il ne fait pas de doute
il n'est pas douteux

3.7.3.4 **in clauses dependent upon verbs of thinking and declaring in the interrogative and/or negative**

verbs of thinking and declaring in interrogative and/or negative		examples
accepter	croire	croyez-vous qu'il vienne?
admettre	dire	je ne dis pas qu'il ait raison
comprendre	penser	
concevoir		

In R3 usage the verbs in the first column may also be followed by the subjunctive when they are used declaratively:

eg   **j'admets qu'il ait raison**

3.7.3.5   **in clauses dependent upon expressions of the following type**

	example
le but/dessein/l'intention est que le fait que	le fait qu'un étudiant soit (R3 + R2) /est (R2 + R1) plus intelligent n'est pas surprenant

3.7.4   Avoiding the subjunctive:

Because of uncertainty over correct forms and grey areas of usage, it is often advisable to avoid using the subjunctive. This may easily be done in certain circumstances:

3.7.4.1   **when the main and dependent clauses have the same subject, it is possible to use a preposition + infinitive rather than the subjunctive:**

prepositions	to replace
à condition de	à condition que
afin de	afin que
à moins de	à moins que
avant de	avant que
de crainte de	craindre que/de crainte que
de façon à	de façon que/à ce que, de sorte que
de manière à	de manière que/à ce que, de sorte que
de peur de	avoir peur que/de peur que
sans	sans que

3.7.4.2 **certain prepositional phrases are available to replace clauses with a subjunctive:**

prepositional phrases	to replace
avant mon départ	avant que je (ne) parte
à mon insu	sans que je le sache
à ma connaissance	autant que je sache

3.8 Pronouns

The following section contains a selection of problems concerning personal pronouns.

3.8.1 Second person pronouns

The following table shows broadly the situation in which *tu* (*toi*, *te*, *ton*, *ta*, *tes*) and *vous* (*votre*, *vos*) are used as modes of address in the singular:

mode of address in singular	
TU	VOUS
used when speaking to:	*used when speaking to:*
young children	
parents	
near relatives	
domestic animals	
	all others
used between:	
friends	
workmates	
soldiers in the same unit	
children in the same school	

However, actual usage is far more complicated than this table would suggest, and is affected by a large number of factors, such as age, personal attitudes, social circumstances, relationships within a hierarchy, etc.

For obvious sociological reasons, the general movement has been away from *vous* to *tu*. Whereas once, probably all teachers used *vous* when addressing older pupils (from the age of 15 upwards), a good number no longer observe this practice; similarly with the priest. However, *tu* is strictly forbidden across the grades/ranks in the armed services. The appropriateness of *tu* or *vous* can often be obscured if, for instance, a child's age is not known. The age of 14 or 15 upwards would, initially at any rate, require the respectful *vous*.

While Protestants have normally used *tu* in their prayers, Catholics are only recently being introduced to this practice. At the same time in certain high-standing, traditionalist families, parents use *tu* to their children, while the latter use *vous* to their parents. This *Vous-Régence* is particularly applicable to the highest echelons of government: former President Valéry Giscard d'Estaing uses *vous* to his wife, children and even his dogs! Similarly the former Prime Minister Raymond Barre. Yet both these distinguished statesmen would say *tu* to a child they do not know.

The point to be remembered is that the use of both *tu* and *vous* contains subtleties capable of expressing strong feelings, likes and dislikes, a sense of distance, superiority, indifference and so on. Thus, a driver, on observing poor driving by an unknown motorist could easily say: '*Tu roules au radar, toi?*' The intimate form puts the guilty driver in his place. Similarly and conversely, the French President, François Mitterand on hearing: '*Allez! on se dit tu*' is alleged to have replied icily: '*Comme vous voudrez!*' Georges Marchais, leader of the Communist Party, always uses *tu* when addressing all his Party colleagues, although of course, he would use *vous* when speaking to journalists, or members of other parties. *Tu* and *vous* can even be used between two people at different times of the day! Two colleagues who run a hairdressing business in Paris use *vous* on the premises and *tu* when they are away from work. The pronoun *tu* would not suit their formal approach to their profession.

The most awkward moment occurs in the actual transition from *vous* to *tu*, that is in passing from the stage of respect to that of friendliness, etc. This is felt especially acutely between the sexes.

Finally, if *A* is addressed in the *tu* form by *B*, he or she should not automatically use the *tu* form in return. Considerations of age dictate the use of the pronoun here.

3.8.2 Third person pronouns

3.8.2.1 *il* or *ce*?

In French constructions equivalent to English 'it's nice to know you', it is sometimes difficult to decide whether to use *il est* or *c'est*, or *à* or *de*. The following table illustrating the possible usages shows that it is a matter of what the pronoun refers to, and at times a matter of register as well:

introducing a new idea or statement		examples
R2+R3	*il est* + adjective + *de* + infinitive	il est difficile de lire le livre
R1	*c'est* + adjective + *de* + infinitive	c'est difficile de lire le livre

with reference to a preceding idea or statement		example
R1, R2+R3	*c'est* + adjective + *à* + infinitive	il a couru le cent mètres en dix secondes; c'est difficile à faire

3.8.2.2   *le*

In addition to its normal function of referring to persons, *le* is sometimes used to effect a link between what is being said and what has just been said, occasionally in situations where no equivalent exists in English:

eg   **il voulait être grand et il l'est** = he wanted to be big, and he is

     pauvre, il risque de l'être = he's in danger of being poor

     grand, il veut l'être = he wants to be important

     dites-le-moi = tell me

     il est plus/moins grand que je ne le pensais = he's bigger/smaller than I thought

     cela va mieux que je ne le pensais = that's better than I thought

     mademoiselle, êtes-vous infirmière? – Je le suis = I am

The pronoun *le* forms an integral part of certain verbal expressions, such as:

l'échapper belle = to have a narrow escape

l'emporter sur qn = to get the better of sb

le prendre de haut = to act arrogantly

se le tenir pour dit = to take it as said

On the other hand, the following examples are equivalent to English expressions with *it*:

$$\text{je} \begin{cases} \text{considère} & \text{difficile} \\ \text{estime} & \text{impossible} \\ \text{juge} & \text{inutile} \\ \text{trouve} & \text{nécessaire} \\ & \text{prudent} \end{cases} \text{de} = \text{I} \dots \text{it} \dots \text{to}$$

3.8.2.3 **on**

On is usually treated as a masculine singular subject pronoun:

eg **quand on n'a rien à faire, on trouve le temps long**

However, it may also be used with reference to feminine or plural subjects and the appropriate agreements of adjectives and past participles (but not finite verbs) are made:

eg **quand on est mère, on est fière des ses enfants**
   on a beau être citoyens, on n'est pas toujours égaux
   on a été sages aujourd'hui? (parent speaking to children)
   on est venus aussi vite que possible (two or more people
      speaking)

On functions only as a subject; when it is required to express a direct object or other complement other forms are used:

complements of *on*		examples
reflexive	se	on se lève, on se lave
	soi (R3 *only*)	on doit aider les plus infortunés que soi
		de temps en temps on doit prendre une décision soi-même
non-reflexive	nous (*including speaker*)	on voit bien ses cheveux gris quand elle est près de nous/vous
	vous (*excluding speaker*)	

In R1 speech it is not uncommon for *nous* to be used in apposition to *on*:

eg **nous autres Anglais, on le fait d'une autre façon**

The possessive adjective associated with *on* is the *son*, *sa* series:

eg **on entre, on enlève son chapeau et ses gants**

Often in R3 usage, for the sake of euphony, the form *l'on* is preferred. It should scarcely be necessary to point out that *on* is used much more frequently in French than *one* is in English (which is more or less restricted to R3 usage in that language).

3.8.2.4 **soi**

Soi, the strong form of the reflexive pronoun, is used only with certain indefinite words and expressions such as *on*, *chacun* and impersonal *il*:

eg **il faut/on doit le faire soi-même**
   chacun pour soi

NOTE: the strong form used with reflexive verbs is *lui* (*-même*) and not *soi*:

eg **l'enfant a réussi à se laver lui-même**

3.8.3 *en*

En functions in two ways:

---

adverb of place	pronoun:
	with partitive value
	used with verbs, past participles, adjectives, nouns,
	numerals + *de*

---

en as adverb: eg **il sort de la ville : il en sort**
                     il vient de Paris : il en vient

en as pronoun: As a pronoun *en* seems to have a number of different values, ranging from reference to specific objects to an extremely indeterminate use, merely providing a weak link with what has been said previously. This use often has no equivalent in English: consequently corresponding English versions are given below where appropriate. Some of the following examples, graded according to the degree of explicitness of reference of *en*, contain fixed expressions.

    eg   **voici une fourchette – Servez-vous-en**
          quel est son prénom? je ne m'en souviens pas
          voici un cadeau pour votre fille – Je vous en
             remercie
          est-ce que tu as fini tes devoirs? – J'en ai fait
             les deux tiers
          j'ai congédié le premier; il s'en est présenté un
             deuxième
          est-ce que tu as cueilli toutes les pommes? – Non,
             il en reste les trois quarts
          l'histoire de Matthieu et de Sylvie est fascinante
             – on devrait en faire un livre
          je suis enfin arrivé! – J'en suis content/heureux/
             fâché/ravi/désolé
          s'en prendre à qn
          s'en rapporter à qch
          s'en remettre à qn
          en vouloir à qn

NOTE: no agreement is made between *en* and the past participle in compound tenses conjugated with *avoir*, since *en* is not a direct object:

    eg   **elle a des robes comme j'en ai eu**
          c'est le type de jeune fille comme j'en ai connu par le passé

Strictly speaking *en* is not used with reference to people, but such examples as the following are normal despite the censure of the purists:

eg **est-ce qu'il y a des médecins? – Oui, il y en a**
   il en a fait son premier ministre

In a comparative expression involving quantity *en*, as well as an expletive *ne*, is required in the subordinate clause in R3 speech:

eg **il ne faut pas donner à l'événement plus d'importance**
   qu'il n'en a

In R1 and R2 speech, when highlighting of an object indicating quantity occurs by moving it to the head or end of the clause, *en* is required before the verb:

eg **du papier, j'en ai trouvé**
   il y en a, des livres

3.8.4 *y*

Like *en*, *y* functions both as an adverb and as a pronoun:

adverb of place	pronoun: used with verbs, past participles, adjectives, nouns, numerals + *à*

y as adverb
eg **je vais au collège: j'y vais**
   êtes-vous arrivé? – Oui, j'y suis arrivé

y as pronoun
y does not have the range of values of *en*:

eg **je pense à ce que vous avez dit: j'y pense**
   est-il décidé à le faire? – Oui, il y est décidé
   je n'y réussirai pas
   je n'y vois pas clair

As with *le* and *en*, *y* forms part of a verbal expression:
il y va de ma vie

3.9 Usage with names of countries

The following table illustrates the usage of prepositions with respect to names of countries:

	M names beginning with cons	M names beginning with vowel	F names
position in	au	en	en
examples	il est au Portugal	il est en Iran	il est en France

	M names beginning with cons	M names beginning with vowel	F names
movement towards	au	en	en
examples	il va au Portugal	il va en Irak	il va en France
movement away from	du	d'	de*
examples	elle vient du Danemark	elle vient d'Iran	elle vient de Belgique

de la is no longer used in this context, except in:
il vient de l'Inde

When the country is qualified by an adjective the following usage is observed:
dans la France contemporaine
dans le Japon moderne

When referring to the north or south of a country, one usually says:
il est dans le nord/sud de la France

Less common is:
il est dans la France du nord
NOTE: il est en Italie du Nord is much more common than
il est dans le nord de l'Italie

For usage with names of islands, see the individual islands listed below. For names of towns with distinctive French forms, see 2.7.2.

3.9.1 France

Regions

gender	il est/va	examples	exceptions
F (the majority)	en	en Normandie en Bretagne en Bourgogne en Provence	none
M	dans le	dans le Poitou	en Anjou

Departments

gender	il est/va	examples
M	dans le	dans le Jura dans le Gard dans le Var dans le Lot
F	dans la/en	dans la/en Gironde dans la/en Charente
	en	en Vendée en Saône et Loire en Côte d'Or
F pl	dans les	dans les Bouches du Rhône dans les Alpes Maritimes

Mountainous areas: il est/va + dans:

  eg dans les Alpes (du Nord, du Sud)
      dans les Vosges
      dans les Pyrénées

Names of towns beginning with a definite article: the article combines with *à* and *de* as in normal circumstances:

  eg il est au Havre, au Mans, au Creusot, à la Rochelle
      il vient du Havre, du Mans, du Creusot, de la Rochelle

Movement away from regions, departments and mountainous areas

gender	preposition	examples
M	du	il vient du Jura
F sg	de	il vient de Normandie, de Vendée
F pl	des	il vient des Alpes Maritimes

Contrary to English, names of inhabitants of regions and towns are very common in French:

eg	Poitou	Poitevin
	Bretagne	Breton
	Franche-Comté	Franc-comtois
	Auvergne	Auvergnat
	Normandie	Normand

Apart from the usual *Parisien*, *Marseillais*, *Lyonnais*, *Toulousain*, *Nantais* and *Strasbourgeois*, here is a small selection from a vast number of less easily recognisable ones:

Besançon	**Bisontin**
St Etienne	**Stéphanois**
Evreux	**Ebroïcien**
Lisieux	**Lexovien**
Pont-Saint-Esprit	**Spiripontain**

All these nouns may also be used adjectivally.

NOTE:

La Côte d'Azur = the French Riviera
La Riviéra = the Italian Riviera

Although *Comté* is masculine one says *La Franche Comté*; the adjective is *franc-comtois*.

Below is indicated how the name of each country is used. The classification is by continents except in the case of France, which has been treated separately.

NOTE: with nationality a capital letter is used, while with a pure adjective a small letter is used

> eg **elle est Française**
> **une ville française**

3.9.2 Europe

il est/va	elle vient	adjective
en Albanie	d'Albanie	albanais
en Allemagne de l'Est	d'Allemagne de l'Est	allemand
en République Démocratique Allemande (RDA)	de la République Démocratique Allemande	allemand
en Allemagne de l'Ouest	d'Allemagne de l'Ouest	allemand
en République Fédérale Allemande (RFA)	de la République Fédérale Allemande	allemand
en Andorre	d'Andorre	
NOTE: à Andorre = *Andorra the capital*		
en Angleterre	d'Angleterre	anglais
en Autriche	d'Autriche	autrichien
aux Baléares, à Majorque	des Baléares, de Majorque	majorquin, espagnol
en Belgique	de Belgique	belge
en Bulgarie	de Bulgarie	bulgare
à Chypre	de Chypre	cypriote, chypriote
en Corse	de Corse	corse, français
en Crète	de Crète	crétois

il est/va	elle vient	adjective
au Danemark	du Danemark	danois
en Ecosse	d'Ecosse	écossais
en Eire, en République d'Irlande	d'Eire, de la République d'Irlande	irlandais
en Espagne	d'Espagne	espagnol
NOTE: au pays basque	du pays basque	basque (une Basquaise)
en Finlande	de Finlande	finlandais/finnois (2.3)
au Pays de Galles	du Pays de Galles	gallois
en Grande-Bretagne	de Grande Bretagne	britannique
NOTE A: dans les Iles britanniques		
NOTE B: Counties: dans le Kent, etc.		
except en Cornouailles		
en Grèce	de Grèce	grec (F grecque)
au Grœnland	du Grœnland	danois
en Hollande, aux Pays Bas	de Hollande, des Pays Bas	hollandais, néerlandais
en Hongrie	de Hongrie	hongrois
en Irlande du Nord	d'Irlande du Nord	britannique, irlandais
en Italie	d'Italie	italien
NOTE: au Vatican		
au Luxembourg	du Luxembourg	luxembourgeois
NOTE: à Luxembourg = *Luxemburg town*		
à Malte	de Malte	maltais
en Norvège	de Norvège	norvégien
en Pologne	de Pologne	polonais
au Portugal	du Portugal	portugais
au Royaume Uni	du Royaume Uni	britannique
en Roumanie	de Roumanie	roumain
en Russie, en Union Soviétique, en URSS	de Russie, de l'Union Soviétique, de l'URSS	russe
NOTE: en Prusse	de Prusse	prussien
en Sardaigne	de Sardaigne	sarde, italien
en Sicile	de Sicile	sicilien, italien
en Suède	de Suède	suédois
en Suisse	de Suisse	suisse (une Suissesse)
en Tchécoslovaquie	de Tchécoslovaquie	tchèque
en Turquie	de Turquie	turc (F turque)
en Yougoslavie	de Yougoslavie	yougoslave

NOTE *the following compound adjectives:*

anglo–français	hispano–français
franco–anglais	germano–russe
franco–britannique	russo–allemand
franco–espagnol	

3.9.3 Afrique

il est/va	elle vient	adjective
en Afrique du Sud	d'Afrique du Sud	sud-africain
en Algérie	d'Algérie	algérien
en Angola	d'Angola	angolais
au Bénin	du Bénin	dahoméen
au Cameroun	du Cameroun	camerounais
en Côte d'Ivoire	de la Côte d'Ivoire	ivoirien
en Egypte	d'Egypte	égyptien
en Ethiopie	d'Ethiopie	éthiopien
au Gabon	du Gabon	gabonais
au Ghana	du Ghana	ghanéen
en Guinée	de Guinée	guinéen
en Haute Volta	de la Haute Volta	voltaïque
au Kenya	du Kenya	kenyien
au Libéria	du Libéria	libérien
en Libye	de Libye	libyen
à Madagascar	de Madagascar	malgache
au Malawi	du Malawi	malawi
au Mali	du Mali	malien
au Maroc	du Maroc	marocain
à (l'île) Maurice	de l'île Maurice	mauricien
(*but often, although*		
mistakenly, aux îles		
Maurice)		
en Mauritanie	de Mauritanie	mauritanien
au Mozambique	du Mozambique	mozambiquais
en Namibie	de Namibie	namibien
au Niger	du Niger	nigérien
au Nigéria	du Nigéria	nigérian
en Ouganda	d'Ouganda	ougandais
en République	de la République	centrafricain
Centrafricaine	Centrafricaine	
à la Réunion	de la Réunion	réunionnais
au Sénégal	du Sénégal	sénégalais
en Sierra Leone	de Sierra Leone	sierra-leonien
en Somalie	de Somalie	somalien
au Soudan	du Soudan	soudanais
en Tanzanie	de Tanzanie	tanzanien
au Tchad	du Tchad	tchadien
au Togo	du Togo	togolais
en Tunisie	de Tunisie	tunisien
au Zaïre	du Zaïre	zaïrois
en Zambie	de Zambie	zambien
au Zimbabwe	du Zimbabwe	zimbabwéen

NOTE: l'Afrique du Nord *refers mainly to* le Maghreb, ie le Maroc, l'Algérie, la Tunisie. *Its southern equivalent is* l'Afrique Australe (*Southern Africa*), *not to be confused with* l'Afrique du Sud (*South Africa*).

NOTE: *the following compound adjectives:*
afro-asiatique
égypto–israélien
israélo–égyptien

3.9.4 Asie et Australasie

il est/va	elle vient	adjective
en Afghanistan	d'Afghanistan	afghan
en Australie	d'Australie	australien
au Bangladesh	du Bangladesh	bengalais
en Birmanie	de Birmanie	birman
au Cambodge	du Cambodge	cambodgien
au Kampuchéa	du Kampuchéa	
en Chine	de Chine	chinois
NOTE: sino- *in* *compound adjectives*: *eg* sino-vietnamien		
en Corée du Nord, du Sud	de Corée du Nord, du Sud	nord-coréen, sud-coréen
en Inde	de l'Inde	hindou, indien; *the latter is the more correct term*
NOTE: aux Indes *is outmoded as a political expression, but is still used*		
en Indonésie	d'Indonésie	indonésien
au Japon	du Japon	japonais
au Laos	du Laos	laotien
en Malaisie	de Malaisie	malaisien
au Népal	du Népal	népalais
en Nouvelle-Calédonie	de Nouvelle-Calédonie	néo-calédonien
en Nouvelle Zélande	de Nouvelle Zélande	néo-zélandais
au Pakistan	du Pakistan	pakistanais
aux Philippines	des Philippines	philippin
à Sri Lanka	de Sri Lanka	ceylanais
en Tasmanie	de Tasmanie	tasmanien
en Thaïlande	de Thaïlande	thaïlandais
au Tibet	du Tibet	tibétain
au Vietnam	du Vietnam	vietnamien

NOTE: il est/va en Extrême-Orient il est/va en Asie du Sud-Est

3.9.5 Moyen-Orient

il est/va	elle vient	adjective
en Arabie Séoudite	d'Arabie Séoudite	séoudien
NOTE: Saoudite *is more common, but is refuted by purists*		
en Irak	d'Irak	irakien
en Iran	d'Iran	iranien
en Israël	d'Israël	israélien
NOTE: Israël *is not normally preceded by a definite article*: eg le premier ministre d'Israël; Israël est un petit pays		
en Jordanie	de Jordanie	jordanien
au Liban, au Liban-Sud	du Liban	libanais
en Syrie	de Syrie	syrien
au Yémen, au Yémen du Sud	du Yémen	yéménite

NOTE: il est au Proche-Orient, au Moyen-Orient

3.9.6 Amérique du Nord

il est/va	elle vient	adjective
au Canada	du Canada	canadien
au Québec	du Québec	québécois
aux Etats-Unis	des Etats-Unis	américain
NOTE: *in speech often* aux USA		

NOTE: For individual States, the usage is:
dans l' before vowel or mute **h**
au before M beginning with cons
en before F beginning with cons
eg **dans l'Ohio, dans l'Utah**
    au Nevada, au Texas
    en Californie, en Caroline du Nord, du Sud
Other states with distinctive French forms:
    Dakota du Nord, du Sud, Floride, Georgie, Louisiane, Nouveau Mexique, Pennsylvanie, Virginie Occidentale
NOTE: **un Peau Rouge, un Indien** = a Red Indian

3.9.7 Amérique Centrale

il est/va	elle vient	adjective
aux Antilles (= *West Indies*)	des Antilles	antillais
au Costa Rica	du Costa Rica	costaricain
à Cuba	de Cuba	cubain
à la Guadeloupe *but* en Guadeloupe *is becoming more common*	de la Guadeloupe	guadeloupéen
au Guatémala	du Guatémala	guatémaltèque
à Haïti	de Haïti	haïtien
au Honduras	du Honduras	hondurien
à la Jamaïque	de la Jamaïque	jamaïquain
à la Martinique *but* en Martinique *is becoming more common*	de la Martinique	martiniquais
au Mexique	du Mexique	mexicain
au Nicaragua	du Nicaragua	nicaraguayen
au Panama	du Panama	panaméen
NOTE: à Panama = *in Panama City, the capital (not to be confused with* Paname, *a popular term for Paris)*		
à Porto Rico	de Porto Rico	portoriquain
en République Dominicaine	de la République Dominicaine	dominicain
au Salvador	du Salvador	salvadorien
NOTE: à San-Salvador = *in San-Salvador, the capital.*		

3.9.8   Amérique du Sud

il est/va	elle vient	adjective
en Argentine	d'Argentine	argentin
en Bolivie	de Bolivie	bolivien
au Brésil	du Brésil	brésilien
au Chili	du Chili	chilien
en Colombie	de Colombie	colombien
en Equateur (= *Ecuador*)	d'Equateur	equatorien
en Guyane	de Guyane	guyanais
au Paraguay	du Paraguay	paraguayen
au Pérou	du Pérou	péruvien
en Uruguay	d'Uruguay	uruguayen
au Vénézuéla	du Vénézuéla	vénézuélien

NOTE: il est en Amérique du Nord, du Sud, en Amérique Centrale
NOTE *also the compound adjective*: latino-américain

3.9.9   Seas and Oceans

	preposition	examples and comments
seas	dans la/en	dans la/en Mer du Nord, dans la/en Mer Noire, dans la/en Mer Caspienne, dans la/en Mer de Chine, dans la/en Mer du Japon, dans la/en Manche,
		en Méditerranée is preferred to dans la Méditerranée
oceans	dans le	dans l'(Océan) Atlantique dans l'(Océan) Pacifique
	dans le/en	only with Océan Indien

Useful geographical phrases:	sous les/aux Tropiques sous la ligne du Cancer/du Capricorne	à l'équateur au pôle nord, au pôle sud

Vocabulary list

Words and expressions contained in Sections 2.1 to 2.4

abaisser 50, 52
abîmer 108
abonné 112
aborder 70
abords 95
absorber 50
abstraction, faire –
  86
abuser 47
accomplir 31, 34
accomplissement
  31, 47, 97
accord 31
  être d' – 31, 70
  tomber d' – 70
accorder 82
s'accorder 70
accroissement 50
accroître 50, 87
s'accroître 50, 87
achèvement 31
achever 31, 50
actuel 31
addition 72
affaiblir 33, 50
s'affaiblir 50
affiche 93
affronter 50
âgé 94
agenda 31
agent de police 98
agonie 31
agoniser 31
agrandir 50, 87
agréer 31, 70
agrément 31
agriculteur 78
aide 36, 37
  venir en – 85
aider 85
aigle 37
aimé(e), bien – 90
aine 33
air 40

aire 40
aise, bien à l' – 47
alentours 95
alité 48
alléchant 71
allée 31, 96
allocution 107
allumer 44
alpestre 50
alpin 50
s'altérer 31
amant 90
amener 50, 73
ami(e), petit(e) –
  90
amoureux/euse 90
amusant 44
amuser 33
an 50
ancien 94
angoisse 31
année 50
annonce 32
  – publicitaire 93
annuel, congé – 86
anoblir 50
anse 84
antique 94
apercevoir 51
s'apercevoir 51
aplanir 51
aplatir 51
apogée 110
apparaître 63
apparition 51, 70
appeler 74
application 47
appointements 96
apporter 51, 73
appréhender 44
apprendre 109
approcher 51, 70
s'approcher 51, 70
approvisionner 99

âpre 85
aquarelle 95
arc 51
arche 51
argent 34, 91
  – comptant 91
argenté 51
argentin 51
argument 51
argumentation 51
arôme 107
arrêt, maison d' –
  98
arrêter 44
arrivage 51
arrivée 51
assassinat 44
assembler 51, 82
assises 80
assistance 36, 47
assister 44, 85
assortiment 105
astucieux 107
atelier 35
attacher 51
attenant 92
attendrissant 48
attentif 51
attentionné 51
atténuer 33
attractif 51, 71
attrayant 51, 71
au-dessous 51, 112
au-dessus 51, 94,
  95
audience 47
augmenter 87
auprès 52
auto 32
autochtone 92
automobiliste 34
avance 52
avancement 52
avancer 70

s'avancer 70
avare 52
avaricieux 52
avertissement 32
avide 83
avoisinant 92
bâcler 108
bagne 98
baiser 52
baisser 50, 52
bal 40, 47
balancer 32, 44,
  110
balle 40, 43, 47,
  52, 71
ballon 52, 71
ballot 52
banc 52, 104
bandit 44
banlieue 95
banque 47
banquette 52, 104
bar 40, 47
barbouze 98
baril 52
barque 73
barre 40, 47, 52
barreau 52
barrière 81
barrique 52
base 80
bassin 88
bateau 73
bâtiment 44, 73,
  74
bâtisse 74
batterie 105
se battre 52, 79
bazarder 110
berge 71
besogne 87
beugler 52
bibliothécaire 34
bibliothèque 34